Bullying
Cyberbullying

Bullying and Cyberbullying

What Every Educator and Parent Needs to Know

Second Edition

ELIZABETH KANDEL ENGLANDER

Harvard Education Press

Cambridge, Massachusetts

Paperback ISBN 978-1-68253-861-6

Library of Congress Cataloging-in-Publication Data is on file.

Published by Harvard Education Press,
an imprint of the Harvard Education Publishing Group

Harvard Education Press
8 Story Street
Cambridge, MA 02138

Cover Design: Ciano Design
Cover Image: skynesher/E+ via Getty Images
The typefaces in this book are ITC Stone Serif, ITC Stone Sans, and Filosofia.

Contents

The Bullying Enigma in 2023

Before 2020: Adults are concerned about kids' use of screens.

Since 2020: Research indicates that children's use of screens may have doubled.

Before 2020: Adults are worried cyberbullying will increase.

Since 2020: During the global coronavirus pandemic, cyberbullying rates may have decreased or only increased slightly.

Before 2020: Professionals can help children with mental health concerns.

Since 2020: This remains true, but we also need to teach children how to help support and promote their own mental health.

Since 2013, the degree to which the world (and thus life for children) has shifted, frankly, cannot be overstated. The most obvious earth-shaker has been the global coronavirus pandemic, which exacerbated several trends we were already seeing among children in 2019, including the relentless and inexorable climb in the use of digital technology. Consider that almost a decade ago, when the first edition of this book was published, a study of third graders at the Massachusetts Aggression Reduction Center (MARC) found that 19 percent owned their own cell phones. By 2017, that proportion had increased to 41 percent.[1] During the most challenging years of the global coronavirus pandemic (2020 and 2021), various studies similarly estimated that children's screen time had increased by 65 to 70 percent, and even as much as 100 percent.[2]

Although we know that technology is a central part of bullying today, digital communications aren't the only changes in the last decade that have affected children's social and emotional development. Other, possibly equally profound, factors have had an impact, including the shock of the pandemic.

THE EMOTIONAL AND SOCIAL IMPACT
OF THE PANDEMIC

The global coronavirus pandemic has been and continues to be, arguably, the most important social and developmental influence for this generation of children. At the time of this writing, 6.6 million human beings have died from COVID-19, the disease caused by the 2019 coronavirus.[3] Children were comparatively less affected by death, but many lost loved ones and caregivers to this illness. Social interactions, a central focus of childhood, were cut off during the various lockdowns in different countries; children didn't go to school and couldn't play with peers. In March 2020, in response to the global pandemic, a national lockdown was announced. It encompassed the entire United States and much of the rest of the world. Overnight, all workers (except for those deemed *essential*) were told to work from home or to take a leave from their employment. Schools closed their physical doors and shifted gears abruptly, as teachers began the novel task of teaching online. Most students were already spending a great deal of time online, but with the advent of online schooling, their screen time increased substantially.

Even children who attended schools that remained fully open during 2020 and 2021 found that their unscripted interactions—free play, parties, recess, and outside activities—were all greatly reduced, and their screen time increased. A decrease in social skills accompanied this change.[4]

This social isolation and the reality of living through a global pandemic seemed to affect mental health more than it affected bullying and cyberbullying, at least directly. Levels of bullying appeared to decrease, whereas cyberbullying remained relatively stable or changed only minimally.[5] In contrast, researchers found significant increases in mental health problems among children, notably anxiety and depression.[6] This increase in mental health challenges is probably one of the reasons why we're not making as much progress in reducing bullying and cyberbullying as we'd like to be making.

WE'RE STILL NOT AS EFFECTIVE AT REDUCING BULLYING AS WE'D LIKE TO BE

A charitable interpretation of current social relationships between children might conclude that we've made, at most, modest progress in reducing bullying and cyberbullying. In a study of almost two thousand youth between 2020 and 2022, fully 60 percent reported that adult-led bullying and cyberbullying prevention programs in their schools were either useless or invisible.[7] Changes in the nature of bullying and cyberbullying can probably account for some of this. Although the dramatic increase in digital forms of bullying was clearly evident by the first edition of this book, since 2016, bias-based bullying has begun to increase as well, posing distinct challenges for children, schools, and parents.[8]

As with all complex problems, it's tempting to point fingers when we think about who is to blame for bullying continuing to be such a significant social problem. And as I noted in the introduction to the 2013 edition of this book, almost anything you pick up on bullying and cyberbullying will, in fact, point a finger at someone, or some group. In 2019, an article reported that New York, Maryland, and Pennsylvania were all considering legislation holding parents responsible for their child's bullying behaviors.[9] Conversely, parents have also, at times, felt that schools were primarily to blame for children being chronically bullied. One media story described a parent who held her daughter's school responsible for the child's suicide following bullying.[10] A similar story reported that another set of parents asserted that their child's school ignored state law and didn't notify them, possibly contributing to their son's suicide.[11] Finally, virtually everyone points the finger at technology as an influence that has hampered healthy child development, made supportive social friendship bonds more difficult for kids to achieve, and provided an unparalleled platform for social cruelty.

Yet blame games are not always productive, and they can even be counterproductive by keeping a great deal of attention and energy focused on ineffective solutions. Some parents almost certainly fail to rein in, or even reinforce, their child's aggression. But is singling out parents the way to end bullying? Does anyone think that merely advising children to abandon video games and social media is likely to be effective? Do the schools, and the kids, hold no responsibility? As usual, the truth is likely to be much more complicated.

On top of this counterproductive blame game, when it comes to bullying, emotions tend to run high, and muddy the waters. Many parents face their children's bullying experiences through the lens of their own painful childhood memories. We all remember the cringe-worthy times we faced peer cruelty. The difficult question is whether those experiences help or harm us. Surely *some* unpleasant social experiences, and some unpleasant people, are a necessary prerequisite for learning to cope with the social challenges of adulthood. In 2013, I noted that we can't require kids to like each other, and that means sometimes they won't. Still, we can (and should) require them to behave decently toward each other. In addition, an obvious difference clearly exists between transient and more minor social challenges—for example, someone who embarrasses you once versus someone who's waging a campaign designed to destroy you psychologically.

So, we have programs that, too often, are ineffective; instead of seeking more productive responses, we might retreat to finger-pointing; and to top it all off, our own emotions and experiences make it hard for us to approach bullying and cyberbullying calmly and logically.

As in the first edition, my purpose in this book is to help educators sort through the thorny issues that complicate our efforts to understand bullying and cyberbullying, and to suggest practical and realistic ways to address these behaviors effectively. Despite the plethora of publications in this field—many of which offer valuable insights according to their different areas of emphasis—I've been struck by how unusual it is to find approaches that not only are both concrete and genuine but also cover the entire spectrum of online and offline bullying behaviors. I don't think these social problems between children can be addressed without a solid understanding of child development, how children actually bully today, what goes on in schools, and how digital behaviors emerge during childhood and interrelate with (and sometimes determine) in-school socializing. Bullying is a complex puzzle because solving it needs *all* of these pieces. And that's exactly the perspective that I present in this book.

Let me introduce myself by saying I'm not a university professor, *or* a professional trainer in bullying prevention, *or* a researcher in bullying and cyberbullying, *or* a parent of three kids, *or* a teacher. I'm all of those things. And each role I play adds an important skill and dimension to the mix. First and foremost, I teach at a state university in Massachusetts where I run the Massachusetts Aggression Reduction Center (MARC), where I (with my colleagues and students) conduct research into bullying and cyberbullying.

MARC is also a founding organization in the Social and Emotional Research Consortium (SERC), in which states pool research data to enrich our knowledge base. I'll talk a lot more about the findings of this research program later in the book. (Appendix A gives methodological details about the research cited in this book. Appendix B provides more information about MARC and SERC.)

It's important that I don't only conduct research. I also do a great deal of work in the field with teachers, children, parents, administrators, and community members. MARC delivers programs, trainings, and services to teachers, students, and parents in hundreds of schools each year (during the pandemic, MARC's programs were used in all fifty US states). Along with other MARC faculty, I deliver, or supervise the delivery of, virtually every one of those services. I've written and tested four evidence-based curricula (a fifth and sixth are in progress) as well as the training materials for the college students we train to work with kids in dozens of schools every year. (You'd be amazed at what school-age kids will discuss with college students, whom they generally revere—it gives us wonderful insights.) I've also trained tens of thousands of teachers, administrators, and staff in hundreds of schools. Finally, I've spoken to and worked with parents organizations in hundreds of communities. I think it's being heavily involved in *both* research and fieldwork that makes my perspective particularly useful. Because parents are such an important part of this mix, my additional perspective as a parent of three children makes my approach to the whole issue more realistic and grounded.

In addition to this combination of experiences, I'm something of a rare bird in that I'm interested in both child development and digital communications. I've been studying child development and aggression, and the difficulties that occur during childhood that result in violence or abuse, for more than thirty years. But my second area of interest—which, until about 2005, had absolutely nothing to do with my first—has always been the impact of technology on human beings and communications. These interests remained entirely separate until, a few years into the twenty-first century, digital communications began to consistently emerge as the newest and most insidious form of aggression on the planet (and a growing problem among children). Virtually overnight, my two areas of study merged.

Let me also introduce a few caveats. I'm not an attorney or a licensed therapist, and so I won't be dispensing legal, clinical, or therapeutic advice in this book. Thank goodness.

THE AGENDA

The first thing I do, in chapter 1, is to summarize some of my research findings about patterns of behavior among bullies—in particular the emergence of "gateway behaviors" that are particularly difficult to monitor and assess at school. This chapter provides guidelines for assessing ambiguous behaviors and discusses why the dynamics of bullying become more fluid in the context of cyberspace.

Chapter 2 sorts through the wildly varying estimates of the prevalence of bullying. How common are these behaviors, really? Which children are most at risk? And what strategies can educators use to reduce risk and enhance resilience?

In chapter 3, we'll take a close look at the bullies. In the past, bullies have tended to be children with low status and poor social skills, but today, evidence shows that even popular children engage in bullying. The chapter discusses the impact of electronic devices on the development of children's social skills, and traces the plume of influence from electronic communications that colors so many social interactions between young people today.

In chapter 4, the focus shifts to cyberbullying and how online behaviors influence (and typically exacerbate) in-person conflicts. We'll talk about some of the distinctive—and confounding—features of cyberbullying, and why it creates such a powerful sense of anxiety and helplessness among victims. In this chapter, I also outline some of the challenges in addressing online behaviors with tech-savvy kids.

In chapter 5, I go over new research findings about some of the unique problems that digital communications have brought us: sexting, self-cyberbullying, and other risky online behaviors from elementary school through high school.

Last but not least, in chapters 6 through 8, I employ all these points to develop practical ways to address these issues—an area that is no less fraught than looking at the incidence and causes of bullying. What do we actually do in the moment, when we see these problems? Chapter 6 discusses the "nine-second response" and other formal and informal approaches educators can use to address various kinds of bullying behavior. Chapter 7 draws on student surveys to suggest ways educators can empower bystanders and other peers to encourage prosocial behaviors and a positive environment. Finally, chapter 8 uses survey findings from parents to decipher their perspectives on bullying and cyberbullying and uses that data to suggest tips for working effectively with parents.

FRAMING THE ISSUES

Before we start, let's discuss a few key points that are often not well understood but that help clarify everything that follows.

- First, the chronic overuse of the term *bullying* produces a set of problems that impede our prevention efforts.
- Second, bullying is an abuse behavior and needs to be understood as such.
- Third, bullying is not always so easy to recognize; teachers and administrators today sometimes struggle because they need better information about what to look for.
- Fourth, bullying in school is not separate from what happens online; we may tend to think of bullying and cyberbullying as distinct and unrelated events, but in actuality, they're neither.
- Fifth, bullying is also not a problem that adults alone should fix; children *do* need to learn how to address meanness, as they're a key part of the solution to this problem.
- Finally, when it comes to educating children about their social lives, we need to rethink how we convey these messages.

Overuse of the Word Bullying

Bullying is a term that's being, well, bullied. It's been rendered essentially powerless by being constantly kicked around. The term is often used to describe any type of nastiness, or, even more commonly, virtually any situation that involves a mean-spirited attack or hurt feelings. Accidents, fights, assaults, quarrels, malice, and differences of opinion are all mistakenly called "bullying" at times. The criterion for bullying isn't simply *anything that hurts another person*, although it's often confused for exactly that. Precisely defined, *bullying* is calculated, ongoing abuse that is aimed at a less-powerful target.[12] Certainly, a single incident of cruelty between two children can develop into bullying or abuse by becoming repetitive. Problems that happen between children of relatively equal power can also change and develop into a situation in which one child predominates. We should not, however, be too quick to label every one-time incident, and every equal-power fight, as bullying.

Why focus on the overuse of the term? Calling every sniffle a "cold" has no real impact; however, calling every hurt "bullying" harms not only the targets and the bullies, but ultimately, all the people and the entire psychological climate in a school.

Children can avoid responsibility

One of the ways that bullying can be distinguished from other conflicts is that it's largely a one-way street when it comes to responsibility. The first problem with overuse of the term is that by permitting children to blithely frame many interpersonal difficulties as bullying, we're encouraging (or at least allowing) them to abandon any consideration of personal responsibility in situations in which they may bear some blame. A child who has been fighting or victimizing others and knows that he or she will get some or all of the blame may be strongly tempted to assume the role of a victim of bullying and thereby avoid the penalty.

Let me emphasize (for those preparing to send me nasty emails) that I am absolutely *not* saying that children who are targets of bullies should take responsibility for their own victimization.[13] I am suggesting that it's prudent to ask a few questions to determine if a child is truly a victim of bullying before accepting that an abusive situation is happening. The desire to avoid responsibility for misbehaviors is completely normal and trying to avoid punishment is one of the more understandable motivations for lying among children—who some experts estimate tell (on average) approximately one lie every ninety minutes by the age of six.[14] But adults, eager to be advocates for a child's well-being, may hear the word *bullying* and abandon any meaningful investigation. Their emotional response (often predicated on their own childhood experiences) kicks them immediately into protective overdrive, in which gear few or no questions are asked.

One could argue that children won't be motivated to call a situation bullying when it's not, because being a victim of bullying is a stigma. That may be true with peers, but when it comes to adults, using the term can actually be advantageous—it gets everyone's attention. Sometimes what they're really saying, as your blood pressure rises, is "I need you to sit up and take notice of what I'm telling you. This is important!"

If everyone's a victim, then no one's a victim

The second problem with overuse of the term is that by calling everything bullying, we greatly water down the very real and occasionally extreme distress that victims and targets of bullying experience. As a teacher, you've probably had your share of students and parents who pointedly identified even mild issues as bullying. But bullying isn't any old meanness that saunters down the sidewalk. Students who are subjected to bullying in school or online are not just living with perpetual fear; they feel unable to defend themselves, they endure wound after wound, and yet they live in a world that doesn't defend them (or worse—doesn't even care to try). It's not just that the bully doesn't care—bullying can leave a victim with the sense that the world doesn't care.

It shouldn't be too much of a stretch, therefore, to realize that bullying can lead to learned helplessness, loss of motivation to try to learn, and loss of friends and support systems. For children who are vulnerable, the unremitting nature of this cruelty can contribute to depression and violence.[15] Bullying appears, in some cases, to be a contributor to children committing suicide and homicide (particularly when children have other psychiatric risk factors).[16] Such extreme consequences don't occur in most cases, but predicting which few children will react more severely is difficult and tricky.

The more commonplace (and less visible) reactions that victims experience in response to bullying are still important, yet risk being ignored when the term is used in situations characterized by little or no impact. Even in the absence of an outward manifestation of harm, being deliberately isolated and laughed at cruelly *every single day* can be devastating socially and academically, because the target must both endure the present and constantly dread the future, hovering like the sword of Damocles. It's this unrelenting cruelty and the callous nature of such an environment that is watered down when we include every social slight or quarrel under the bullying rubric.

Even worse, the weakening of the term can mean that children take bullying much less seriously. Watering down the seriousness of bullying is exactly the opposite of what we want—but when we allow the overuse of the word, we contribute to that diminution.

Bullying is an Abuse Behavior

Probably the single-most-common confusion I see in the field is the mix-up between bullying and fighting. Fighting or quarreling is an equal-power conflict. Bullying is an abuse behavior that, like all abuse behaviors, occurs between a powerful aggressor and a target who lacks the power to fight back.[17] In fact, some researchers have argued that what we call "bullying" would be better described as "peer abuse."[18] Like all abuse victims, targets of bullying can behave in some characteristic ways—for example, they may outwardly minimize bullying and refuse adult help, because their primary fear is retaliation. Few police officers today, called to a domestic abuse situation, would accept a beaten wife's reassurance that she is "just fine" and simply turn around and leave. We understand that an abused wife fears retaliation and thus minimizes her distress; we understand that she's not saying that it's just fine to be beaten. Targets of bullying who tell adults "we're just goofing around" or "I don't mind, we're friends" may likewise be trying to minimize their own victimization. When adults attempt to mediate situations characterized by an imbalance of power, bullies and abusers who are succeeding in their dominance over their victim also show characteristic behaviors. They have a strong incentive to feign cooperation during a mediation, but this doesn't always mean that once out of sight, they'll truly comply. Understanding that bullying is an abuse behavior can be a key factor in interpreting these reactions correctly.

We Lack Information About Identification and Responses

Many, if not most, of us saw or experienced bullying as a child, and it's natural that as adults we should be on the lookout for the kind of overt, often physical bullying behaviors that we saw when we were young. But a glance at newer data shows us that bullying today, in the majority of cases, does not involve physical contact.[19] My own studies, along with a number of others, show the overwhelming tendency to now use psychological methods, including those I call *gateway behaviors* (more on this in chapter 2). Because so much of bullying today is psychological, we need to know much more accurately what to look for, and what to respond to.

Related to the issue of what to look for is the profound impact of the digital revolution upon the lives of children today. This constant digital communication is juxtaposed with what is actually a pretty low level of knowledge (and sometimes, maturity). Children may easily learn which buttons to push, but they often fail to understand the *impact* of electronic communications—despite their myriad and apparently effortless use of electronic devices. The fact is that digital devices change *how* we communicate, not just how often we communicate. I'll talk about this in the second half of the book in much more detail. For now, I'll point out that children easily absorb cognitive patterns that help them effortlessly use new technology; yet at the same time, they are less conscious of what information is missing in digital communications, and how the thinness of that interaction can contribute to social problems that are manifested both online and in school.

It's safe to say that both the growth in nonphysical bullying techniques and the proliferation of electronic communications have had an enormous impact on children and their bullying behaviors. The bad news is that we are only now—after more than a decade and a half of ravenous digital consumption—beginning to understand these issues. But the good news is that data are clear and consistent about the kind of behaviors we need to look for in school. In addition, the struggle that children appear to be having with technology is *not* a technological issue per se. Children need help in understanding how to send and interpret accurate communications. Estimating the impact of what you write (or post) is a skill related to *life experience*—happily, it's not a technical skill.

Formal discipline cannot be the only response

You can't respond to bullying if you don't know what to look for. We all know how to respond to the more obvious, "old-fashioned" type of bullying: if we see children in a physical altercation, we pull them apart, investigate, and discipline accordingly. But what if the problem isn't so apparent? How do you discipline someone who uses a psychological tactic that isn't against any rules (like rolling their eyes or ignoring someone)? How can schools discipline if the bullying is *only* happening online (i.e., out of their jurisdiction)?

When we're upset, in a bullying case, it's tempting to focus solely on formal discipline. It's absolutely true that formal discipline may play a key role in responding to an incident of bullying.[20] But discipline alone is *not enough of an answer*. For one thing, it is a *reaction*; it is not a method of *prevention*. We cannot depend on it to address every need. In addition to the use of formal discipline, we need to know what should precede it to prevent both bullying and cyberbullying.

Bullying and Cyberbullying: Neither Separate nor Equal

Because of the obvious ways that cyberbullying is separate from bullying, it can be challenging to see how they impact each other. But by now, many adults realize that bullying and cyberbullying are not two different and unrelated types of bullying. Every year that children grow, the proportion of cases that involve both bullying and cyberbullying increases.[21] To appreciate the interaction, though, it can be helpful to begin with the many ways that digital communication changes how we communicate and thus, in turn, changes the social interactions that ensue both online and offline. Kids don't see the school hallways and cyberspace as separate; for them, messaging and social media are just other ways of talking, and the internet is just another place where they see their friends. The profound impact that using technology has on cognitions and emotions is an area of knowledge that we're only just beginning to mine. The fact that this issue is still being defined, twenty years after the birth of social media, is reflected in the uncomfortable truth that researchers have yet, as of 2023, to arrive at a widely agreed-upon definition of *cyberbullying*.[22]

Teaching Children to Address These Issues on Their Own

Deciding when to react, and how not to overreact, to children's interactions—in person or online—definitely can be another challenge. On the one hand, it's clear that bullying and cyberbullying are behaviors we must address with children. On the other hand, it's an indisputable fact that occasional and mild mean behaviors are an inevitable part of life, and every child must learn to cope with such problems successfully. Actually, uncomfortable as it is, we *want* children to be exposed to mild meanness, because they must have practice in dealing with unpleasant people. We can always help children learn to cope with cruelty, but how can they do this if adults intervene in every incident, no matter how minor? If we accept that some things should be left to the kids to resolve, then what should trigger adult intervention? Every hurt feeling? Surely not. Seriously hurt feelings? Probably, but the nature of our intervention may depend on the circumstances. Repetitively hurt feelings? More likely. How can children learn to control these behaviors between themselves, if adults shoulder the entire responsibility for prevention? When mean behaviors are relatively mild, do we address the target, the aggressor, both, or neither? It's clear that adults have to correct antisocial behaviors, protect children from egregious harm, and help children cope emotionally when a peer is mean. But it can't just be about what we, the adults, need to do. We need to think about ways to empower kids to be coleaders in addressing bullying and cyberbullying—and part of that strength must come from being an active part of the solution.

Both the Message and the Messenger Matter

Information doesn't occur in a vacuum, of course. The context of the message and the messenger determine the relative impact of a communication. When issues are viewed by children as being of concern only to adults, and not to peers, the "gag factor" may enter into play (i.e., it may be more socially advantageous for children to disparage the message rather than to agree with it). Choosing a messenger with high status (i.e., one whose message is socially advantageous to adopt) can definitely increase effectiveness. Put plainly, a high-status peer can influence values about social interactions better than the vast majority of adults.[23]

Kids and the gag factor

Many bullying prevention programs are probably more effective than children give them credit for; even programs that middle schoolers contemptuously dismiss may be planting seeds that bloom at some later point. But it's still true that the most effective antibullying messages are those that genuinely reflect children's and teens' perspectives and experiences. That's the reason that programs led by kids, for kids, are among the most successful.[24] At MARC, we train graduate and undergraduate students to work with kids in grades K–12 under the assumption that a message they bring will be more genuine and more powerful than that message from any older adult—even the "coolest." However it's done, though, it's important to try to get past students' sense that adults do not understand, and cannot speak to, their life experiences.

This is never more important than when discussing digital life with kids. A cringe-worthy example is a well-intended, adult-led discussion about misusing email (which most kids don't use with peers) or expressing puzzlement about the appeal of social networking. You might as well wear a blinking neon sign that reads, *I Don't Get It.* Even when adults do "get it," having high-status peers deliver the message can endow it with more oomph.

Misleading slogans

Of course, ultimately the message matters as much (if not more) than the messenger. Most educators today have heard (and probably repeated) the mantra, "Tell an adult." I realize that this slogan is intended to be helpful, and sometimes it probably is; but I also see a number of significant problems with it. First, the word *tell* is a loaded word for children, with all of its implications of tattling. The slogan itself utterly fails to acknowledge the serious difficulty of violating one of the core tenets of childhood: *never snitch.* Another problem with this mantra is that it has been overused past the point of saturation. "If I hear 'tell an adult' one more time," an especially articulate seventh-grade boy once told me, "I'm going to throw up on the shoes of the self-righteous grown-up who says it."

Widely used slogans like this aren't just ineffective; if they simply didn't work, I wouldn't mind them so much. But their shorthand, catchall use can actually undermine more important prevention messages. Instead of asking children who witness bullying, "How can you help?" the "tell an adult" mantra, used in isolation, says to all bystanders, "Never mind helping. You can abdicate all responsibility here. Just pass the buck to the adults." The incredibly important role of other children thus actually may be *undermined* by the widespread adoption of such brief but catchy slogans. If we emphasize to students that adults are the answer, and that children are not, and perhaps should not be involved in addressing bullying, then we've essentially told children that we don't expect them to hold much responsibility in their own community.

Finally, a third (pretty major) problem is that, used in isolation, the "tell an adult" mantra implies that telling an adult is a strategy that will succeed. According to research, that isn't necessarily true (more on this in chapter 7).[25] It's painful to think, and to write, but I've seen too many cases of bullying to imagine that adults can always solve these problems for kids. I don't like feeling helpless. But honesty compels me to conclude that adults probably cannot always guarantee a resolution when children face such situations—and that makes me careful not to recommend *only* "telling an adult."

A similarly ubiquitous slogan is to "involve bystanders." But not all bullying episodes include bystanders. And when they do, are they the only peers who matter? What about the children who may not have actually witnessed bullying, but who knew about it, or who befriended (and thus empowered) a bully? What about the target's friends, or other friendly allies? The focus on *bystanders* doesn't always include them.

Of course, the idea that those who are physically present could actually stop or intervene in the bullying and report to adults is an appealing one. But although we tend to assume those strategies are helpful, hard data have made researchers question their actual success. This suggests to me that we may lack traction with this problem because we need to better understand the circumstances in which either intervening or reporting to adults actually helps with bullying situations. Although a great deal of the discussion about bullying prevention does emphasize intervening or telling an adult, I think we need to understand more before we can truly and effectively empower those bystanders and peers.

Bias: The issue that is sometimes missing

All bullying isn't the same. In fact, kids who are targeted because of bias or prejudice are significantly more traumatized by a bullying incident.[26] Moreover, bias-based bullying is clearly on the rise. The Federal Bureau of Investigation (FBI) measured a 25 percent increase in hate speech in K–12 schools in 2016, and a second, similar, increase in 2017.[27] My research also showed a significant increase; between 2014 and 2019, I recruited subjects each year to study the perceived motivations of any "bully" who targeted them. These motivations were classified as either "not bias-based" (e.g., if someone reported being targeted because they were dating the aggressor's ex-boyfriend); "bias-based" (e.g., if a subject was targeted because of their race); or "possibly bias-based" (e.g., if a subject reported being targeted for unclear reasons that might or might not involve bias, such as "because of the way I looked"). Like the FBI, I found that in 2014 and 2015, approximately one-third of the incidences reported involved "bias" motivations (i.e., race, ethnic identity, religion, sexual orientation, immigrant status); but by 2019, that proportion had increased to 49 percent. This increase almost certainly accounts for part of the reason we aren't as effective as we'd like to be; thus, learning more about bias-based bullying is essential today.

WHAT CAN THIS BOOK DO FOR YOU?

This book is different because it needs to be. Let me begin by telling you what it *won't* do. It won't show you instant solutions, or one simple step that will always work. It won't turn you into an expert in social media. It can't make all adults—or all children—behave themselves. This book *will*, however, be *directly useful*—offering perspectives that are concrete, grounded in research, up to date, practical, and realistic.[28]

One of the paradoxes I've discovered in working with parents and educators is that our childhood experiences with social cruelty can cause us to misdirect our responses to the bullying we see between students. Painful memories of being bullied may spur adults to seek simple, immediate solutions—but such a complex problem defies simplicity and takes time to solve. While I'm not going to review each and every potential theory, overall, the book should give the reader a good grasp on the complexity of the issue. With so many different facets, laying the entire problem at the door of a single factor can be tempting, but such an approach isn't likely to result in an effective response.

The pain of bullying is real, and pain always impels us to seek a rapid response. But changing a school climate isn't typically a fast operation, and social factors may work against us. For example, one type of bully today is a student who is popular and socially powerful. This fact often leaves students with the (sometimes correct) impression that being cruel is one way to increase social status. Because of the ingrained nature of this belief among kids, and because living with abusiveness leads to the general expectation that abusiveness and aggression are normal life circumstances, truly changing a school's psychological and social climate is, by necessity, something of a journey. I don't have any magic tricks to reveal, but the knowledge and behaviors that educators need to make a real difference can be found here. Expecting rapid, easy transformation is rarely if ever in the cards.

Ultimately, we can and should still expect to teach children that general civility is a centrally important social behavior. We hear a lot about respect, but I would argue that respect can be viewed as a positive sense of another person's value, a feeling you have inside of you for someone else. I don't see how we can require children to *feel* certain things. I do know, though, that we can require them to *behave* respectfully—that is, to adopt certain social manners that facilitate peaceful interactions and arrest hurtful behaviors. Requiring children to behave civilly, even if they don't like someone, does not mean that we don't care how they feel. It means that we're teaching them to care how *other* people feel.

But to teach kids successfully, we need to know what to look for; how to respond to it in a way that prevents both bullying and cyberbullying; how and when to wield formal discipline; and how to encourage appropriate assertiveness and self-efficacy in children, while at the same time, promoting those positive emotional connections with adults and peers that are so protective.

During the past thirty years, I've studied children, their social lives, their abusiveness toward each other, and the intersection between their face-to-face contact and their digital interactions. In making these studies, both anecdotally and in research, I've begun to better understand how to help others understand the phenomenon that we call bullying and cyberbullying. The goal of this book is to help *you* understand it, too. Read on.

CHAPTER 1

The New Face of Bullying

Understanding "Gateway Behaviors"

Bullying can be a single incident (laws in New Jersey, New Hampshire, and Australia).

Bullying is not generally considered a random act or a single incident.

—Special Edition School Bullying[1]

IDENTIFYING BULLYING: SIMPLE ON PAPER, DIFFICULT IN REAL LIFE

You may already have run across one or another of the classic definitions of bullying, most of which refer to three characteristics that are generally agreed on as present in bullying cases.[2] These three characteristics, in and of themselves, aren't complex:

- *Power imbalance*: The child who is the bully wields greater power—usually as a result of high social status.[3]
- *Repeated occurrence*: Bullying happens repeatedly—it's not a one-time encounter, not even a one-time cruel encounter.
- *Intentionality*: Bullying is not an accident or an incident misinterpreted as an act of cruelty. Bullying is a dysfunctional relationship between two children. These children may or may not "know" each other in the traditional sense, but they do interact repeatedly.

Power imbalance. Repetitive. Intentional. In theory, once you know these three characteristics, you should be able to identify bullying immediately. But the usefulness of this abstract approach is limited. None of these elements is actually so clear and simple in the field, although all three are often presented as though they were. Clues can help reveal a *power imbalance*, if you know what to look for (more on that later). *Repetition* is easy if you see bullying repeatedly, but if you see it once, how do you know whether it's the first time or the hundred and first time? *Intention* is an internal process, not outwardly visible, and different children interpret the intentions of others differently. It's also true that before even trying to judge power imbalance, repetition, and intention, you first have to recognize that a behavior could be bullying. It was easier to spot the overt physical manhandling that used to characterize bullying; today, students are safer physically, but recognizing the new behaviors is more challenging.

IT'S NOT THE BULLYING OF TWENTY YEARS AGO, PART I: GATEWAY BEHAVIORS

In decades past, kids who bullied tended to be physically large, relatively weak academically, and not particularly admired by other kids in school.[4] Bullying frequently involved overt physical altercations during child-only interactions that happened away from the purview of adults. But the world has changed, and although today's adults may have grown up in a world in which bullying was more likely to involve a blatant, physical behavior, their children live in an environment in which they are more closely supervised and in which unconcealed physical threats or attacks are much less likely to be tolerated. Today's digital communications also provide a ready staging area for bullying and aggression. Because of all this, bullying today has evolved predominantly into forms of psychological, social cruelty, which as an attack method has the advantage of requiring neither a large physique, personal physical risk, nor child-only privacy away from adults.

The difficulty is that many adults may notice only obvious behaviors, like the physical bullying of yesteryear, and subsequently they miss what's happening right in front of them—dismissing it, despite the best of intentions, as something much less serious. When the overt behavior lacks drama, it's understandable to assume it has little impact. Adults may fail to realize that contemporary bullies tend to perfect understated methods for demonstrating dominance and contempt for their target *without* drawing obvious attention from adults by breaking concrete rules. Old-fashioned bullying is risky today. Threatening someone with a fist will almost certainly bring detection and punishment, and the reduced time spent away from adult supervision means fewer opportunities to jostle others. However, bullies can still reliably put targets in their place in full view of peers and adults by using subtle behaviors such as whispering about them right in front of them, snickering as they walk by, or rolling their eyes when they voice an opinion in class. These rude, socially malicious behaviors are definitely *not* always indicators of bullying (only when they're intentionally and repetitively targeted at a less powerful peer), but regardless of their purpose, they can be done anywhere. In 2019, I studied 1,404 schoolchildren in grades 3 through 5. In that study, the playground was the most common site of in-school bullying, but the classroom was a close second.[5] Stan Davis and Charisse Nixon's subjects also reported that the classroom was a frequent location for bullying.[6] The more that gateway behaviors move into the mainstream rooms and hallways of schools, the more normal they feel to the children and adults who occupy those spaces.

Today's increased supervision of children, despite being well intentioned and probably keeping children safer in many ways, may have unwittingly contributed to the normalization of bullying behaviors by requiring bullies to adopt methods that can be used in more public areas. These changes also mean that adult advice on handling bullies may not only be outdated but also counterproductive. A generation or two ago, it wasn't unusual to advise children to hit a bully, to demonstrate that you weren't an easy target. Hitting a bully back may have been a viable option in 1975, but today, a target who hits back is liable to immediately land in hot water and could then occupy the unenviable position of being in trouble with both the bully *and* the adults.

Rates of Gateway Behaviors Versus Physical Bullying

I call these psychologically contemptuous, rude behaviors *gateway behaviors*, because they're used as "beginning" or low-level, low-risk ways of asserting power or expressing contempt. Left unchecked, bullying behaviors can escalate, both in frequency and in quality.[7] The research findings agree with fieldwork observations—today, gateway behaviors are used substantially more often than other, more obvious types of bullying behaviors. In all my research over the last decade, subjects have been much less likely to report being victimized by a physical bully than by a bully using gateway behaviors.[8] In fact, only about one in ten victims have reported being physically bullied; the rest were victimized through psychological weaponry, including cruel digital behaviors (which, for obvious reasons, are always psychological).

In the course of my career, I've been asked several times why we should characterize any laugh or eyeroll as "bullying." Isn't this precisely the overuse of the term that I often warn against? It's a good point, and it's important to remember that gateway behaviors are used in all kinds of unpleasant social interactions, including to show someone you're mad at them or because you're in a bad mood. By themselves, gateway behaviors don't always mean it's a bullying situation. For these behaviors to be counted as *bullying*, they must meet the three criteria and also be rated as significantly upsetting.

Although not all gateway behaviors are bullying, most bullying does appear to involve the use of gateway behaviors. Data are consistent year to year. In 2012, only 6 percent of subjects reported being victims of physical bullying while in high school, but 34 percent reported being victims of distressing rumors or lies and 32 percent reported being victimized through pointed, public exclusion.[9] Other recent studies have found similar proportions of physical versus nonphysical bullying.[10] The Youth Voice Project found that psychological bullying was much more common than physical bullying in a sample of thirteen thousand students.[11] A study I conducted between 2020 and 2022, of 2,427 youth in Massachusetts, Colorado, and Virginia, found that while "only" 11 percent reported being physically victimized by bullying during high school or middle school, 25 percent reported being moderately or severely cyberbullied online.[12] There seems to be little doubt that physical bullying is taking a back seat in this century.

Taken individually, gateway behaviors seem common and innocuous; it's certainly true that having teachers fill out a three-page bullying report form every time a seventh grader rolls her eyes would bring every middle school in America to a screeching halt. *Gateway behaviors in and of themselves don't constitute bullying.* Infrequent use of such behaviors in a nonsystematic way is just evidence of the periodic meanness between children that everyone must learn to deal with. But it's the *continually repeated* and *targeted* use by powerful peers, with the intent to demean and harass, that truly creates bullying victims. Being targeted frequently and repeatedly was, in fact, the factor most strongly associated with being particularly vulnerable to bullying in the 2012 Massachusetts Aggression Reduction Center (MARC) freshman study. Anecdotally, not a few teens have told me that they'd rather just be hit. "At least that way you get it over with," one teenage boy pointed out to me, "but this just goes on and on. It never stops and no one notices it and you have to feel like c**p every single day."

All freshman subjects in the 2012 study were asked which type of bullying they felt was the most serious. It's interesting that subjects who had never been victims rated physical and psychological bullying as having a similar impact (or physical bullying as more serious); but subjects who had been targets rated psychological bullying as far more severe. Similarly, to the adult eye, gateway behaviors may appear mild and even insignificant, but they're clearly quite significant when continuously aimed at a much less socially powerful peer.

This evolution toward the use of gateway behaviors as preferred bullying tactics didn't come out of nowhere. As noted earlier, it's not just that adult expectations around supervision and aggression have changed; children are also raised notably differently today, with two particularly important changes. One is the reduction in child-directed playtime spent only among other children and away from the direct coaching of adults; the other, the obvious influence of digital communications. It's possible that the changes in the way that children are being raised have affected their social skills, including their willingness to be socially cruel.[13]

How Do I Tell if It's Bullying?

As I have pointed out, it's virtually impossible that every gateway behavior used in your school is a manifestation of bullying. Much of the time, these behaviors are used to be mean in passing or even just to tease. So, how do you know when you're seeing true bullying? I'll tip my hand by saying that, first, you don't always *need* to know if something is definitely bullying; and second, no hard-and-fast rules will allow everyone to reliably detect intention, repetition, and a power imbalance. My point is that it's easy to list *abstract* characteristics of bullying, but when we're looking at actual people, such a list is not terribly useful. You may see a cruel act without knowing if it's the first time it's happened or the hundredth, or whether the behavior is the result of carelessness or deliberate intent.

Candidly acknowledging the limitations inherent in the formal, abstract definition does not imply theoretical weaknesses, but it does reveal the need to operationalize the concept and make it much more useful in real life. As I'll discuss next, while it's difficult to judge an internal process like intention, clues can help detect other characteristics, such as repetition and power imbalance.

Assessing power imbalance

As previously noted, it used to be that seeing a physically large child manhandling a smaller classmate was a pretty obvious indication of bullying. But because most children's power today is derived from social status (not physical size), it's important to consider any known differences in social power (popularity and social status) between the children involved.

A recent meta-analysis of eighteen studies found that bullies were more popular than other kids, but they were also at risk for being socially rejected.[14] In my research, subjects who reported that they were able to exploit bullying successfully for their own social gain rated themselves as significantly more popular than other children.[15] Thus, the first possible red flag is the existence of social differences between the two students: either one student is much more popular than the other, or the alleged target may belong to a socially vulnerable group. Popular kids and groups vary from school to school, but vulnerable categories of kids are more consistent to identify. For example, special needs children who are mainstreamed, especially those with emotional and behavioral disorders, are often vulnerable, with low social power.[16] Among older children, it's common for students who identify (or who are identified, accurately or not) as gay, lesbian, bisexual, transgender, or queer (LGBTQ) to be socially vulnerable and subjected disproportionately to bullying, and these youth were particularly vulnerable during the pandemic.[17] Consistent with other research, in the 2020–2022 Social and Emotional Research Consortium (SERC) study of 2,427 youth, LGBTQ subjects were about twice as likely to report being victims of bullying, compared with students who did not identify themselves as LGBTQ (although because of low numbers, that difference wasn't statistically significant).[18]

Another red flag that reveals a possible power imbalance is the way a target responds to adult offers of help. Bullying targets, like other abuse victims, tend to respond in characteristic ways.[19] You might expect that a child who is being targeted by a bully would gratefully welcome adult offers to help with the situation. But children who are being bullied, similar to adults who are being abused, may simply fail to respond at all when approached by adults (even with offers of support); they may minimize a situation ("we were only goofing around") or even defend the bully by begging a teacher to avoid a consequence ("don't get [the bully] in trouble"). Adults are often reassured (sometimes falsely) by these responses and accept them as proof that bullying isn't occurring, instead of seeing them as a possible indicator that the target does not feel free to speak candidly, especially in front of a bully. Probably the most powerful tip-off is when the adult has a strong sense that bullying is going on— perhaps he or she saw something actually happen, or knows that these two kids aren't really friends, and that one is much more socially powerful than the other—but both students deny there's a problem. A suspicious denial doesn't necessarily mean that there is a problem. Similarly, though, it doesn't always mean that there *isn't* a problem. In an unequal-power conflict, one student is much too fearful to blame the more powerful peer.

Power imbalances may sometimes reveal themselves, but intention is a purely internal process, and thus isn't likely to be apparent. When children are being mean, they use visible behaviors to hurt others (such as a cutting remark or snarky laughter). The difficulty is that they also use similar behaviors in much less insidious circumstances—when they're teasing or being mean just once. It's thus often hard to tell when someone is bullying, because a bully may use the *same behaviors* as someone who's just teasing or being occasionally mean. The differences are internal (the student's intent to wage a repeated campaign). So when adults see cruelty such as gateway behaviors, how can we assess intent, and thus know that it's bullying?

Assessing intention

Intention, because it's an internal process, is probably the most difficult element to judge from overt behavior. Even if we had some way to literally view an aggressor's intention, the perceptual differences between targets could result in one interpreting a behavior as intentional meanness, and another experiencing the identical behavior as benign. I vividly recall a little girl telling me that a boy in her tennis class was being deliberately mean. "How do you know he was trying to be mean?" I asked. "He was lobbing a ball at me when we played," she replied. She was interpreting lobbing as intentional spite. Other children might see this only as reflecting their opponent's lack of skill.

Consistent with these field observations, my research also noted that assessing intention in a strictly objective manner is probably impossible. In the lab, I found that different people attributed different intentions to the exact same behavior. In my 2012 freshman study, I showed subjects a picture of two girls laughing. Only 12 percent of nonvictims felt that the girls were probably bullying someone; but 22 percent of the victims in the study attributed the laughing to bullying. Of course, it's not only that students might attribute a mean intent to a neutral action; the other side of that coin is that some children fail to register cruelty even when it is intentionally directed at them. Either way, judging intention from external behavior seems, at best, an iffy business.

Assessing repetition

Perhaps you've decided that, indeed, red flags merit further investigation into a situation, or maybe it's just your sixth sense that's tingling, and you want to explore a student's circumstances further. Perhaps parents, or others, have reported a situation to you and your job is to figure out if it is, indeed, bullying. The logical next step is to consider whether the situation has occurred only once or is being repeated.[20] As I've noted, most researchers studying bullying regard "true" bullying as an ongoing, abusive relationship between children.[21] This is a frequent source of confusion, especially for parents, who may label any hurtful behavior as bullying. Although one-time actions aren't technically bullying, they can be a first step toward a new bullying campaign, and parents have a legitimate need for reassurance that any hurtful act should, and will, be taken seriously. For these reasons, Davis has argued that whether or not an incident is bullying shouldn't be the primary consideration in formulating a response, particularly an initial response.[22]

It's also important to distinguish, when possible, between problems that are ongoing but detected only for the first time, and problems that are genuinely one-time incidents. Just because an incident is the first time a child has *reported* bullying doesn't mean that it's the first time it has happened.

The bottom line: The child may know things that he hasn't disclosed to you, and he may be the only source likely or able to divulge that information. The only way to tap that vein is to develop enough of a connection with the student that he is likely to tell you the entire history. If you suspect that a child may be experiencing repeated episodes of cruelty, but you're not sure whether the child would divulge such information to you personally, the most responsible course of action is locating an adult who can be comfortably confided in. That person may or may not be you. (Don't misinterpret this as a criticism. The chemistry that unfolds between you and the children you teach is not entirely in your control.)

Dealing with Gateway Behaviors

Combining the predominance of gateway behaviors with our general inability to know the internal characteristics of bullying (like intention) reveals the difficulty of knowing when you're seeing bullying. True, gateway behaviors are used to bully, but they're also used to tease and to be mean just once. So how can an adult tell the difference? It's those covert factors (repetition, power imbalance, and intention) that differ between teasing and bullying situations—not the overt behaviors. If you see a student being denied a seat at a cafeteria table, you probably won't be able to tell whether it's the first time this has happened. Similarly, you may not know if the kids are simply mad at each other that day, or if an ongoing campaign is being waged. Sometimes you may observe clues about a power imbalance, and sometimes you may see repetition. But much of the time no such clues are in evidence. If you ask the child who was denied the seat, she's likely to say that it's okay with her, or not a big deal. Ask the kids at the table, and they're apt to deny the whole thing. Report the incident as "bullying," and you'll be asked for evidence of repetition, intention, and power imbalance—evidence you likely can't produce. The fact is, you simply saw a mean act; categorizing it on that basis alone is almost impossible.

Even though you may not be able to definitively label a situation as bullying, teasing, or just being mean, the good news is that you can still respond effectively. The solution is to focus on what you can see—the behaviors—instead of what you can't see—the internal motives and feelings. When the outward behaviors that you notice are breaking a school rule, you know what to do: follow the school's protocols (e.g., send them to the principal's office). So far, so good. Gateway behaviors are trickier precisely because they *don't* break school rules. In those cases, the student is obeying the letter of the law but is still behaving in a *socially inappropriate* way—and it's the inappropriateness of that behavior that calls for a brief but effective response. Consider this: it's fine (even nice) for kids to laugh along with peers, but it's socially inappropriate to laugh pointedly *at* someone. My argument is that because of the strong connection between social behaviors and social climates, socially cruel behaviors absolutely require a response, *regardless* of intent. Yet it's still true that exclusion and eye-rolls, by themselves, are small transgressions. So even if they're sometimes used to bully, why focus on them?

The best analogy I can think of is littering. Imagine that you're sitting on a beautiful beach, enjoying the sun, the waves, and the white sand. Now imagine that that same beach is covered with litter. Even though the positive elements are still present (waves, sun, sand), you wouldn't be able to enjoy them anymore; instead, you would be entirely focused on avoiding touching the disgusting garbage that's all around you. Gateway behaviors are the litter of the social climate. Regardless of intent or purpose, they shouldn't be happening, because they make the psychological landscape dirty and unpleasant. In chapter 6, I talk about exactly what you need to do when responding, and why educators need to respond even to behaviors that don't overtly break any rules.

One final point about the deceptively "minor" nature of gateway behaviors: Although an action may look like "no big deal" to an outsider, from the perspective of a targeted child who knows that it is a bullying situation, any adult's lack of response can feel like a callous emotional betrayal. This difference in perspective between students and educators isn't confined to physical encounters. What happens in a digital environment can, similarly, feel incredibly hurtful to children, while barely registering for many adults.

IT'S NOT THE BULLYING OF TWENTY YEARS AGO, PART II: CYBERBULLYING

Almost two-thirds (65 percent) of the subjects in the 2012 freshman study told us that during their time in high school, no adult even asked about the possibility of cyberbullying when discussing a bullying situation with them. In the 2019 freshman study, students were reporting that they heard from adults about digital technology; but the most common messages they heard were simply dire warnings about not limiting their future opportunities or being careful about privacy. The possibility of online bullying, emotional intensity of digital interactions, anxiety in social media use, or conflict in gaming were much less likely to come up. It's true that many younger teachers today grew up taking the cell phone for granted, but they still typically lack the completely cyber-immersed childhoods of today's students. For anybody over twenty-five (as of this writing), perceiving how much face-to-face behaviors can intersect with those perpetrated with a keyboard or touchscreen may not be intuitive. Even in 2023, I am often asked to speak on bullying *or* cyberbullying, as though these were two completely separate and different events. Even though interacting in person obviously isn't the same as typing messages to someone or posting a comment on a website, one type of communication can affect the other. But the question isn't only whether bullying and cyberbullying are disconnected from each other, we also need think about how digital environments change how we communicate, and how those digital communications feed, interact, and interplay with in-school encounters.

Gateway Behaviors in Digital Environments

Obviously, no direct physical bullying occurs online or through texting, but serious threats still contrast markedly with a general plethora of mildly nasty or thoughtless remarks. For example, a cyberbully could threaten to hurt the target or someone close to the target (a family member or a friend) or get someone into serious trouble (e.g., reporting the target for a crime he or she didn't commit). Comparing serious and milder threats online in the 2020–2022 freshman SERC study shows the same pattern that's seen in face-to-face events: only 22 percent of the students reported that they had received a *serious* threat online (either in middle or high school), and explicit online threats of physical violence were reported by only 6 percent of boys and 5 percent of girls. We found significant gender differences: 14 percent of boys received a serious threat, compared with 60 percent who experienced a milder action, such as name calling, mean comments, or embarrassing photos posted online. Among girls, 26 percent reported serious threats, compared with 42 percent who reported milder problems. Youth who were not cisgender (e.g., transitioning or gender fluid) reported the most problems online: 60 percent reported a serious threat, and virtually all reported a milder online problem. Overall, like bullying in school, cyberbullying appears to be dominated by incidents that, taken individually, represent less extreme but still hurtful behaviors. Also like more traditional bullying, it may be the accumulation of individually small actions that cause some of the more serious harm. Moreover, it's clear that different types of youth experience very different types of cyberbullying, and again like bullying in school, some are clearly more vulnerable than others.

How Do I Tell if it's Cyberbullying?

When you see a situation unfold in front of you in school, clues can help alert you to a power imbalance between two children. Furthermore, children's social status—and thus their social power—in school tends to be a relatively stable characteristic. This helps us detect and assess power imbalances in general. In a digital environment, the power imbalance between actors is rarely stable, and thus is often challenging to pin down. What's not always simple in person is often even more complicated online.

In a commonly cited digital power grab, the online attacker remains anonymous. Anonymity is frequently cited as a preferred mechanism for gaining power over one's victim, and it's true that an anonymous cyberbully can cause a lot of distress. But it may actually be a relatively unusual way for bullies to gain power, at least during adolescence. In my study of twenty-seven thousand schoolchildren, I found that by high school, three-quarters (74 percent) of cyberbullying victims *knew* the identity of their cyberbully; anonymity may be theoretically desirable as a power mechanism from a bully's point of view, but in practice, it seems to be unusual between teens.[23] More recent research on 1,103 youth found that anonymity is only a factor in cyberbullying among teens who are morally disengaged; for most youth, it's not so relevant.[24] Thus, relying on anonymity as an important source of online power may be a red herring.

One of the fascinating things about digital environments is how much online power is fluid and changeable. As I pointed out, social power in school tends to be a stable quality; popular first graders usually grow into popular fifth graders and popular tenth graders.[25] But in cyberspace, power differentials can shift quickly and dramatically. Thus, even if a situation at school seems to involve a stable power imbalance, the roles can change once the students go digital. In fact, cyberbullying is not always clearly associated with social status at all.[26] A study of 899 children between eleven and sixteen years old found that a subject's social group status may be more predictive of cyberbullying then their individual social power. It's not only that power online becomes more complex; it's also that digital incidents themselves can shift in character. Almost half of the subjects (46 percent) in 2011 reported that once bullying went digital, the incident shifted to a more equal-power fight.[27] Online, students were more apt to use tactics they might have felt too timid to use in person, such as seeking revenge, fighting back, getting their friends to help them, or simply "deciding that the bully didn't really have any power over me." Because that online change in power, in turn, can affect what's happening at school, adults need to be conscious of these situations, which means routinely inquiring whether a problem between students has migrated into cyberspace. The older your students are, the more likely their answer will be yes.

Is Cyberbullying Actually Bullying?

Before we continue, it's important to note that the harassment that occurs online may often not fit our traditional three criteria for bullying (repetition, intent, and power imbalance).[28] It's not only that power imbalances can shift unpredictably online; the difficulty is also that although the target may *experience* those three criteria, an alleged cyberbully may never have *intended* them. To illustrate what I'm talking about, imagine a more traditional (in-person) bullying scenario. A boy is bullying a target in a school hallway; he does this every day just before recess. The three elements of bullying can be identified here: the interaction is repeated; the bully knows and sees that he has an audience, which enables him to demonstrate his superior power; and clearly he's not being cruel by accident. His victim would likely completely agree with this assessment.

At times, digital behaviors closely resemble in-school bullying in that aggressor and target largely agree on intention and outcomes. Imagine, for example, a student who sets up a social media group committed to "The Group Who Hates Sally Smith." That aggressor clearly intends to be hurtful; the group regularly updates with new content, so she intends the hurt to be repetitive, and because she invites others to become "members" of the group or web page, she's clearly looking for the audience to admire her power. But many other times, what the so-called cyberbully actually intends is much less clear, and the target may experience the harassment completely differently. Suppose a student posts a maliciously funny image on Facebook about another student. In this case, the aggressor, who's trying to be funny, sends the image to two of his buddies. They think it's hilarious and forward it on to dozens of other students. You could certainly argue that the creator of the meme *should* have realized that his snarky picture could get sent to many other people, but this action still probably wouldn't meet the criteria for bullying. The creator's intention wasn't to demonstrate his power or dominance, and although the picture was forwarded repetitively, he sent it out only once. He may not have even intended it to hurt the target, if he believed that the target would never know. However, the subject of that image might indeed experience what happened as bullying—the humiliating picture was sent and seen repeatedly and was certainly sent on purpose. The object of the "joke" is likely to feel markedly powerless as well, because once out on the internet, that image is essentially uncontrollable.

In 2022, a SERC study of 2,427 youth in Massachusetts, Colorado, and Virginia began to explore a new way of defining "cyberbullying," using criteria that took into account intention and severity to better understand what kids experience online. That research, analyzed by members of the Consortium, identified four different types of cyberbullying:

- minor—cruel online acts are perceived to be without intent to harm and aren't really significant (e.g., when something is unintentionally embarrassing);
- moderate—the action has intent to harm, but the digital action isn't serious (e.g., spreading a rumor online);
- severe—the action is both clearly intentional and serious (e.g., betraying secret, humiliating or very confidential information); and
- repeated severe—the severe action is part of an ongoing campaign (e.g., repeatedly attacking someone online is the most serious way possible).

This taxonomy appears to more accurately identify youth who suffer the consequences of increasingly serious forms of cyberbullying, and it avoids some of the problems inherent in attempting to use the definition of traditional bullying for online behaviors.[29]

Because the intent to hurt or bully can be absent or not apparent in a digital environment, the essential lesson is that it's critically important for children to understand the dynamics of communication in that type of environment—and how easily casual digital actions can escalate out of their control. From our perspective as adults, and as part of our attempts to understand bullying and cyberbullying behaviors, it behooves us to realize that the intent and effect of behaviors we call cyberbullying may be out of sync between the alleged bully and the target. Cyberbullying may have an impact on the victim that's similar to bullying because it may be experienced similarly, but the cyberbully and the bully may be two very different sorts. Assessing for cyberbullying, therefore, relies heavily on the subjective experience of the target—and we need to keep in mind that the *existence of a cyberbullying victim won't always imply the coexistence of an intentional cyberbully.*

WHAT COMPLICATES OUR ABILITY TO ELIMINATE BULLYING

Having laid out the process for detecting and discussing bullying and cyberbullying, I offer a caveat. In spite of our desire to make everything right for children, the truth is that certain factors limit our power to address abusive behaviors between them. Children interact both with and without adults present; our grown-up perspectives and judgments aren't always spot on; and the hard fact is that children need to experience some small degree of meanness to learn to cope with it. The reality of these limitations means that it's important to understand where the lines are drawn, what we can and cannot promise, and how to be genuine about those limits when we talk to children.

The Child-Only World

To completely understand the dynamics of bullying, adults would need full knowledge of 100 percent of the behaviors that happen between children. That's clearly unrealistic. As we've seen, even in closely supervised environments, many behaviors occur that adults may not recognize as bullying. Children also interact with each other in a child-only world, where adults don't rule and are often unaware of what happens.

That child-only world isn't a place, so much as a sort of alternative plane. Vivian Seltzer at the University of Pennsylvania has referred to this as the *peer arena*.[30] These child-only peer interactions are *influenced* by adult values and rules (children do carry their internalized beliefs with them between both worlds), but they are not entirely governed by them.

Children know that regardless of what happens in the adult world, they will still have to deal with interactions in the child-only world by themselves, without adult protection. We can supervise—to a point—when children are in the "adult" world. We can tell a child to stop bullying another child; we can watch and listen and supervise. But inevitably, those children will at times interact without our supervision. They'll pass each other in the hallways; they'll sit within view of each other in the same classroom; they'll interact on the playground and on school grounds after school; they'll see each other as they walk home, or ride the bus, or interact online. Even if the children are kept physically distant from each other, their friends and cohorts, and online interactions, may well form a link between the two players.

The bottom line: It's always possible that what appears, in our world, to be a one-time, unintentional event can actually be part of a pattern of intentional cruelty, the majority of which occurs in the child-only world where adult detection is unlikely. It's also theoretically possible to stop bullying where *we* live, while doing little more than slowing it down (if that) in the child-only world. It's true that children today spend less time there than did previous generations; one typical study found that mothers estimated they had more than twice as much unsupervised playtime as their own children.[31] In 1969, 42 percent of American children walked or biked to school alone and were unsupervised by adults; today, only 11 percent do.[32] Despite more recent adult efforts to support "risky" play (e.g., climbing and running), the child-only world is still diminished.[33]

The Issue of Perspective

Apart from child-only interactions, another complication arises in detecting bullying: the difference between child and adult perspectives. Adults may see a single incident of teasing as benign, not realizing it is part of an extremely hurtful pattern. Conversely, adults may perceive as "mean" behaviors that are regarded with indifference by their subjects. For example, about ten years ago, I was analyzing some data on online bullying with students and noticed that the boys were reporting situations that appeared to be cyberbullying at the astounding rate of *98 percent*. Recognizing what was obviously some sort of mistake, I explored the issue with a group of male students. They readily acknowledged regularly encountering what appear to be quite callous and cruel comments during online game play. The interesting twist was how they interpreted that type of chatter: instead of viewing it as bullying, they saw it as a type of game-related trash-talking, similar to the remarks often flung across basketball courts and in football lineups. Research I conducted on this, as well as studies done by other researchers, found that 75 percent of subjects reported that trash-talking definitely happens during online game play, but this isn't a personal attack akin to bullying.[34] Rather, it's a game-playing strategy and would happen to *anyone* the person was playing against.

This example brought home to me that sometimes a huge difference exists between what adults and kids perceive as bullying. However, the issue of perspective can be tricky. The circumstances may indeed not feel mean at all to the child, as in the gaming scenario. But a child who is a target may deny the problem for a variety of other reasons, which are not all simply a matter of perspective: they may fail to interpret the meanness correctly; at times targets (e.g., special needs children), fail to recognize that the behaviors aimed at them are actually abusive. Or they may downplay the seriousness of the situation and, like other abuse victims, may even side with the bully—not because the situation isn't serious, but because they greatly fear retaliation. These latter situations are clearly different from the gaming example. Sometimes "it's okay" means that it's truly all right; at other times, however, a reassurance might just reflect a lack of understanding or the possibility of retribution. The point is that if it appears alarming to you, a student's assurance that it's all fine doesn't completely rule out a problem.

This fact can render these situations confusing. Generally speaking, the first priority in responding is to be sensitive to the tendency of targets to downplay bullying situations in their efforts to protect themselves. But at the same time, keep a corner of your mind open to the possibility—especially in gaming situations—that what appears awful to the adult eye might not be experienced as abusive by the students. The trick, it would seem, is to utilize your rapport with the student to separate *false* minimization because of fear of retaliation from minimization because of a true lack of impact, either from genuine indifference or from a failure to appreciate the situation. Look for hints and consider histories that will allow you to decide if a lack of impact is real or feigned. The absence of factors such as strong self-confidence, a myriad of other support systems, or even special needs that affect social skills may suggest that a false minimization is happening and intervention is called for.

Learning to Navigate Social Challenges

We may wish we could ensure safety 100 percent of the time, including in that child-only world, but it's a wish we would probably regret if it were granted. Difficult as it is to acknowledge, child-only interactions have value as well as risk for most children. In the adult world, children are essentially powerless; it's in that child-only world where they get to flex their muscles and practice coping with explicit power differentials. It's true that someone has to be on the losing end of that interaction, and completely understandably, no one wants to see a child suffer. But if children were to grow up with literally no experience of meanness (either in themselves or in other peers), they might never develop the social coping skills needed to successfully navigate around it. These more challenging social exchanges probably help many children develop better skills for coping with social encounters. It is even theoretically possible that children's extreme reluctance to report to adults what happens in child-only exchanges essentially compels them to learn advantageous social skills.

What's so emotionally painful is that not all children benefit from the same kinds of life lessons. For example, children who have been previously abused may learn, from an episode of peer abuse, not to cope effectively but rather just to assume their role as victim. For some children, a typical peer interaction isn't going to be the setting in which they learn how to cope. For many others, it will be.

UNDERSTANDING THE BEHAVIOR ISN'T ENOUGH: WE NEED TO UNDERSTAND THE PLAYERS

When you throw a baseball, you throw a round white ball, and the catcher receives a round white ball. Every ball is white and round, and every pitcher and every catcher deals with the same thing. But when it comes to social behaviors, the pitcher can throw one thing and the catcher can catch something entirely different. What a target experiences from a bully depends both on what's actually being thrown and how the catcher interprets it. One boy may construe a spoken "Hi!" as friendly; another may see it as mocking. One girl may laugh along if others laugh at her; other girls might glower or become upset at precisely the same behavior.

Everyone knows that different people interpret or experience social behaviors differently. So, as this chapter has shown, when it comes to understanding bullying and cyberbullying, the recipient's perspective matters a great deal. We may know what the ball looks like now (e.g., gateway behaviors, cyber behaviors), but how often are these behaviors used to bully, and how often do intentional slings and arrows really hit their mark? Some targets become victims, just as a bully has intended; others are much more resilient. In the next chapter, the focus shifts from the ball (the actual behaviors) to the catcher. We need to look at not just what percentage of kids are bullied but also at how many of those kids are resilient, and what makes them that way. Meanness will always be with us, to some degree. We can't construct a world in which every child, no matter how vulnerable, is spared that. But we can try to construct children who are more resilient. In the real world, empowerment of targets is probably our most formidable defense.

CHAPTER 2

How Common Are Bullying and Cyberbullying, Anyway?

Parsing the Numbers to Identify—and Help—Children at Risk

The scope and effects of bullying are underestimated.

—Safe and Caring Schools[1]

Bullying is more common than previously thought.

—Ashley Psychology Center[2]

The level of playground bullying is being exaggerated.

—Anushka Asthana[3]

In 2006, an article in a medical journal discussed a concept known as "disease mongering."[4] The trouble emerges, the authors wrote, when a disease becomes widely covered in popular media, and competing estimates about its frequency can lead to an exaggerated sense of danger. Although the authors were writing about a different problem, bullying might be a victim of the same syndrome. Contributing to the possibility that some dangers may be underplayed while others are overestimated is the wide variety of estimates produced by different studies. Consider the following:

- A large study of thousands of children found that between 2005 and 2014, all types of bullying (including cyberbullying) appeared to decline.[5]
- In contrast, between 2016 and 2019, researchers at the Cyberbullying Research Center found that school bullying had increased. In their

2016 study, 39 percent reported being bullied at school; that increased to more than half of students in 2019.[6]

- During the global coronavirus pandemic, bullying declined and cyberbullying seemed to remain stable, with little or no change.[7]

It's definitely enough to make one's head spin, but let's put it through the juicer.

HOW OFTEN ARE KIDS ACTUALLY BULLIED IN PERSON?

Victimization rates for traditional bullying aren't really all that disparate. With the exception of a few extreme outliers (which typically use methods, such as self-selected subjects or specific groups), most percentages reported range from 23 percent to 32 percent of students reporting being bullied over one year.[8] But taking this estimate at face value misses an important point. It's clear, by now, that not all children experience bullying and cyberbullying alike. Some groups are decidedly more vulnerable (as I just noted). Tuhin Biswas's review pointed out that as well—that is, different areas of world appear to experience different rates of bullying, with Eastern Mediterranean and African nations reporting the highest rates. My point is that averages, whether it's within a school or within a nation, don't tell us everything. It's imperative that we explore, within any school or institution, *who* is most vulnerable and address the needs of those students.

Victimization rates may vary depending upon the age of the child as well. Most research is conducted on bullying among adolescents. In elementary-age student populations (as I noted), special needs children may be particularly vulnerable. One meta-analysis found that children with neurodevelopmental disorders do appear to face an elevated risk of bullying victimization.[9] Overall percentages are not, however, markedly different from somewhat older youth (at least among older elementary school-age children). My study of 1,404 children in grades 3 to 5 found that in 2019, 35 percent reported being bullied at school. Linda Beckman's review found that prevalence rates among elementary school-age students usually reached about 40 percent.[10] Having said that, a number of researchers found that during the pandemic rates of bullying among younger children declined, just as they did among older students.[11]

One of the most challenging groups to study are children in the early elementary years. In my own research of grade-school students, I don't examine K–2 children largely because their lack of literacy skills means that interviews are the only reliable method for measurements, and such interviews require more resources than typically are available. I do, however, have data from a pool of 1,940 parents, measured during 2011.[12] In that survey, 6 percent of kindergarten parents, 7 percent of first-grade parents, and 19 percent of second-grade parents reported that they were aware their child was being, or had been, bullied at school or online (and as we'll see, cyberbullying can indeed start this early). Although I prefer to emphasize statistics that come directly from the subjects, in this case, parent reports may be a reasonable approximation of the truth. The youngest children are actually the most likely to report everything to their parents, so parents of very young children may have, relatively speaking, the most accurate knowledge about their child's victimization.[13]

HOW OFTEN ARE KIDS ACTUALLY CYBERBULLIED?

Measuring cyberbullying prevalence is more confusing, because researchers don't have a widely agreed-upon definition.[14] As a result, estimates tend to range from the single digits to about half of youth, depending on the definition of cyberbullying used, the age of the child, the way the question is worded, and the time span studied. Researchers at the Cyberbullying Research Center point out that when they ask about lifetime prevalence, about 36.5 percent of teens say they have been cyberbullied. In contrast, when they ask about the past thirty days, only about 17.4 percent of teens report being bullied.[15]

The actual questions asked influence the results as well. Sometimes researchers simply ask, "Were you cyberbullied?" That question probably results in the lowest rates, given that some children may not identify online incidents as cyberbullying.[16] Other researchers list a few specific types of cyber behaviors, such as "texting cruel remarks" or "posting mean comments." My own research (which found 41 percent victimization rates) added to this list pressured or coerced sexting, posting false stories or lies, disseminating personal data that the target didn't want revealed, and being stalked electronically.[17] It stands to reason that the more types of cyberbullying a survey includes, the higher the likelihood that the subject will say "yes" to at least one of them. The tricky part is being aware of different types of cyberbullying, as children rarely discuss these with adults. Because our knowledge of cyberbullying is only developing, and the potential types of cyberbullying are changing constantly, it's particularly difficult to keep track of different ways that a subject might have been victimized. Through the Massachusetts Aggression Reduction Center's (MARC's) exposure to children both in the field and through research, we have been able to pick up on the many different types of cyberbullying and thus include them in our research.

As it is in the case of bullying, most studies of cyberbullying have focused on older children; I found lower rates among elementary-age kids, similar to other findings that include younger age-groups.[18] However, the gap between younger and older kids, at least when it comes to cyberbullying, may be narrowing. In 2012, I found that 15 percent of children in grades 3 to 5 reported being victimized by peers online; but by 2019, that number had risen to 28 percent.[19] This coincides with the increasing rates of cell phone ownership in primary grades, and the statistical association between that ownership and cyberbullying.[20]

The bottom line: Studies that ask briefer and more general questions, that include younger children, and that study shorter periods of time are the most likely to have the lowest estimates of cyberbullying. Having said that, cyberbullying is clearly an issue in elementary school, as it is among older children. As younger and younger children acquire digital devices and spend time online, we need to be cognizant that their social interactions are going to be affected.

But It's Really Not Just One or the Other

Statistics such as these may reflect a prevailing tendency to view bullying and cyberbullying as separate; but other data (including some of mine) suggest that these behaviors tend to be fundamentally interactive and related. Especially for teens, bullying and cyberbullying often happen in tandem, and kids seem to view the digital world as just another place where they see their friends. If we compare the incidence of these two types of bullying in the same sample, the data shows that the older children become, the more bullying and cyberbullying intersect. Across many years and different samples, this trend has remained stable. In my study, most elementary school bullying happened only in school; but reports of in-school-only incidents reduced steadily across the grades until, by high school, only 8 percent of teens reported them. This tendency, for bullying to occur less and less exclusively in school as children progress through their school years, is echoed in other studies as well.[21] And this trend associating increased age with higher proportions of bullying online appears to continue into college: when I looked at the nature of bullying in college, I didn't find even one case that occurred only in person.

Most High School Bullying and Cyberbullying Isn't Static

Even if the records of bullying frequency were more consistent, the figures themselves wouldn't necessarily paint a useful picture. In other words, rather than just knowing the one-size-fits-all number, it can be more interesting—and useful—to know how bullying and cyberbullying *progress and develop, wax and wane* as children travel through their school years. Isn't it likely that the social lives of ninth graders are very different from the social lives of twelfth graders? Suppose a student *is* being bullied or cyberbullied in ninth grade—is that bullying, or the impact of it, likely to remain consistent, or is it more likely to dwindle over time? When working with a student who admitted to being bullied, I was interested in knowing how unusual that student's experience was (relative to his or her peers), and what that student could reasonably expect in the near future. This is one of the issues I've been studying among students reporting on their high school years.

In a nutshell, my study found that bullying and cyberbullying usually do not persist across all four years of high school.[22] In fact, only 4 percent of the subjects in my study reported being victimized across all four years. Therefore, a student who reports being bullied throughout high school is much more unusual, and may be struggling much more, than one who reports being targeted during one year only. Being targeted at some point during only one year was actually the most common type of victimization, and that year was most likely to be ninth grade. Among the students who are targeted in ninth grade, about half will be targeted only in that year; the other half will be targeted in both ninth and tenth grade. If they are targeted in tenth grade, it's very unlikely that this victimization will continue into eleventh grade. As students progress through high school, it becomes less and less likely that any bullying victimization will be sustained. Even between eighth grade and tenth grade, researchers have noted a decline in bullying rates.[23]

Moreover, in my study, most students who were bullied throughout high school reported that it bothered them less and less as they progressed through the years. In fact, 45 percent of students said that bullying was less and less likely to bother them, versus 15 percent who said it bothered them "more and more." This suggests that younger teens may be more vulnerable than older teens to problems like bullying and cyberbullying.

Let's sum up: Probably between a quarter and a third of children report being targeted by bullies in a given year. It's harder to know how common cyberbullying is; the more specific and numerous the data about cyberbullying, the more frequently events will be reported. It does appear clear that as children grow, digital bullying occupies an increasingly larger proportion of all bullying incidents. Among high schoolers, incidents of bullying and cyberbullying seem to occur more often, and are more traumatic, earlier (e.g., in ninth grade). But regardless of average prevalence, and how it's measured, one of the most important takeaways is that some children are clearly more vulnerable than others. Children with special needs, LGBTQ youth, and younger students are among those who appear to be disproportionately affected by both bullying and cyberbullying. And the research conducted during the global coronavirus pandemic reinforced this conclusion.[24]

DISTINGUISHING THE ACTION FROM THE IMPACT

When my oldest child was about three years old, he was diagnosed with a type of disability that affected his ability to pronounce some words. This persisted through childhood, and he was occasionally mocked for his mispronunciations, but at least some of the time he was (luckily) unaware of the teasing. Is bullying really *bullying* if the subject doesn't understand, or doesn't care, what's going on? In the vast majority of studies, statistics on bullying and cyberbullying never take into account the impact—or lack of it—on the target.

Taking impact into account can be useful for a few different reasons. First, it's interesting to compare children who correctly perceive and are *very* affected by bullying with those who similarly perceive it but who aren't particularly troubled. (We call these children "resilient," while understanding resiliency is a key goal in bullying research.) Second, we know that bullying increases the risk of a host of bad outcomes for the target (e.g., depression, academic trouble, social problems), but we also know that it doesn't increase those risks equally for every target. Put simply, bullying affects different children differently. It's not enough just to know how many kids bully or are bullied. We also need to know which bullies and which targets are at risk for escalating difficulties, and how some children develop resiliency in the face of cruelty. Ultimately, because we can't make the world a uniformly kind place, we want all children to be able to withstand at least some of the minor cruelties that life will inevitably throw their way.

Resiliency and Vulnerability

I think any educator who has considered it readily perceives that bullying doesn't affect all children equally. In psychology, we conceptualize these differences as *resiliency* and *vulnerability*.[25] Langevin describes *resilient* children as those who are bullied but do not internalize that bullying.[26] Bowes et al. define it as when children do better than we might expect, given their bullying victimization.[27] Why are more resilient children able to "shrug off" peers who try to abuse them, whereas others are devastated?

There are different ways of measuring and considering vulnerability or resiliency. One method is to compare *bully/victims* (students who are bullies at times and targets at other times) with those who are identified as only victims or only bullies. There's little doubt that bully/victims are vulnerable children. They are at significantly higher risk for anxiety and depression and are likely to be at higher risk for aggressive, homicidal, and suicidal behaviors. They also have more problems with externalizing (blaming others or circumstances inappropriately) and internalizing (blaming oneself even when not responsible).[28]

A second method (possibly a better one) is to compare targets of bullying who report being the most upset with targets who feel very differently. In the 2020–2022 Social and Emotional Research Consortium (SERC) study (of 2,427 youth from Massachusetts, Colorado, and Virginia), subjects reported that in elementary school, bullying was more likely to affect them. More than a quarter (27 percent) said it bothered them, while only 10 percent said it didn't. By high school, the picture had changed: only 13 percent said it really bothered them, and about the same proportion felt resilient. A 2007 survey by the National Crime Prevention Council also classified about half of bullying targets as resilient and half as vulnerable.[29] A study measuring children's responses to a variety of potentially abusive home situations noted that a similar proportion (about half) were resilient.[30]

In the 2012 MARC freshman study, targets of bullying and cyberbullying were separated into three groups: just victims, just bullies, and both a bully and a victim. About 13 percent of subjects reported being both a bully and a victim in high school; 17 percent of students reported being just bullies, and another 18 percent were just victims. Again, other research has found similar proportions.[31] Being vulnerable was clearly associated with being a bully and a victim. Of all the vulnerable targets, almost half (48 percent) were both a bully and a victim. In contrast, only 9 percent of resilient targets were both a bully and a victim.

Identifying Victims Who Are Most at Risk When Bullied

What does identifying *vulnerable* or *resilient* children, or vulnerable bully/victims, have to do with measuring the frequency of bullying and cyberbullying? It's really a matter of economies. Ultimately, the answer to bullying is to address the entire broader community, but we also need to channel special resources toward the children who are most at risk for serious difficulties. We may know that from 13 to 24 percent of students may be at higher risk of more severe problems, like violence and mental illness, if they are bullied. So how can we identify these vulnerable children and accord them some extra attention and care?

Do different kinds of bullying result in resiliency or vulnerability?

Some types of bullying and cyberbullying have been found to be much more common than others. In general, for example, gateway behaviors (both in person and online) were much more frequent than physical bullying in a variety of studies.[32] The question remains, however: are some specific types of bullying not only more *frequent* but also more *upsetting*? We know that some kids were more upset by the bullying they experienced—they were vulnerable, in other words. But were they more upset because they experienced particular types of bullying?

If a type of bullying determines vulnerability or resiliency, then we would expect to see a pattern whereby, for example, vulnerable targets were more likely to be associated with some particular type of bullying. Overall, however, that's not the pattern that emerged from either the 2012 freshman study data or the 2020–2022 SERC study. In both studies, vulnerable and resilient subjects alike reported being on the receiving end of the same types of bullying behaviors. For example, both groups reported that the most common type of behavior used to bully them was "name calling," with "spreading rumors" and "eye rolling" as the next most common behaviors.

This doesn't mean that the nature of the bullying is always irrelevant. Some compelling research has found that *bias-based* bullying (i.e., bullying that focuses on the target's race, ethnic group, or sexual orientation) is closely linked with more negative outcomes, avoidance, and fear as well as with more serious psychiatric outcomes (such as suicidality).[33] Bias-based bullying is reported by more than one-third of bullying victims and is correlated with physical health effects as well as psychological trauma.[34] It may be that some students who are repeatedly subjected to bias-based harassment respond both to the content of the harassment and to its repetitive nature.

Is vulnerability related to more frequent bullying?

Perhaps what makes vulnerable subjects feel less able to shrug off bullying isn't being victimized in a specific way, but simply being victimized more frequently. All bullying, by definition, is repeated, but there's repeated and then there's incessant (in other words, the frequency of events still varies). In fact, the frequency of being bullied *did* emerge as important in determining vulnerability versus resiliency in the 2012 freshman study. How upset youth were by the bullying was strongly correlated with number of times being bullied, both in school and online.[35] Resilient subjects were more likely to report being bullied once or twice, but vulnerable subjects were more likely to report being bullied more than twice. If the subject was both bullied frequently *and* targeted by both friends and nonfriends, they were overwhelmingly characterized as vulnerable (see more about being bullied by friends in the next section).

The bottom line: It seems to be the frequency of bullying, rather than the type of specific bullying behavior, that distinguishes vulnerable from resilient children. These vulnerable children are, perhaps, simply being worn down by frequently repeated abuse.

Ways We Can Help Children Be More Resilient and Less Vulnerable

We can capitalize on several differences between vulnerable and resilient targets.

1. Talk about the issue of bullying between friends

We talk to kids a lot about bullying these days, but how frequently do we bring up the issue of bullying specifically as it pertains to friendship? Although it's always a reprehensible behavior, bullying takes on added emotional significance and impact when it happens between people who are supposed to be able to trust each other. Friendships are supposed to be the port in a storm—not the storm itself. Indeed, Hodges's and Boulton et al.'s data showed that even one good friendship that does not involve bullying (particularly a "best" friend) can be deeply protective against being bullied by others, and other studies have concurred.[36] In the field, I often run across adults who assume that their students don't need to talk specifically about bullying and friends because students (particularly teens) presumably understand that friendship carries with it certain obligations of loyalty and kindness. But that assumption may not always be correct. The data in my freshman study showed that many kids revealed being bullied by a "friend"—but real differences existed in the type of friend. Children who were resilient were more likely to be bullied by a friend who was *not* a close friend (e.g., either an acquaintance from school or a more casual friend who was not part of their closest circle of friends). Children who were vulnerable, in contrast, were more likely to be bullied by a close friend.

If, by directly addressing bullying by friends, we could reduce its incidence, we might also reduce the proportion of vulnerable targets.

2. Be sensitive to signs of emotional distress or struggle

Not surprisingly, vulnerable children in this study were more likely to report that during high school they struggled with anxiety or depression. Certainly, many teens experience anxiety or depression, but resilient children were closer to the norm on these variables. Vulnerable subjects were significantly more likely than resilient targets to have problems with anxiety, depression, or controlling their temper during high school. What we don't know, however, is whether the anxiety and depression made vulnerable children feel the impact of bullying more deeply; if the more frequent and impactful bullying resulted in these emotional difficulties; or if some other factor caused both to occur together (e.g., perhaps having fewer friends caused both the depression and anxiety and the more impactful bullying among vulnerable targets). The data on percentages, unfortunately, don't permit us to draw conclusions about which factor caused which.

Other research can offer guidance, but still no firm conclusions about causation. Several studies have found an association between being bullied and anxiety and depression, and it seems plausible that emotionally compromised children are disproportionately targeted.[37] But other research has found that, at least sometimes, a third factor may determine if bullying causes emotional distress. For example, in 2010, researchers compared children with different genotypes (genetic patterns) and found that only children with a certain genotype had an increased risk of developing emotional distress following bullying.[38] That study found that, among those with the vulnerable genotypes, bullying clearly caused emotional problems, rather than vice versa.

Ultimately, whether bullying causes anxiety or depression, or vice versa, probably isn't the most important question. Likely both are causal, but regardless of which causes which, the association suggests that the risk of depression is elevated among both bullies and targets.[39] If adults notice behaviors that suggest a student might be feeling excessively anxious or depressed, and then refers that student for evaluation to the psychological staff at school or to his or her pediatrician, their intervention could reduce the vulnerability of that child to bullying.

3. Be on the lookout for signs of dating or family violence

One of the great injustices of life is that once you're a victim of abuse, you're statistically more likely to be revictimized. A large body of research has documented this phenomenon, noting that once a victim has been abused, the probability of future abuse rises.[40] Several theories support the reasons for this association, including post-traumatic stress disorder and learned helplessness.[41] Perhaps people who conclude that they're powerless (i.e., are convinced that abuse cannot be stopped or helped) become more attractive victims to future bullies.

In the 2012 freshman study, I examined two types of possible prior victimization: bullying by siblings, and threats or aggression in prior dating relationships. Bullying by siblings appears to be more common. Across all subjects, I found that 20 percent reported that they had a sibling who sometimes or often bullied them. The more vulnerable bully/victims were the most likely to report this (29 percent), relative to either bullies (23 percent) or victims (21 percent) alone.[42]

Previous victimization in a relationship (threatened or real domestic or dating violence) largely followed the same pattern as sibling bullying. Compared with victims, bully/victims were more than twice as likely to report being bullied by a date (15 percent versus 6 percent) or by someone they were trying to break up with (14 percent versus 2 percent). Vulnerable victims in general reported prior victimization in greater numbers, but bully/victims were more strongly associated with these problems than other types of victims. In any case, being on the lookout for signs of prior abuse or bullying could be useful in getting targets the support they need to decrease their future or present vulnerability to bullying and cyberbullying.

4. Don't dismiss "tattlers" by refusing to hear them out

One mantra about bullying that I frequently hear is "tell an adult." Unfortunately, society's strong disapproval of "tattling" may make this directive problematic and possibly even detrimental to a child. If an adult decides that telling is "tattling," the child who alerts an adult to a bullying situation may be dismissed as reporting false or insignificant information, or possibly exploiting a valid complaint to further a third agenda (e.g., to get someone in trouble because they are mad at them, or to make themselves look good in adult eyes). Children may thus become bewildered, hurt, and distrustful when an adult turns around and reprimands them for doing precisely what they've repeatedly been urged to do.

Another difficulty is that adults may not be particularly good at judging what is tattling and what isn't. In the 2010 Youth Voice Project, Stan Davis and Charisse Nixon reported data that revealed that adults do not use the "don't tattle" admonition as fairly and objectively as they believe they do.[43] For example, in that study, students of color and special needs students were more likely to be told not to tattle, when compared with white and typical (i.e., not special needs) students. (One could conceivably argue that special needs students might be more likely to "tattle" because of cognitive or social skills limitations, but clearly no such argument could be made because of a child's racial or ethnic background.)

In my research, I found that both resilient and vulnerable children were told "don't tattle" at similar rates in elementary school, but by middle and high school, vulnerable children were being told not to tattle at much higher rates. It may be that vulnerable teens are less able to effectively communicate their concerns, or perhaps the more frequently bullied, vulnerable children also report more frequently, and as a result, adults are less likely to regard any single report as significant. In any case, I think it's safe to conclude that using "don't tattle" is a questionable teaching mechanism. Certainly, some issues can and should be put off for a more convenient time, but students who seek to report should ultimately get a hearing—especially because they're relentlessly encouraged to do so. Nevertheless, it's indisputably true that children don't always report with the purest of motives, and we do need a better mechanism for detecting and responding to such behaviors.

5. Give children who report attention and reassurance

Although resilient and vulnerable children reported to adults at similar rates, resilient subjects were more likely to characterize reporting as an activity that made them feel better. This effect may be due in part to characteristics in the reporter, but the Youth Voice Project did find that adult behaviors affected a child's experience during reporting. In that study, Davis and Nixon found that adults who made children feel better listened to their report closely without jumping to conclusions or rushing the interview, and also reassured children that they were worthwhile.[44] My own research has similarly found that listening to and following up with children who report was most effective, in the victim's view, even in cases in which the adult could not entirely "fix" the problem.[45]

6. Advocate for children who need help developing stronger social skills

The development of social skills, with its significant impact on learning and development, is an area of learning that education can no longer afford to ignore.[46] Not surprisingly, popularity and strong social skills appear to the related. Recent research has found that popularity predicts aggressive behaviors among elementary school students.[47] Social skills also appear to help children shrug off bullying to a considerable extent. It may also be true that being able to brush off bullying increases one's popularity. In any case, resilient subjects rated themselves as significantly more popular than those who were vulnerable Resilient subjects rated themselves, on average, a 6.7 out of a possible 10 in popularity; vulnerable subjects rated themselves almost a full point lower, 5.8 out of 10. In the 2020–2022 SERC study, 25 percent of vulnerable subjects rated their popularity as "low," compared with 18 percent of resilient subjects.[48]

Although many victims in the 2012 study gave the impression of having weaker social skills, an analysis of the data showed real differences between bully/victims and other victims. The bully/victims evidenced the weakest social skills, as measured by a reliable scale (Cronbach's alpha [standardized items] = 0.972) that included items such as, "Do you have one or a few close friends you feel you can count on?" and "Did you have small problems with friends that frequently 'blew up' into large fights (and that were not resolved successfully)?" The strongest social skills were noted in those who were uninvolved in bullying or cyberbullying (i.e., they were neither victims nor bullies). Among bullies and victims, the strongest social skills were, in order, as follows: bullies, victims, and (with the weakest skills) bully/victims. Bully/victims were least likely to prefer face-to-face communication, bullies and victims preferred it more, and uninvolved subjects preferred it most often. More than half (60 percent) of male bully/victims reported feeling "different" in high school, versus only 31 percent of bullies and 35 percent of victims. Almost half (47 percent) of female bully/victims were bullied by a friend, compared with only 28 percent of victims.

As I noted earlier, both vulnerable and resilient subjects reported that they were, at times, bullied by friends. Resilient subjects were more likely to be bullied by someone who was *not* a close friend, whereas vulnerable subjects were more likely to be bullied by close friends or by both close and not-close friends.

7. Pay more attention to students who are less strong cognitively and academically
Research conducted decades ago noted that bullies in general were children with weak academic skills.[49] Today, either the population of children who bully has changed, or researchers have become more skilled at identifying a broader range of students who engage in these behaviors. Bullies may be anywhere on the spectrum of academic achievement. But because so many adults (parents or educators) continue to associate bullying with poor grades, they may reject out of hand any suggestion that a high-achieving student could also be a bully. To more clearly describe which bullies are

higher achievers and which tend to struggle academically, I undertook in the 2012 study to compare more resilient bullies and more vulnerable bully/ victims on measures of academic skills. Because this sample was composed of students attending a moderately competitive college, their high school performance wasn't highly variable (i.e., the sample didn't include students who did very poorly in high school or, for the most part, students who excelled). A second measure—the presence or absence of an Individualized Education Plan (or IEP)—proved a better way to study academic ease or struggle. (All special needs students are put on an IEP; thus, being on an IEP is a good measure of having a documented disability or other special needs.) In studying this issue, I took a distinct approach. Although plenty of other studies have found correlations between being a special needs student and vulnerability to bullying and cyberbullying, I assessed both whether or not students were on an IEP during their K–12 years, and if so, *when*.[50] Using this data, it was possible to identify three IEP patterns. Subjects who remained on an IEP for all grades between kindergarten and high school were classified as type 1; subjects on an IEP in elementary school, but not in middle or high school, were type 2; and subjects who reported being on an IEP only in middle and high school were designated type 3.

Generally, both resilient and vulnerable targets reported similar rates of being on type 1 and type 2 IEPs. Resilient subjects were slightly more likely to be on a type 1 or 2 IEP, but the difference was not great. More interestingly, only 8 percent of resilient targets were on a type 3 IEP, compared with 31 percent of vulnerable students. It's hard to say exactly what cognitive vulnerability being on a type 3 IEP suggests, but because this IEP begins during preadolescence or adolescence, it may reflect previously undetected cognitive or learning difficulties, or emotional and behavioral problems that emerge at adolescence. Being on a type 3 IEP should potentially be considered a risk factor for other coexisting vulnerabilities, including a particular vulnerability to bullying and an inability to regard bullying as an unimportant or insignificant event.

Like other vulnerable subjects, male bully/victims were far more likely to be on IEPs, and especially on type 3 IEPs (23 percent) compared with bullies (9 percent) or victims (6 percent). This pattern wasn't true for girls, but other research on both girls and boys has found higher academic achievement among bullies who had higher status, which is the group consistent with these bullies (see previous discussion regarding popularity and vulnerability).[51]

Cognitive patterns seen in vulnerable children can extend beyond academic skills. For example, bully/victims also appear to interpret and perceive their school environments differently. In my research, bully/victims consistently rated their school environments as more hostile. They were least likely to characterize the adults at their school as consistently caring about bullying, and they were least likely to say that the adults at their school were responsive when they saw obvious bullying. They were most likely to state that they were bullied "continuously" during high school, and they found reporting to adults during high school a more negative experience. Almost a quarter of bully/victims (22 percent) felt that reporting to adults actually made a bullying situation worse; in contrast, only 2 percent of victims felt that way. Vulnerable bully/victims were least likely of all subjects to say that reporting would "usually" help a bullying situation. Bully/victims were by far the most likely group to say that their school's climate actually *encouraged* bullying (36 percent versus 17 percent of victims and 13 percent of bullies), and they were slightly more likely to believe that bullies were kids whom adults "tended to like" (37 percent versus 26 percent of bullies and 28 percent of victims).

We still can't point definitively to cause and effect. Perhaps more vulnerable victims attended schools with more negative social climates. Or, perhaps their schools weren't actually different, but these victims may have had a stronger tendency to perceive their ambiguous school climate as more negative. Either conclusion is possible, but the latter explanation is probably more plausible. Hostile interpretations of ambiguous situations have long been noted in aggressive children, although it is fascinating to ask why some aggressive children (in our study, the bullies) do not appear to show those cognitive misinterpretations as widely.[52]

Risk Factors Beyond Direct Influence

Although the preceding list shows what we can do to detect and influence risk situations, we may not be able to directly influence some of the differences between resilient and vulnerable children. But it's good to know about them anyway. Although we may not be able to change these factors, knowing them can help us evaluate risks and thus intervene appropriately.

8. Public bullying might affect targets more

Subjects who were vulnerable were more likely to report that other peers were aware of their victimization (presumably, either by having seen the bullying directly or by being told about it). Among resilient targets, about half said peers were aware of their harassment; for the more vulnerable targets, this figure was about 75 percent. Digital technology can also enhance the sense that "many others" are aware of one's victimization.[53]

These findings could be due to vulnerable students being subjected to more public bullying, but it's also true that vulnerable targets were more likely to actually tell peers what was happening. (Vulnerable children reported more often to peers, although both vulnerable and resilient children reported to adults at similar rates.) It's possible that public bullying is more humiliating and could increase targets' sense that the bullying is damaging their general social reputation and status. This could remain true even if the victim is the person who actually reveals the bullying to others.

9. Boys are generally more resilient

In the freshman study sample, girls were significantly more likely than boys to report feeling vulnerable—a result consistent with findings from the grades 3–12 study in schools and with the more recent SERC research.[54] More than half of the girls (54 percent) scored as vulnerable, compared with only 26 percent of the boys. Previous studies have found that girls are more vulnerable to bullying and cyberbullying victimization in general, possibly because of their more frequent use of technologies that may increase the frequency of being bullied.[55] As we saw earlier, higher frequencies mean more vulnerability. Compared with boys, girls also have an elevated tendency to bully friends—another factor that may increase their vulnerability.[56]

10. Less-stressed families equals greater resilience

I did find a slight (but not strong) effect for family size and vulnerability to bullying. Parental stress is linked to a host of behavioral issues in children, and bullying and cyberbullying may not be exceptions. In this sample, vulnerable children were slightly more likely to come from larger families, where parents have more children to attend to and less attention and energy to devote to each child. Resilient targets were also more likely to have been raised in suburban (versus urban or rural) settings, which tend to be more affluent, with more resources for children.

SHIFTING OUR FOCUS TO THE BULLY

So what have we learned thus far? Bullying is neither a rampant epidemic nor a rare event, but whether it's more or less common is not the only important question: rather, asking what helps targets be more resilient can be a key factor in developing the skills needed to deal with cruel social behaviors. Even if we were to successfully reduce bullying to a much rarer event, we would still want to know why some children are able to cope successfully and others aren't. But we're still missing one piece of the puzzle.

In the last chapter, I used the analogy of a pitcher throwing a baseball to a catcher to describe how, when we examine social behaviors, a ball isn't always a ball. In that chapter, we discussed the nature of the baseball and what it looks like (e.g., gateway behaviors, cruel behaviors online); in this chapter, we begin to get the idea that targets (i.e., the catchers) may have certain characteristics that influence how they interpret the ball. That is, children have cognitive and emotional styles and experiences that affect how they deconstruct the social behaviors lobbed at them by peers. But the bullies (the pitchers) also merit some examination. What are their motivations? What kind of pitch will they throw? Is bullying the result of profound changes in our society? Are children today being raised differently? And what does the research conducted on bullies reveal about their motives? You may be surprised to read how the bullies view their intentions. Read on.

CHAPTER 3

Why Do Children Bully and Cyberbully?

The Impact of Digital Technology on Social Behavior

So, why *do* children bully and cyberbully? The question invokes impassioned debate, probably because the causes of antisocial behaviors—including bullying—aren't simply of academic interest; the answers have broader social and political implications. For those who believe that certain children simply choose to bully, the response to bullying is obvious: reward positive behaviors and deter them from that negative choice, often through punishment. Yet those who believe that children who bully are at the mercy of their genes or their dysfunctional environments may feel that punishment is inappropriate—even unjust.

Complicating this tangle of opinions is the fact that bullying has always been around, yet it has also indisputably changed. Bullying is more common and more varied today than ever. So the question might better be put: Why has bullying changed from a marginal behavior to a more pervasive problem? If you read enough, you'll run across a number of opinions:

- *Nothing has actually changed*: Proponents claim that the entire problem has not really changed but has been blown out of proportion into an "epidemic" by theorists, the media, and overprotective parents; or that cyberbullying is just another type of bullying, with no unique features; or that bullying behaviors and frequency have not really changed.
- *Children today are more troubled*: American media decried the decline in adolescent mental health during the global coronavirus pandemic. Indeed, research suggests significant recent increases in poor mental health and depression among teens, especially among those who already suffered from depression before the pandemic.[1] Even before 2020, some youth trends alarmed experts, including increased

screen-time use and declining social skills; the pandemic does appear to have exacerbated those trends.[2] Having said this, it's important to note that indicators suggest that in some ways, adolescents are doing quite well. Parental illness, sibling death, expose to domestic violence, physical abuse, sexual abuse, and bullying all declined during the first two decades of the twenty-first century (prepandemic), whereas parental substance abuse, divorce, and incarceration increased.[3] I think it is fair to say that the mental health dust from the "explosion" (i.e., the pandemic) has not yet fully settled. It may take several more years before we fully understand how children's mental health has been affected.

- *Changes in society are the root cause*: This perspective generally focuses on social changes such as mothers working outside the home, drug abuse, or supposedly eroded values. These problems might be related to bullying, but they're probably not primarily responsible, having emerged on the scene decades before the current situation. (I'll return to these issues a bit later.)
- *Teachers are apathetic or unprepared*: This argument is difficult to sustain; teachers today go through more training and more effort to achieve their positions than ever before. The global coronavirus pandemic challenged teachers as never before, requiring them to shift their teaching to an online model virtually overnight. A study of educators in 2021 from 15 states found that an unprecedented percentage reported considering leaving the field of education because of the pandemic's stressors.[4] It seems likely that teachers who have remained in the classroom are truly dedicated professionals.
- *The internet has promoted irresponsibility and maliciousness in children*: Internet communications and social websites are of course partly responsible for a change in bullying patterns. But remember that while cyberbullying may be a real problem, its more traditional first cousin is still very much in the picture.

When it comes to how and why bullying has changed, I'm not going to pretend to have all the answers; but one glaring difference is that in past decades, bullying appeared to be a behavior usually engaged in by "at-risk" children. Studies from more than thirty years ago found a pattern of strong associations between bullying, academic problems, and social difficulties.[5] More recent data paint a different picture. The 2012 Massachusetts Aggression Reduction Center (MARC) freshman study and other research revealed the emergence of two types of children who bully. One type, the bully/victims (bullies who are also victims), resemble the more "traditional" at-risk kids; but another type, the "just" bullies (who are *not* also victims), appear to be children who evidence fewer risk factors in general.

These two groups seem to be different socially and academically. As noted in chapter 2, bullies rate themselves as significantly more popular than bully/victims, and they have stronger social skills. They're more likely to prefer face-to-face communication (36 percent versus 23 percent for bully/victims) over digital communications. Bully/victims, in contrast, are more likely to be on an Individualized Education Program (IEP; 35 percent versus just 14 percent for bullies). Bully/victims see adults as being less responsive to, and less caring about, bullying and cyberbullying. The long-term outcomes for these two groups of bullies are different as well. While in college, 45 percent of bully/victims were targets of bullying, but only 12 percent of bullies experienced college victimization. Of these, 22 percent of bully/victims, but only 6 percent of bullies, were vulnerable (significantly affected by college bullying). In short, with their higher likelihood of academic and social problems, bully/victims appear to resemble the group of "at-risk" students who have long been studied as bullies. In contrast, those who are simply bullies, with their popularity, higher social skills, and better functioning with adults, seem to resemble more closely the students who, in the past, would have been less likely to be bullies in the first place.

Or would they? Although I've suggested that two significant changes may be in play—that bullying is more likely to involve psychological methods, and that the better-functioning "just bullies" weren't involved in bullying several decades ago—other interpretations are definitely possible. Maybe in the older studies, high-functioning bullies were actually around and operating, perhaps using these psychological bullying methods regularly, but they simply went unnoticed. Perhaps adults weren't able to see them as stereotypical "bullies" because of their better social functioning and assumed that bullying happened only through physical behaviors. I tend to shy away from this interpretation, simply because it's hard for me to imagine that parents, educators, and researchers universally failed to observe that psychological bullying was present and being wielded by higher-functioning kids.[6] It seems more likely to me that both high-functioning bullies and psychological bullying were present forty years ago, but they were simply the exceptions and not the rule (whereas today the opposite appears to be true). In the end, though, with the exception of cyberbullying (which is clearly a recent phenomenon), we can't definitively say if *how kids bully* and *who bullies* has changed, or if it's just that we're finally noticing these elements. I would estimate the answer is a little of both.

In either case, it is a matter for concern that abusive behaviors are currently being committed by children and teens who should, by any reasonable measure, be capable of internalizing our values about aggression and abuse, but who are rejecting everyday opportunities to behave prosocially. One of the uncomfortable things about today's bullying is the sense that even when we provide children with every privilege, they may still opt to engage in destructive antisocial behaviors. As an unsettling case in point, consider the maelstrom surrounding the suicide of Rutgers University freshman Tyler Clementi. His alleged cyberbully was no misfit; rather, he was a privileged child coming from an apparently happy home life, of sound mental health, and enjoying many advantages in life. He had no obvious reason or rationale for allegedly attempting to either spy on or publicly humiliate his roommate. In any single case, we may wonder if the bully had a pathological personality; but that doesn't wash when you're considering a problem that happens as frequently as this one. They can't *all* be sociopaths.

DO STUDENTS BULLY BECAUSE
OF CHANGES IN SOCIETY?

If behaviors used to be one way, and now they are different, then something causal must have changed. As noted, a host of reasons have been offered. Could toxins in our water and air contribute to some kind of problem with central nervous system development that makes kids more susceptible to aggression or abusiveness? Has the development of the internet and electronics fundamentally changed how children grow up today? Could people be worse parents than they used to be? Could this generation of children be more bombarded with violent media?

Some factors in society have indisputably changed. More families need two working parents to stay in the middle class, and more children attend daycare at a younger age; but research on family factors and bullying suggests that such social changes are less important than both the style and methods of parenting, and sibling relationships and bullying.[7] Furthermore, many of these social changes predate the changes in bullying that we've observed. It's not that something that's been around for more than forty years *couldn't* be involved, but to be a credible and central cause, such shifts would probably need to be combined with a more recent development. It has also been observed that social factors, taken by themselves, often can't entirely explain behaviors. Consider, as an example, violent media. We have particularly seen an increase in violent video games, and a large body of research has associated violent media with an increase in aggression, at least among some children. These findings have led to the theory that an increase in aggression and bullying could be due solely or primarily to the increasingly aggressive games children play. Yet this theory, placed beside the reality we see among children, cannot satisfy by itself. Many boys who play violent video games are not aggressive, and furthermore, a great deal of the bullying and cyberbullying problems seen today occur between girls, who are much less likely to play such games.

In short, simple, single-cause answers often don't entirely fit. As with any complex problem, there are multiple causes, and for different children, different types of influences will prove important. One child may be affected strongly by his or her parents' divorce, whereas another child (perhaps even a sibling) may be much less affected. One child may strongly benefit from a stay-at-home parent, while another child may benefit more from the peer socialization advantage of daycare programs.

So let's try to improve the question: Not, What causes bullying? But instead, What new or changed factors are *contributing* to the new and different bullying and cyberbullying that we see today? What, if any, significant changes in the last decade could account for why psychological bullying may be the preferred method, and why higher-functioning children may be becoming more involved in bullying and cyberbullying?

The Impact of Electronics on How Children Grow Up

Plenty of parents today (myself included) grew up addicted to their favorite television show. But children's television viewing habits during past decades are legitimately different from those of today, not to mention the many different screens children now use. These differences may be real factors in altering how children are growing up and how their social environments are changing.

New devices: It's not just the television anymore

In the 1970s, the average home had one television set (perhaps two) showing three or four channels. Today, television ownership is actually declining in the United States, from an average of 2.8 televisions in 2021 to 2.5 in 2022.[8] This decline is probably attributable to the increased use of media-streaming services. By 2017, American households had an average of 7.3 internet-connected devices (computers, laptops, tablets, cell phones, smartphones, iPods, music players, e-readers, gaming systems).[9] Thirty to forty years ago, the family likely watched their one television set together; today, family members scatter, each to his or her own screen. Nielsen statistics gathered in late 2011 and early 2012 suggest that for the first time, the "other" screens began to actually displace television time in American families.[10]

The interactive nature of screen-watching

But screens aren't only more numerous; they are also increasingly focused on interactive technology. I grew up as a television consumer, subject to mass media campaigns in the form of television commercials; I remember singing along to their familiar jingles. But television was one-way. I couldn't alter or affect what was shown. Commercials weren't aimed at my personal interests or shopping patterns, and I contributed none of the content that we all watched. Today, many of the most popular internet sites and electronic activities are infrastructures into which users pour their own content, often for the amusement or interest of others.[11]

The number of hours spent screen-watching

In the 1970s, Americans spent (on average) 2.9 hours per day watching their television screens. This average increased slightly to 3.1 hours by the 1980s and then skyrocketed to 6.3 hours by 2004. Although television watching actually decreased thereafter, the total time watching screens kept increasing, to 7.6 hours by 2010.[12] Today, teens spend up to nine hours a day with a screen.[13] During the pandemic, screen-watching was estimated to increase by 65 percent to 100 percent (depending on the study).[14] Any activity engaged in for this amount of time every day is likely to leave a mark.

The issue with screen-watching today isn't only the time spent; it's also the type of screen encounter. Some screens show images (television, video online, photo-sharing applications, or video phone calls), whereas others show only or primarily use text (messaging, blogging). Some screens are passive (YouTube, television) whereas others are interactive (gaming, sharing and posting content, social media apps, and websites). It seems reasonable to assume that these different digital experiences have, in turn, different impacts.

Of course, children of different ages are affected differently, both by the type of screen exposure and by time exposure. Preteens and young teenagers rack up more than eleven hours a day, including one and a half hours spent in texting activities. However, this number really isn't a fair comparison; in the 1970s, we wrote on paper (versus on a device), and although teens couldn't post or send text messages, they did spend hours talking on the telephone. In 2023, we read, write, have meetings, consume media, conduct video calls, and chat on a screen, but it's hard to know what category all of those different screen hours belong to. If a fifteen-year-old is reading a newspaper article on the internet, how could that screen activity possibly equate to playing a video game? Does reading on a tablet differ in any fundamental way from reading on paper? Some studies have found comprehension differences, whereas others, including a randomized single-blind experiment, found no significant differences.[15] Some activities may not have substantially changed, even though the vehicle has.

Displacement of more direct person-to-person contact
Some things are learned through the medium of the screen; other things are *not* being learned, as we forgo other activities to be with our beloved screens. Time spent with digital electronics is time that children don't spend playing or interacting with others face to face. Popular forms of communication, such as messaging, online gaming, sending texts, and blogging, deprive users of opportunities to practice reading nonverbal cues and body language. Several studies have found that kids who engage in less media time have better social skills and healthier social relationships.[16] Face-to-face contact promotes the development of social skills by requiring people to confront and cope with socially awkward situations. These situations range from mildly embarrassing (e.g., introducing yourself to someone you want to date) to truly challenging (e.g., defusing a playmate who's becoming increasingly frustrated and angry). Although these uncomfortable moments can also occur online, a digital encounter doesn't give you the chance to study complex body language or facial cues to see if, for example, your social strategy is working. (Even common video platforms, such as through Zoom or FaceTime, don't typically have the quality and detail needed to pick up nuances.)

To visualize how being deprived of in-person interactions might affect coping skills, imagine a situation in which one girl says something mean to another girl. The target might decide to cope by arranging with a friend to grin and whisper together immediately after the comment, thus making the mean girl feel discomfited and uneasy. That strategy probably couldn't be conceived, carried out, or evaluated in a digital environment. But forming an effective strategy in dealing with a "small" awkward situation like that can pave the way for the ability to deal with more serious social problems. Perhaps, a year or two later, the grinning-and-whispering strategy will be used again by one of the participants to deal with something more serious, like bullying. But without the chance to practice (in person), kids may never master such a skill, and feel less able to cope if bullying does happen.

Of course, digital communications can (advantageously) permit us to smooth over some of life's socially awkward moments. If you want to have some fun with this concept, tell your students how uncomfortable it *used* to be to ask someone out on a date: how you discussed it ad nauseam with your friends, debated tactics, prepared scripts, and so on. This will strike them as hilarious—that you couldn't just shoot off a casual text. But avoiding awkward moments has a cost, too. The awful clumsiness of asking people out on a date is one of those situations that forces us to cultivate our social skills. Absent those uneasy but important social moments, children today may find themselves with many fewer opportunities to smooth off their rough social edges. The global coronavirus pandemic exacerbated this trend, and the teachers I studied in 2021 identified social skills as the most blatant deficit among children returning to the classroom.[17]

Impact of Electronics on Bullies' Methods and Motives

It's easy, in the middle of all the bad news, to forget that many kids don't particularly want to bully. They don't want to be cruel, or are too timid, or feel that bullying is fundamentally wrong. Still others probably view cruel behavior as occasionally justified, but they don't see themselves as "bullies" per se. The point is that it's not as though some children simply wake up one day and decide to become bullies. Rather, given the right set of circumstances, some children who wouldn't otherwise bully might be drawn into it.[18] And the digital world does, sometimes, provide the "right set" of circumstances. How does the emergence of online and digital communications make bullying easier?

The more obvious stuff: It's quicker and easier

It's obviously far easier to send a message to many people at once electronically than it ever was with paper and pen. It's a cinch to forward embarrassing messages or photos, and it's the work of a moment to post or share anything you receive or read. This makes it easy to send communications, but it also makes rumors—even casual ones—potentially more widespread, and thus more damaging. Subjects I studied in 2011 often reported feeling anxious about not being connected via their cell phone (even for one hour), and the number-one issue that caused this anxiety was the possibility that they would miss a rumor spread via a text message.[19] Whether they are *catastrophizing*—that is, imagining rumor-mongering dangers where none or few exist—or whether an errant rumor could genuinely get around all too easily is still up for study. In 2013, I studied a new group of subjects, of whom 39 percent opined that a hypothetical rumor, begun electronically, would spread to about one hundred students in *less than 15 minutes*, and 64 percent felt it would spread to a hundred students in less than one hour. Only 10 percent of subjects felt that ignoring the rumor was the best way to squash it, and 48 percent felt that a quick response would result in the least social damage.[20] Data seem to suggest that the anxiety kids feel about the extremely rapid spread of damaging rumors may actually be justified.

Lack of visual and auditory cues that normally suppress aggression

Digital environments may, at times, unwittingly promote "negligent" cyberbullying. In person, a series of interpersonal cues generally functions to discourage people from being too hurtful, especially when they're just being careless. For example, seeing the wounded look on a friend's face after thoughtlessly blurting out how ugly their sweatshirt is will usually cause the careless speaker to stop what they're saying. In a digital environment, however, those cues are absent, and someone being thoughtlessly cruel is liable to continue nattering on, oblivious. Does careless cruelty constitute "intent"? In a way, yes (the remarks aren't true accidents), and in a way, no (seriously hurting the recipient's feelings is probably not the primary goal). Perhaps we can christen a new type of digital abuse: *negligent cyberbullying*. This type of bullying doesn't reflect the essential personality of the child involved; it just represents an environment in which that person isn't getting the feedback he or she would normally receive and that would normally stop the casual cruelty.

It's important to note that the lack of immediate visual cues can also embolden digital users in a positive way. Online, where discouraging feedback cues (e.g., scowls, disapproving or disgusted looks) are absent, users may be able to express important, sensitive thoughts or feelings that they otherwise feel too intimidated or fearful to discuss. For example, LGBTQ youth can find important and meaningful social support online, when they cannot always find such support in their communities.[21] Thus, the lack of negative feedback cues can be powerful and positive. In my relentless focus on the problems with digital environments, it's easy to forget how much good they can do, and how empowering they are, for so many people.

Lack of tone: It's easier to misunderstand what's being said

Although the lack of punctuation and grammar in messaging is usually bemoaned by educators as evidence of the destruction of the English language, another problem with this writing style has emerged. Punctuation and complete sentences aren't just academic exercises; they're part of the way that writing conveys tone, and thus meaning. For example, consider the phrase: "I'm *soooooo* going to kill you." Most readers would conclude that the person who wrote that is emphatically saying that they're not, actually, going to kill you. But if you write the phrase without emphasis or punctuation, it may look like this:

im so going to kill you

and then it would be much harder to know if the writer is being threatening or humorous.

The difficulty with conveying tone in brief digital messages hasn't gone unnoticed. Scott E. Fahlman is a computer scientist at Carnegie Mellon University who claims to have invented the sideways "smiley" emoji: which looks like this ":)".[22] He thought up the emoticon to compensate for the difficulty in conveying tone in digital communications that couldn't otherwise be identified as sarcastic, friendly, and so on. The widespread use of emojis suggests that many users perceive how difficult it can be to convey tone in an electronic environment.

That suggests, in turn, that it's fairly easy to misunderstand a digital communication and inadvertently start the preteen equivalent of World War III. Imagine a scenario in which a twelve-year-old girl receives this message from her friend: "omg I cant believe he dissed u like u wr so ugly." (Translation: "Oh my god I can't believe he disrespected you like you were so ugly.") Assuming the friend was trying to be supportive, you could take the message "like you were so ugly" to mean, sarcastically, "Of course you weren't ugly!" But if the indignant, supportive sarcasm doesn't come across clearly in the message, the recipient might well conclude that her friend was literally calling her ugly. And thus the battle is engaged, and all because the brief nature of messages doesn't promote a clear transmission of tone.

Social media provides lots of information and, sometimes, more fuel for the fire

The final way that kids who aren't likely to bully in person might become engaged in it online is simply through increased opportunity. Among elementary-age children, simply owning a mobile digital device (especially a smartphone) increases the probability that they will be either a bully or a victim online, presumably because ownership increases their digital opportunities.[23] Why does owning a smartphone increase the odds of trouble with peers online? Perhaps it increases the use of social media. A 2010 study found that people who regularly visit social media sites post more about themselves, and they post it more often.[24] This means more information and more data to read about someone, which increases the likelihood that a reader might run across some fact or thought that they feel inclined to challenge, negate, or even use in an attack.

The Disappearance of Children's Play

Regina M. Milteer has argued that the role of play in children's lives is so central that play should be an integral part of the very definition of childhood.[25] Despite this, the role of play in early childhood education has changed dramatically in the last decade or so, with the emergence of a trend toward formal academic structure over more traditional, play-based preschool and kindergarten.[26] Although most proponents of academic early education acknowledge the more obvious benefits of play (e.g., healthy exercise, creativity), the conclusion that play is also linked to both academic and social success is somewhat more controversial, at least among policy makers. Evidence suggests, however, that formal academically oriented early education does not appear to increase academic outcomes in the long run and, in fact, may damage both social and academic development. Joan Almon studied twenty three-year-olds who, while in preschool, had taken part in an experiment in which they were separated into two different groups: one preschool group was taught using more formal academic techniques, whereas two other preschool groups participated in a play-based program.[27] Although academic achievement didn't ultimately differ between the two groups, by adulthood, the academic group had a much higher rate of social and emotional problems, such as a lack of personal relationships, higher arrest rates, a need for special education services while in school, and problems at work. Almon argued that such evidence suggests that replacing preschool play with formal education not only lacks benefits—it is actively harmful.

But *how* is play (during preschool, kindergarten, or after school) related to bullying? Apart from its link to social skills (e.g., higher social skills mean more friends, more self-confidence, higher status), imaginative play promotes a child's sense of power and control, which is critical for resiliency.[28] Researchers have noted further that one important purpose of play is to teach children skills that are useful in more challenging social situations, such as bullying.[29] These *social coping skills* may be positive (such as trying to befriend someone who is being mean) or negative (such as using lies to distract or displace the attention of a bully). Although bullying-prevention programs typically don't promote negative tactics (adults usually view them as socially undesirable), in the real world, learning tactics such as dismissal, trickery, and deception can be powerful strategies, and targets can and do use them to defend themselves. Indeed, learning to run social minefields is a critical element in play, and any strategy (short of cruelty or violence) that empowers a victim or prevents bullying should not be dismissed out of hand without due consideration.[30]

Changes in the Nature of Friendship

The changes in the way children grow up today may also be affecting their ability to form positive, enduring, and protective relationships. Many studies have confirmed that good friendships and social support during school years protect children against bullying.[31] Could deterioration of the ability to form friendships—meaningful, intimate relationships—be increasingly common and thus account for some of the bullying and cyberbullying problems?

As discussed earlier, several factors, including higher use of digital communications and paucity of playtime in early childhood, are associated with social skills problems and with some negative and unfriendly social behaviors.[32] The global coronavirus pandemic, at least temporarily, increased screen use and decreased social skills in children.[33] Social skills difficulties, in turn, are related to a lack of stable and positive friendships during childhood and beyond.[34]

An ongoing thread of research has found that friendships are protective and particularly important for girls. Traditionally, research studying gender and friendships has found that girls' friendships are more intimate, more intense, and more emotionally supportive than boys' friendships.[35] This tendency toward greater intimacy and support in friendships has been found to extend through the lifetime of females.[36] Despite these well-documented tendencies, the girls in a 2019–2021 study of 1,404 elementary school children reported that, if they were targets of bullying, the bully was more likely to be a friend of theirs compared with the boys (60 percent versus 37 percent).[37] This confirms earlier data from the 2012 freshman study, which reported that, if girls bullied others, they were far more likely to victimize their friends. In contrast, boys reported that they were most likely to victimize acquaintances, rather than their closest friends.[38] In the field and in the lab, one intriguing (and common) mechanism for the between-friends bullying has really stood out. Girls seek support from each other when they're upset with someone and, today, when seeking such support from friends, will often message them repeatedly.[39] Although it's normal, and actually desirable, to seek support when upset, doing so *through texting* exposes the upset girl to repeated written messages about her hurt or angry feelings. One effect of reading these repetitious messages seems to be to "prime" users to feel the negative emotions increasingly intensely.[40] Thus, this effect is called *cognitive priming*.

Cognitive priming implies that if upset individuals access friends' emotional support by *talking* with them, their feelings may be calmed; but if they gain that emotional support by repeatedly text messaging their friends, doing so may actually *escalate* or inflate their feelings. A teen may be a little upset with a friend who stains a borrowed sweater; but after reading and rereading messages about her frustration, she may find that her feelings have escalated into much more intense anger. In the 2012 freshman study, girls were more likely than boys to report that they went online or texted friends when they felt upset about something (90 versus 71 percent). When upset, girls were much more likely to prefer sending and receiving text messages (83 percent versus 53 percent of boys).

I discuss the cognitive priming effect more in chapter 4, but for now, my point is that while texting may make girls feel better able to access support when they want it, the written, repetitive nature of texting may artificially heighten their negative feelings and thus cause more conflict in their friendships. That anger and conflict, in turn, can trigger bullying and cyberbullying episodes between friends. Bullies frequently cite anger as an important motive for pursuing a campaign against a peer (as discussed in the next section). Conflicted friendships can also leave girls without the deep emotional connections that can be so protective. When asked about their friendships in high school, both boys and girls in my research similarly described their friends as fun and able to talk about personal things, but the boys were much more likely to describe their closest friends as very loyal, always friendly, and able to work out problems or fights. It's possible that cognitive priming has affected at least some girls' friendships, but if so, it's an issue that could probably be mitigated, at least partially, through simple education and awareness.

WHAT DO BULLIES TELL US ABOUT THEIR MOTIVES?

In studying how subjects perceive the motives for bullying, I separated two distinct motives. First, subjects were asked about the general motive for bullying. Is the bully usually angry? Seeking power? Trying to look popular? Second, I asked about the "trigger," or the *immediate* motive, a bully had for choosing that target. Was the bully angry at the target or in a fight with them? Was the choice of a target motivated by the target's characteristics?

In the Abstract, They See Power as the Ultimate Motive

When asked about the overall motive for bullying, most subjects (73 percent) reported that bullying is not about anger; it's about power and control, and demonstrating to targets, bystanders, and others that they have that power and control. This helps explain why the *power imbalance* discussed earlier is central to the concept of bullying. This finding aligns well with other research, which has similarly found that children in general see bullying as an expression of the power dynamic.[41] A minority of the subjects felt that bullying was fundamentally about anger.

The trigger for the bullying they saw—the rationale for victim choice—was usually seen as a characteristic ("something about") the target. Slightly less than half of the subjects felt that was the most important immediate reason. Smaller groups of subjects fielded different explanations. About a sixth felt that the bully usually disliked the target (possibly because of some characteristics, but this was not explored explicitly), and another fifth felt that most bullies select a target because they're in a "minor" fight that has escalated out of control. Although opinions weren't universal, the trend favored the pursuit of social power as the primary rationale for bullying.

In Their Own Situations, They See Anger as the Primary Motive

In the abstract, subjects viewed bullying as a confirmation of power over targets with vulnerable characteristics; however, when bullies were asked about their own motives for bullying, most described the cause as their anger at the target or, less often, "showing the target that I didn't like them." This was true for both male and female bullies, who viewed their bullying more as an exchange between them and someone they were mad at or pointedly disliked, rather than as a move for power and status. They usually didn't see the target as having certain characteristics that provoked an attack.

A lot of the aggression and meanness expressed in the 2012 freshman study sample was about being "mad." Both one-time cruelties and repetitive bullying situations were attributed to anger about 70 percent of the time, and bully/victims were only slightly more likely to attribute the bullying to being mad, in comparison with bullies. Interestingly, anger was cited much less often by cyberbullies; only 51 percent of cyberbullies said their motive was anger, in comparison with 75 percent of in-person bullies. Demonstrating popularity was among the *least* cited reasons given by both bullies and bully/victims as their primary motive for bullying.

These findings appear to contrast strongly with the general views about bullying expressed by the study sample, but other studies have also associated bullying with anger.[42] Moreover, anger has been statistically associated in a host of studies looking at other types of abuse (e.g., spouse and child).[43] It has been fingered as a contributing cause in psychological dating abuse (a behavior I consider closely related to bullying).[44] Although in my research anger was less often associated with cyberbullying than bullying, it was still the top reason cited by both types of bullies, and other research has yielded similar results.[45] But how do we reconcile the widespread perception that bullying is really all about power, with the findings that anger is also involved?

Do Bullies Really Feel Anger as a Motive?

Bullies report anger as the motive for their behavior, but it's hard to know, frankly, if that answer is straightforward. Bullies may genuinely feel anger toward their targets, but they could also be faking or exaggerating their anger. The loosening of self-control typically experienced when angry could be a convenient justification for their behaviors; rather than struggle to control their anger, bullies might welcome it as an opportunity. So I perceive two uncertain dimensions: Is the anger genuine? Or is it being used as an excuse for bullying?

It does seem likely that at least some bullies and aggressors genuinely feel anger, even when it's unwarranted. Many social encounters are unclear, requiring some type of judgment on the part of the participants (e.g., interpreting the meaning of others' social behaviors), and researchers have noted across many studies that children who tend toward bullying and aggression sometimes exhibit markedly hostile and angry interpretations when faced with ambiguous situations.[46] These overly hostile perceptions have even been noted in aggressive children before the development of any aggression, suggesting that they are a genuine cognitive problem and not a justification, at least for some children.[47] In other words, solid evidence suggests that some aggressors may see justifications for anger where most of us see none and that this tendency appears to have its origins in cognition (not in emotions per se).

The second dimension is the possibility that bullies may be conveniently using their anger (real or faked) to justify their abusive behaviors. While bullying behaviors may increase status, bullies may also encounter the attitude (among adults and children) that it's socially unacceptable to bully someone for their characteristics. Citing anger avoids that problem.

I explored this issue in the 2012 freshman study by asking eighteen-year-old subjects to look back on any cruel behaviors they had engaged in during high school and to justify or explain them. Subjects could characterize their behavior as either essentially excusable or, alternatively, as wrong or thoughtless. I hypothesized that a subject who sees his or her behavior as excusable would view it as provoked or appropriate under the circumstances. What I found pretty much fit the theory that repeat bullies are more likely to view bullying behaviors as appropriate, given their perception of the circumstances. Those who were mean once (not repeat bullies) were more likely to say that they "weren't thinking" or what they did "wasn't ideal." Repeat bullies, in contrast, were more likely to characterize their behavior as "understandable and justified" or to feel that they had "no other options." In the 2020–2022 Social and Emotional Research Consortium (SERC) study, we found some gender differences in these tendencies. Female bullies were more likely than male bullies to feel that others didn't understand their point of view, or that even though they engaged in bullying behaviors, they were actually the victims.[48] Overall, it may be that bullies sometimes sincerely view their own behaviors as more justified by circumstances, relative to other observers.

Anger in other types of abusers has been viewed as a tool that the abuser exploits as a rationalization. Therapists who work with batterers have noted that once anger-management therapy has been completed, some abusers will simply shift to another justification.[49] Another study found that some child abusers used the circumstance that caused their anger as a justification, even if it was a hostile interpretation.[50] It's difficult to say whether feigned or genuine anger is more likely to be associated with severe abuse or bullying.[51]

This issue seems most important when we're considering how to intervene with bullies. Genuine anger problems are very different from a cynical tendency to exploit anger as a rationale. And there's no reason to assume that anger is static. Perhaps some bullying situations begin as anger but continue for other, less impulsive reasons (or just fizzle), whereas sustained bullying situations are more about status. When I asked bullies in the 2012 freshman study why they stopped bullying someone, 59 percent said that they "stopped being mad." But the role of anger in bullying is *there*, in some form, and it does have broader implications. If our prevention efforts don't address the possibility that anger is sometimes the motive, then children who are angry may be inclined to see what they do as definitely *not* bullying. If we present bullying as only about power, that may confirm for some that the issue of bullying doesn't apply to them. It's still essential, of course, to help children develop values that emphasize diversity and inclusivity, rather than inequality and the power some people hold over others. We need to recognize that children who bully, and possibly their friends and closest cohorts, view their bullying situations more like equal-power fights—and thus might not think that the messages of tolerance and respect apply to *their* situations. In their minds, they're not picking on someone because of that person's inferior appearance, ethnic group, or sexual orientation; they're attacking someone because they're legitimately angry.

The bottom line: Anger has something to do with bullying, at least part of the time. It may be an issue only for the kids who are already prone to anger, or it may be the spark that lit the fire, or it may be used as a justification for bad behavior. Whichever it is, we'd better start studying it and addressing it in our discussions with students.

UNDERSTANDING AGGRESSION

All children have the capacity to hurt others. As preschoolers, children not only begin to understand that aggression hurts others but also begin to form intent, which is the basic underpinning of interpersonal violence. It's during early childhood that the capacities for both prosocial behavior and aggression increase dramatically.

Parenting Problems Generally Linked to Aggression in Children

Attachment refers to the emotional bond between child and caregiver, and can be critically important. It's vital to note that attachment problems are not rare (estimates of insecurely attached infants can be as high as 40 percent of all infants) and can happen between babies and responsible, educated, and conscientious parents. Attachment problems aren't inevitably the result of poor parenting, but they can result from stressful experiences (such as a difficult pregnancy or financial problems) that interfere with a parent's ability to feel positively about his or her infant. Attachment is one of the most important processes in a child's life (arguably the most important) and is almost certainly strongly related to a child's tendency to be either prosocial or aggressive. Secure attachment to parents predicts a high level of prosocial behavior, and infant attachment problems sometimes lead to hostile or aggressive behavior during the preschool years. Attachment is also related to social competence as discussed next.

Parenting style during middle childhood and adolescence also has a significant impact on aggressive behavior. The research strongly bears out the relationships between attachment, parenting style, and aggression. One typical study found that parents who maintained a secure attachment and had a positive influence on their young teens had children with more prosocial behavior.[52] In contrast, another study found that parents who exercised a high degree of physical control had adolescents with significantly more behavior problems.[53] Of course, this relationship is never quite so simple and is always a two-way street; different types of children provoke different types of parenting. Parents who feel a need to strictly control one child may not feel that need with other children. The complexity of these relationships reminds us that pointing the finger at parents may not be productive (especially in any individual case); but when we're considering why bullying sometimes occurs, it's important to consider attachment and parenting circumstances.

It's also important to remember that environmental factors don't always increase aggression; these influences work both ways. Mother Nature may have provided for processes that increase the potential for aggression, but other mechanisms also work against it.

Normal Processes That Repress Aggression

Within the first few years of life, the critical process called *socialization* begins, and toddlers start to acquire the rules and values of their society. Although at first young children obey rules because they're afraid of being punished, or because they want to please others, after a while they internalize them—that is, they begin to believe that these rules are correct. Ultimately, socialization is the heart of most law-abiding and peaceful behavior.

Social competence is an ability seen in a child who plays regularly with peers and is liked by them and is related to behavior in preschool years. Children with adequate social competence are able to play in a friendly manner with other children. Such play is critical, because it enables them to learn about many different issues, including the acceptability (or unacceptability) of aggression and violence. Children with high social competence are better able than children with poor social competence to absorb peer lessons about prosocial and aggressive behavior.

CYBER ISSUES: THE CURVEBALL THAT COMPLICATES EVERYTHING

We've got the nature of the baseball (gateway behaviors, cruel cyber behaviors); we see the differences in the catcher (vulnerable or resilient); and we're beginning to get a grip on the pitcher (sometimes angry; sometimes seeking to justify; less play, more screens; worse social skills). Now it's time to extend the analogy. Imagine that as the ball is flying through the air, a bizarre wind shifts violently and skews the ball to the right or left—or even right back at the pitcher. An unpredictable element has been introduced into what was before a fairly predictable pastime.

This unpredictable element is, of course, what happens in cyberspace. That's what's new, and it's affecting the entire game. Some of it is expected but a great deal of it is decidedly not. Students certainly don't always understand these factors. How many adults really do, and how can we teach the children, if we don't fully grasp these issues ourselves? In the next chapter, we consider two important issues: first, how does social behavior shift or skew in digital environments, and second, what kinds of new problems are uniquely associated with the use of electronic communication devices and computers?

CHAPTER 4

How Bullying and Cyberbullying Interact

The Amplification of Conflict in Cyberspace

> *Cyberbullying is no different from any other forms of bullying.*
>
> —Angus Council Anti Bullying Policy[1]

> *Cyberbullying could be viewed as more of a threat than traditional bullying.*
>
> —Charlotte Dodds[2]

In 2013, while writing the first edition of this book, I noted research that suggested—amazingly!—that 34 percent of college students felt that their cell phone was "essential."[3] Predictability, the percentage of teens who deem cell phones *essential* has since risen to 64 percent in a 2022 survey. What's interesting, though, is that 59 percent of their parents now hold the same view.[4]

The central role that connectivity plays in the lives of today's children and teens means it's unlikely that any—even those being cyberbullied—will give up their technology entirely. Indeed, giving up technology, for most children today, would mean an inability to socialize, communicate, and even complete homework. Children (and probably most adults) see technology as a Rubicon from which there is no going back. The necessity and, yes, the advisability of using technology remains strong despite any problems with the medium. When I asked teenage subjects how they would feel if they had to give up their cell phone for *one hour*, the most common answers given were "bored" and "anxious," apart from a fear of not hearing about an emergency.[5]

But the amazing growth in mobile digital devices (and our dependence on them) isn't just happening among adolescents (and older folks). In my 2018 research of 4,584 elementary school kids from five US states, 71 percent of eleven year olds reported owning their own cell phone. That's up from 52 percent in 2012.[6] In the 2019 study of 1,404 elementary school kids, 45 percent of eleven-year-olds reported that they were on social media.[7] Almost all (98 percent) of the 753 eighteen-year-olds in the 2019 freshman study reported that they had accounts on social networking websites.[8] Digital participation during childhood isn't just common—it's essentially *universal*.

Some of the activities children and teens engage in online promote bad feelings between peers; but most do not, and many even promote wonderful insight, involvement, communication, and empowerment. Virtually all youth in the 2019 freshman study were able to cite social media (one app or another) as being a source of positive connections with peers, and LGBTQ youth find support, help, and positive community online when they sometimes cannot find this in person.[9] But, good or bad outcomes, we can't ignore the problems that happen online. And one thing that sometimes happens, as recent news coverage has made clear, is cyberbullying. So the first question to ask here is, Is cyberbullying really different from bullying and if so, how? That's what this chapter is about—exploring what's singular about cyberbullying and cyber behaviors.

BULLYING AND CYBERBULLYING ARE NOT THE SAME, BUT THEY DO INFLUENCE EACH OTHER

By now, most adults who work with children readily perceive the enormous influence of their digital interactions on their everyday lives. In the 2013 edition of this book, I pointed out that the interaction between online and offline still hadn't really penetrated some niches. For example, elementary schools were, in general, less attuned to digital behaviors and their influence on social development and health. "This really isn't my problem," a second-grade teacher once said to me, nervously eyeing a lesson plan about cyberskills. "Can't they just talk about it in computer class?"

By 2023, although things have changed, debate persists. In my 2019 study of elementary school children, 58.3 percent reported that they discussed cyberbullying at school with an adult. In the field, adults working with younger children seem much more aware of the influence of screens in the lives of younger kids today. But that's not the only change I've noticed. Educational efforts do seem to be paying off, at least in past. In my research, the older kids are, the more they seem to realize how much technology influences social relationships. For example, youth in the 2020–2022 Social and Emotional Research Consortium (SERC) study reported that as they went through adolescence, they became more and more likely to use apps for purposes other than socializing (e.g., for news, studying, work) and they became conscious that when they had a problem in a relationship, it was usually better to talk face to face.[10] Thus, it seems that teens, like everyone else, are becoming more aware that the balancing and interacting between digital and in-person communications is something we all need to be mindful of.

This inherent interactivity applies to bullying, as well. My 2012 study of thirty-three thousand students in grades 3–12 found that as children grow, the odds that a bullying incident will occur *only* in school become smaller and smaller; by high school, more than 90 percent of reported bullying happened both online and in school—or only online. Michele L. Ybarra's research found, similarly, a substantial overlap between school and online bullying, even among middle schoolers.[11] More recent research of 1,130 boys and girls in Spain has also found a high rate of overlap between traditional bullying in school and cyberbullying.[12] In the three-legged race of social life, in-school and online interactions appear to have their feet firmly tied together.

Yet despite their interconnectedness, it remains true that in a digital environment, interpersonal dynamics, perceptions, and communication substantially change. And bullying behaviors are affected as much as any other type of behavior.

Cyberbullying: Distinctive? Or Distinctively Similar?

Journalist and pundit Larry Magid has argued that distinguishing cyberbullying from bullying is essentially as pointless as calling bullying with a fist, "fist-bullying" to draw a distinction between it and "regular" bullying.[13] He has a valid point. Separating every mechanical method by which children might abuse one another is unnecessary and renders the entire situation needlessly complex. Although we probably have little reason to distinguish "laughing-at-someone-bullying" and "telling-rumors-bullying," distinguishing bullying that happens *in an electronic environment* from *in-person* bullying might have some utility and does have some basis in research.

By definition, all bullying shares some characteristics: It's more common when adults are not present or not paying attention; it's generally accomplished in front of an audience and with a power-seeking motive; and its goal is cruel dominance (although even these widely held assumptions are sometimes off-base; more on that later).[14] But cyberbullying is also different from bullying, and not only because cyberbullying occurs while people are using a cell phone or keyboard instead of speaking face to face. Some of the differences seem to be largely due to the way that online communications change how we communicate in general. Tripping someone in a hallway versus spitting on them may not differ much in motivation, interpretation, and consequences; but the myriad of ways that bullying can happen in a digital environment presents many possible motivations and consequences. For example, posting something on social media is different from saying it to someone on a video call; and name-calling during a competitive video game is different from showing others a private or embarrassing digital photo. And, of course, all of these are potentially different from bullying in the classroom or in a hallway. Thus, these real differences are worth taking a look.

DIGITAL COMMUNICATIONS DIFFER
FROM NONDIGITAL FORMS

I think it's fair to say, at the outset, that digital technology, which facilitates many types of communication, can also facilitate bullying and social cruelty. This is not to say that technology always makes communication clearer or more productive; in fact, at times, neither is the case. But, for better or worse, it can make communication *easier*.

Ease of Use and Dissemination

Let's begin with the obvious. Using digital communications—text messaging, instant messaging, writing, and posting communications online—is so much faster and easier than writing and sending paper communiqués that many adults and children now see paper letters, newspapers, paper bills, and check-writing as quaint and dated methods of communication. Writing by hand was always somewhat cumbersome and slow, and it hastily began to succumb to modernity as soon as the telephone became commonplace. Writing requires a lot of equipment (paper, pens, typewriters, envelopes, postage stamps); a lot of thought (a good letter requires a knowledge of grammar and spelling, if not elegance of expression); and a lot of time (in the writing, if you stop to choose the right words or rewrite, and in the mailing, as a letter can take days to reach its recipient). Digital devices have relieved us from all of these constraints. We use a single device, and delivery is almost instantaneous, which in turn allows us to shoot off one line of text if we're not up to writing a whole letter, and lets tone and reflection fall by the wayside. (This is not to suggest that digital letter writing is better in every way. Many people still enjoy paper letter writing. Remember how exciting it was to receive a handwritten letter? Also, think of all we know about past generations from the physical letters they left behind. It's not clear how our ancestors will access our digital communications.

Even more salient than ease of use, though, is the different potential for dissemination. One need only compare the trouble and bother of copying and handing out paper notes about, say, the state of your vegetable garden with the click-a-button convenience of posting on social media or texting your friends, to see why the broad dissemination of routine information, once a rarity, is now commonplace. We are swimming (perhaps drowning) in a sea of data and information. But it isn't only real dissemination that affects users; kids may worry about *potential* dissemination, regardless of whether or not the information is actually disseminated. For example, a message that's humiliating can have more of an impact because the target *perceives* that it could be disseminated easily, without knowing if it has been sent out widely. Kevin C. Runions and Michal Bak pointed out that potential dissemination may also contribute to cyberbullying behaviors by facilitating moral disengagement.[15]

Human cognitive processes struggle, unfortunately, to digest and process this extraordinary potential for wide dissemination. Humans have evolved with conversation that most often occurs between two people or a small group of people, and for which wide dissemination is limited and difficult. If you're chatting by the lockers, you're not scanning every potential word with hypervigilance, knowing that any nugget of content might be the joke of the week among your schoolmates on TikTok. Instead, you just talk. You enjoy the emotional connection you're experiencing with your friends and the topic you're discussing. Faithful and accurate replication of your words and mannerisms would be challenging (short of surreptitiously recording you), and even if replication were done well, it would be difficult (without digital media) to spread what you said beyond a few concentric circles of your acquaintanceship.

The trouble is that just as we relax and enjoy our offline chats, so too do we relax and enjoy our online chats and postings without the vigilance and filter we sometimes need to apply to information that could easily be widely disseminated. Ramona Singer accidentally posted a screenshot of her bank account. Chris Evans posted a nude photo of a certain body part. Kim Kardashian tweeted about her "favorite" makeup but misspelled its name. These are just a few of the famous cases of unintended quick-but-regrettable social media postings. Posting or sending something that eventually goes viral (even though you don't intend it to) is the common cold of today's social faux pas.

Hopefully we'll learn, as a society, to adjust our attention when engaging in digital talk. But for now we generally don't watch what we say electronically, and the exposure of pictures and text that are embarrassing and even serious is a preferred method for cyberbullying. In my 2011 study of college freshmen, 22 percent of girls said that someone else had revealed a private fact or photo of them that they didn't want disclosed; the same percentage in 2019 said a serious dissemination problem had occurred online, like someone disclosing a private picture or spreading a vicious rumor to lots of people.[16] This potential for wide dissemination is just one way that electronic communications differ dramatically from talking in person, and an important way that using cyber communication contributes significantly to bullying.

False Sense of Privacy, Anonymity, Disinhibition, and Casual Cruelty

Digital communications can *feel* deceptively private. This is related to the dissemination issue—that is, the feeling that this conversation isn't going further than you and me—but other elements can add to this false sense of privacy. Writing to someone in the safety and privacy of home, enclosed by four walls, can make the exchange feel like it's happening at home and not on the World Wide Web. But while a cozy home may contribute to this feeling, you don't even need those four walls to feel that a digital give-and-take is occurring between just two people. Typing out a message on your cell phone can feel private, even if you're standing in Grand Central Station in New York City during rush hour. If you spoke aloud on the phone, the people milling around you would be able to hear at least half of the conversation, and you might well rein in what you'd say as a result. For example, instead of announcing "I'm pregnant!" you might cryptically impart, in a low voice, "The test was positive." But a written text message feels more private because none of the people physically surrounding you can see the small screen, so they don't have any idea about the content of the message. You can type anything at all. This sense of insulation can, in turn, contribute to disinhibition about what you reveal, and sometimes, to the thoughtless production of casual cruelty.

Anonymity

Much has been made about anonymity and its role in promoting cyberbullying. Many writers cite first and foremost the ability of cyberbullies to be anonymous.[17] Indeed, perceived anonymity appears to be a motivating factor for cyberbullies.[18] It's notable, however, that not all research supports the assumption that cyberbullying is inevitably anonymous. My study of grades 3–12 found that, by high school, about 74 percent of cybervictims *knew* the identity of the cyberbully. Anonymity online was much more common in the elementary years.[19] As the children got older, their online interactions more and more closely reflected and influenced their peer relationships in school.

Disinhibition and lack of nonverbal cues

Communicating electronically makes people less inhibited about both content and tone. People say and do things when online or texting that they wouldn't say or do otherwise.[20] This isn't really news, at least according to the students I study. They clearly grasp this phenomenon, because 90 percent of girls and 75 percent of boys agreed that digital environments lead to disinhibited tone and disclosures.[21]

It appears that the perceived privacy of the interaction and the lack of face-to-face cues generate this disinhibition. The fact that your discussant isn't right in front of you is an important difference between electronic communications and talking. When physical presence is removed, so too is a host of verbal and nonverbal social communication cues, including body language, tone of voice, and facial expressions. As an example of how such cues usually influence our responses, consider the interesting fact that research has actually correlated the scheduling of a school exam with a sudden crisis in the health and, yes, the very *life* of students' grandparents.[22] The result is that almost all teachers have had students pitch to them an improbable "grandparent" excuse for a late assignment or for missing an exam. While we listen respectfully to the story of a grandmother's hospitalization, we usually manage to convey our skepticism through our body language—arms crossed, face attentive but skeptical. Students who watch and note these nonverbal cues often quickly decide to backpedal. Without those feedback cues, however, they remain uninhibited by and unaware of their excuse's implausibility and may simply charge ahead blindly with the sales pitch.

In the case of cyberbullying, the lack of feedback cues in front of us means that, correspondingly, we don't always know when something is hurting another person's feelings. Let's turn the tables on our example. If a student really *does* have a sick grandparent, his visible distress can lead the teacher to accommodate a family crisis. But if the student has simply emailed a note about the situation, the teacher lacks the nonverbal feedback cues that signal distress and might not accept the explanation. Similarly, any exchange that lacks all the detailed and rich nonverbal data could result in a lack of understanding, "negligent" cyberbullying, or nasty remarks that reach far beyond their original intent.

Evidence shows that body and language cues, in person, can reduce aggression. One recent study consisting of four experiments with almost two hundred subjects found that pain cues were most effective at reducing an offender's aggression (versus displays of sadness, or verbal protestations of discomfort).[23] Bullies who are more interested in third-factor goals (e.g., enhancing their social status) or who underestimate the impact of what they do can be made so uncomfortable by the social cues of in-person events that they reduce or even stop aggression. In my research, a substantial proportion of bullies reported were *dabblers*; they only bullied once (i.e., they engaged in one cluster of repetitive attacks on a less powerful person). The most common reason for stopping (38 percent) was because "I started to feel bad about the whole thing" (perhaps these subjects were taken aback by the impact of their cruelty and concluded that it wasn't worth it).[24]

While in-person pain cues may serve to put the brakes on, a digital environment *lacks* nonverbal cues, which may contribute to online bullying by those who typically wouldn't bully in person.[25] A meta-analysis of forty-nine studies looking at the intersections between aggression and social cues revealed that online bullies tend to reduce their focus on the target (who is, after all, not physically present) and increase their self-focus, which could explain an increase in the propensity to be aggressive by reducing any focus on the victim's suffering.[26]

Sometimes third factors (e.g., alcohol use) interact with a digital environment to increase disinhibition even further. That's hardly surprising; alcohol use is related to disinhibition of aggression generally. My own research has found that problems with alcohol are reported more often among subjects who admit to being bullies or bully/victims, both in person and online.[27] Slightly more than a quarter (26 percent) of the subjects in this study said that for them, using substances made them more likely to cyberbully specifically, suggesting that factors that disinhibit people generally may do so electronically as well.

Inflation and Escalation of Emotions

One of the most fascinating characteristics of digital communications is how it can alter your feelings in a way that paper writing generally doesn't.

As I mentioned in chapter 3, even before the widespread use of electronic communication technology, psychologists decades ago had noted that repetitive exposure to emotional materials sometimes "primed" subjects and made them feel emotions more intensely.[28] Once digital technology came into play, it greatly increased the repetitive exposure of individuals to emotion-laden content. Consider a semifictional exchange between teens (not word for word, but based on a real conversation):

TEEN 1: M so mad at C. She wrecked my swter [sent to multiple
     friends via text message]
TEEN 2: dnt blame u she did same 2 me [reply]
TEEN 3: I no u r mad [reply]
TEEN 4: im mad at hr 2

And so on. The point is that each reply text reiterates the emotion (anger) and thus primes and increases the initial sender's feelings. On paper, such a message might go out to only one or two people, who would take days (or longer) to reply. The time lapse would undoubtedly blunt the priming effects, especially in the case of mild emotions like irritation. But through the medium of text messaging, the original sender might receive literally dozens of reiterations of his or her feelings, in writing, within a few minutes or hours. Reading over and over about these feelings is likely to artificially inflate and escalate them.

This can theoretically occur for any type of emotion, positive or negative. Are you interested in someone a little bit before noon? By the evening, you're in love. Are you annoyed with your friend? By the time school lets out, you may be furious. And of course, the kids involved aren't saying to themselves, "Gee, I'm feeling substantially more angry than I did this morning over such a little thing. That's crazy!" Instead, they simply think, "I am *really* mad at her." The more their feelings are primed and reiterated by their support group of friends, the stronger their feelings are and the more justified they feel in experiencing them.

It's ironic that this kind of false emotional escalation can happen when kids are doing what should be a healthy reaction to any distressing emotion, even mild ones. The difficulty is that students (more often girls) are seeking this support in a digital arena, where the dynamics change. I tried to replicate this effect in the lab by introducing freshman subjects to a mildly annoying scenario. After reading about the scenario, half the subjects read one text message from a sympathetic friend, whereas the second half (randomly assigned) read five text messages from friends sympathetically reiterating the subject's annoyance. Subjects who received one text message rated themselves as less annoyed than subjects who received five text messages, although the presented scenarios were identical.[29] As I noted in chapter 3, girls seem to be more likely than boys to experience this phenomenon—a pattern consistent with the fieldwork we do at the Massachusetts Aggression Reduction Center (MARC), where we often speak with teenage girls about this type of difficulty in their friendships.

Another way to study this is through the examination of mild social problems that escalate into serious ones. By 2022, it was widely recognized that social media can exacerbate cruelty and conflict, and experts in de-escalation of conflicts routinely recommended taking the problem offline to facilitate resolution.[30] In 2012, I explored gender differences in this phenomenon by asking freshman subjects about this type of problem with friends during high school. Girls were more likely than boys to say that a minor disagreement with a friend had blown up into a big one. Furthermore, more than half (52 percent) of the girls said that during the blow-up they had been texting many friends. Only 27 percent of boys texted friends in similar circumstances.[31] This probably reflects a generally higher preference for text messaging among girls, relative to boys (33 percent of boys versus 49 percent of girls opined that their favorite method of communication in high school was text messaging.) Lots of other research has also noted that girls have long outpaced boys in texting.[32] This marked preference for texting may help girls communicate more (a good thing), but it may also make them more vulnerable to a digitally fueled escalation in their interpersonal conflicts. In any case, the potential for emotional escalation is one way that electronic interactions clearly differ from in-person ones.

Inability of Targets to Get Away

Earlier in this century, many adults noted that cyberbullying could be worse than traditional bullying, as the target couldn't escape from it even by leaving school.[33] By checking messages or email after school, or playing video games, they might still encounter bullying online. Today, however, youth may struggle to understand the very concept of "getting away" from technology. For many, digital communications are no longer an activity in the same way that, for example, picking up a book is an activity. Reading a book is a discrete activity—one that begins and ends. Fifteen years ago, you sat down in front of your desktop and checked your email—and then you stood up and did something else. But the continuous flow of digital interactions today is more like wearing clothes; something you don't think about yet do it all the time. For the most part, people don't actively *think* about their clothes, but we would all definitely notice if we weren't wearing any. The lives of today's children and teens are so immersed in technology that I don't think it's a situation in which they think of digital communications as "central;" it's more that they simply cannot image life without the ever-present phone in their hands.

But middle-age adults (such as those born before 1975) may have a relatively harder time understanding this perspective, as they may view electronic communication as a more discrete activity, even if it's one engaged in for hours every day. For those who grew up with the landline telephone as their primary means of communication, the fuss over cruelty on screens may seem misplaced. Because of this, I have noticed that some advice given to victims of cyberbullying (e.g., "Just pull the plug!" or "Stop using that app!") can be misguided. I think that many educators today know that such a solution is completely unrealistic, but they still often tell targets to simply block the offending cyberbully (i.e., to disable the bully's ability to send a message or posting directly to them). By blocking one of the key players in the drama (the bully), the victims no longer know what's being said to the wider audience. So they may not want to block the cyberbully; or they may comply with the adult's advice, only to unblock the person soon after.

These actions can be baffling to adults who are trying to help, in much the same way that society used to be baffled by battered women who stayed with their abusive husbands. But behavior rarely occurs entirely without reason. By the 1970s, psychology had begun to acknowledge that battered women were often motivated by fear of retaliation or financial dependence, rather than by masochism, although the standard diagnostic manual used in psychiatry didn't drop the masochism concept until 1994.[34] Just as in the case of battered women, cybervictims have a rational reason to keep communications open with the peers who bully them; generally, they simply feel a strong need to be in the loop.[35] Being excluded from the communications is, for many teens, anxiety provoking.[36] Indeed, teens are so strongly motivated to keep the flow of information going that they may not even tell adults about cyberbullying, for fear their devices might be taken away.[37]

Is Cyberbullying More Severe Than Traditional Bullying?

Another potential difference is the question of whether cyberbullying has more of an impact than traditional bullying, at least for some subjects or in some circumstances. A 2009 study of about seventeen hundred Spanish adolescents compared the impact of in-person and online bullying and found that subjects had a wide range of emotional reactions to traditional bullying, but they tended to have more extreme responses—either disregarding or being significantly impacted—with cyberbullying.[38] During the 2012 MARC freshman study, subjects were twice as likely to categorize the most upsetting and serious threats they received during high school as digital (42 percent) rather than in person (21 percent).[39] More recent research has analyzed the combined impact of bullying and cyberbullying and concluded that cyberbullying rarely occurred in isolation and usually happened in conjunction with bullying in school, and that traditional bullying was the source of most distress.[40] Moreover, different groups may be differentially affected by cyberbullying and bullying; for example, a 2019 study of thousands of youth found that LGBTQ adolescents were disproportionately affected by cyberbullying and bullying.[41] Such findings bring up the possibility that the critical question may not be whether cyberbullying is more impactful than traditional bullying, but rather, whether vulnerable populations are more affected by cyberbullying.

What Do Our Students Need to Learn About Cyber Communication?

To effectively communicate online, students need to learn the following:

1. Talking digitally isn't like talking in person. It is very easy to widely disseminate everything that is said.
2. Talking digitally can make you feel uninhibited and may lead to more thoughtless, casual cruelty.
3. Texting or posting back and forth about a feeling (like being annoyed) can cause that feeling to escalate and might make the situation worse.
4. It's hard to get away from an electronic problem. Understand that and help your friends if they need your support.
5. Sometimes cyberbullying has a bigger impact that bullying in person. Just because it's not face-to-face doesn't mean it doesn't hurt.

CONTROLLING TECHNOLOGY, INSTEAD OF LETTING IT CONTROL US

Growing up during the Cold War, I vividly recall hearing laments about nuclear technology and our collective human failure to control our technological advances. Whether or not nuclear technology is better controlled today is questionable, but the same principle needs to be applied to digital technology. Electronic devices should be used to enhance our lives and to serve us—not enslave us. This is an important concept that children (as well as adults) need to consider, discuss, and study.

I mentioned briefly the anxiety that subjects reported upon having to theoretically give up their devices for one hour. Both teens and adults have talked with me about their emotional response to being alerted to their device (e.g., by vibrating or ringing) but being unable to attend to it (e.g., being in a meeting or in class). One girl described the different possibilities that made her anxious; she talked about worrying that someone could be angry at her or that others could be discussing her and she "wouldn't know about it." This was characterized as a potentially serious, even catastrophic, problem. Almost a third of subjects (32 percent) agreed with the statement, "not answering my phone right away makes me feel anxious." Almost a quarter (24 percent) said they would "worry that a text was about me," and 22 percent responded that "someone could get mad" if they couldn't respond immediately to a text or posting. These anxieties seem to lead some people to feel controlled by their device (i.e., they jump when it calls) and the constant link to a communications network, rather than in control of it. One researcher has coined a name for the fear of being without one's cell phone—*nomophobia*—and has noted the anxiety that accompanies even the *idea* of being without the device.[42]

I'm going to sound like a broken record here, but once again, these issues seem to come down to vulnerability. A study of nomophobia suggested that other mental disorders, like social anxiety, can precipitate symptoms of fear about not having a cell phone.[43] As with other issues, the more extreme problems seem often to be linked to preexisting challenges. This doesn't mean that garden-variety anxiety doesn't exist when it comes to technology, and it certainly isn't confined to children. For adults, this phenomenon may manifest in constant checks for work-related communications, even after work hours. This issue was brought to a head during COVID-19 lockdowns in which millions of workers shifted to working from home. Newly remote workers worried that failing to check email or messages and respond promptly, regardless of the hour, could lead to repercussions in their jobs.[44] Advice abounds online about how to turn off email and message notifications when you want to "turn off" the urge to respond.[45] From a psychological point of view, all of this is intriguing because it suggests that some people cannot or will not stop on their own, but rather require technological help to control their message-checking behaviors.

But can education and awareness address this? Actually, awareness of this anxiety is the first step in controlling and mastering it, and in my fieldwork, I see very little awareness about anxiety around digital devices in general. Kids see them as fun, entertaining, and connecting, but they seem less aware of any impact from being constantly connected. Still, compared with a decade ago, many more adults are aware of the link between digital device use and anxiety. I'm optimistic that once we appreciate the differences between electronic communication and other forms of communication, and how they affect our lives, we will begin to better understand and deal with the incidence and types of cyberbullying.[46]

What Complicates Our Ability to Teach Children About These Issues?

Cyberbullying isn't just different from bullying in terms of the media used. It's also a topic that fills many adults with a particular sense of unease and, sometimes, sheer inadequacy. We see the problem, but can't see ourselves as being helpful in the solution. One of the more persistent myths about children and cybertechnology is the belief that children know "everything" about technology, so adults can't be effective when it comes to cyberbullying or cyber education, because the kids are so far ahead of us. If your teenager is your at-home tech support, then what can *you* possibly teach *her*?

Children themselves largely adhere to this belief. In the 2020–2022 SERC study of 2,427 freshman, roughly half felt they were "consistently excellent and correct" at identifying others' emotions online, like humor, sarcasm, and anger. Less than 10 percent admitted that they "often get this wrong." More than a quarter (28 percent) characterized themselves as "very knowledgeable" about technology in general, although half explained that they were very good at using apps but knew nothing about programming or computer parts.[47] One computer science teacher I read about a decade ago foresaw this trend, pointing out that the largest subset of his students consisted of kids who knew very little about computers, and who didn't particularly want to know more.[48] The limitless sophistication of children's understanding of technology may therefore be something of a myth.

Children are, however, very *comfortable* with technology. Although adults might worry about breaking an unfamiliar device, children generally aren't afraid to pick up new electronic devices and push buttons until they achieve the effect they want. This markedly comfortable use of digital devices is probably due to their superior grasp of the similar logic underlying many different digital devices. For example, most devices have some type of "back" key, and pressing that key causes the same action to occur. Once you know what the back key does on the first device, you can pick up a totally novel second device and understand that purpose of the back key before you even use it. Many of the features and functions on digital devices are consistent in this way. People of all ages actually note these types of patterns in stimuli.[49] Adults' greater life experiences, however, may make them consider both patterns and the possible exceptions to those patterns. Just because both buttons *say* "back," does it mean that they both *do* the same thing? Children, in contrast, tend to accept the consistency of patterns more readily, without considering the possibility of exceptions.[50] When they apply learned patterns to new digital devices, they're usually successful, and these successes increase their confidence in their abilities.

So, an adult may see children fearlessly using different devices and conclude that they're knowledgeable; but in fact, that adult may be confusing the skill of *using technology* with the skill of *using technology wisely*. Some of us will indeed be teaching children how to use technology, but for most adults, our role needs to focus on helping children understand the *impact* of what they do electronically. How can what we type or post be misinterpreted or misunderstood? How can electronic communications be disseminated? When is it appropriate to use more direct interpersonal communications, instead of technology? How does using technology intersect with mental health and relationships?

This education can begin with teaching students about the ways in which digital communications differ from other forms of communication. How we can all use technology is an important part of a healthier lifestyle (psychologically and physically). Today, this is more often addressed in schools and at home, but adults are still hungry for guidance about how to approach these topics with children. Many adults cannot teach children about these issues, simply because they don't understand them themselves. This doesn't represent a failure; it's just too new a field to have generated a broad degree of understanding.

If our goal is to help children minimize abusive interactions, we have to teach them to successfully communicate, and to interpret others' communications, in electronic realms. Despite our anxieties about knowing less than our students, the fact is that their mastery of technological mechanics doesn't always include the impact of using technology to communicate. We need to coach children on how their communications change in a digital environment, and how they can learn to master their anxiety so that their devices don't control them. We also need to explain that what you intend to communicate can be very different from what the recipient subjectively hears and that this is *especially* true in digital environments. If we're to help children control their use of technology, we need to understand what it is they need to know. So, before we can teach them to do that, we have to teach ourselves.

CHAPTER 5

New Times, New Troubles

Sexting, Self-Cyberbullying, and Other Risky Online Behaviors

Sexting Rampant in Social Media Circles

—Njeri Mbugua[1]

Sexting May Be Less Common Among Teens Than You Think

—Kayla McKiski[2]

In the first edition of this book, a decade ago, I made an analogy at the beginning of this chapter that I now find pretty ironic. I noted that in 2010 there were an estimated 112 *million* episodes of drunk driving in the United States, according to a report from the Centers for Disease Control and Prevention.[3] Despite this statistic, I continued, no one had recommended that transportation using automobiles be abandoned. That would have been an absurd suggestion, given that cars overwhelmingly have a positive influence on modern life. So despite the dangers online, should we consider if digital communications might be abandoned?

I concluded (not too surprisingly) that digital technology was worth keeping. Today, however, in 2023, I find that arguing that digital technology has "value" to be a very dated approach. It's like claiming that housing has value—an absurdly obvious statement. Technological communications now hold a central part in the lives of almost all of us. We work online, we socialize online, we explore information online, and (of course) we shop online, for everything from paperclips to houses. Moreover, we know that the question of whether technology use offers significant advantages is moot and that is just as obviously true for children and adolescents as it is for adults. During the 1918 Spanish Flu pandemic, children simply lost a great deal of education as schools closed periodically over more than a year.[4] In contrast, during the 2020 global coronavirus pandemic, electronic communications enabled many of us to remain working and attending school online, and 40 percent of us even used technology in new ways.[5] Even among the slowest adopters of technology (those age sixty-five and older), 61 percent owned a smartphone, 45 percent were using social media, and 44 percent owned a tablet computer by 2021.[6]

So, this particular train has left the station, and the debate is no longer about whether or not digital technology is worth it, in light of the challenges it poses. Instead, we need to focus on how to live with technology in a healthier way: how to use it while promoting our own mental and physical health, and how to be on the lookout for signs of trouble among youth.

Some of the issues that digital technology has brought up are truly new in this century; others are just reiterations of existing problems. Note that the topics covered in this chapter—sexting, self-bullying, and other risky behaviors—are not always about cyberbullying per se. Sexting, for example, can be a form of digital sexual harassment or a form of adolescent sexual exploration within a relationship. Having said this, there's little doubt that some of these more peculiar online behaviors can be related to cyberbullying or to digital abuse in general. Understanding these behaviors can help us identify and perhaps reduce problems and bullying online, so it's worth taking some time to look at a few of the more prominent oddities. In this chapter, I provide some data and perspective on sexting, how and why kids cyberbully, how the very young use technology, and how children view the very fluid issue of "privacy."[7]

I also share some research about what kids get away with in school; how they illicitly use cell phones; and why children might seek the anonymous opinions of total strangers online as a strategy for obtaining candid, honest, and constructive feedback (and end up making themselves vulnerable to abuse). These issues seem to be risk factors rather than causes of cyberbullying—they may increase the likelihood of bullying online, but they don't seem to single-handedly and reliably cause cyberbullying to occur.

SEXTING

Sexting can be variably defined as "the electronic sending of pictures depicting nudity," the sending of pictures depicting "partial nudity," or "sending or posting sexually explicit pictures *or* writing." The 2020–2022 Social and Emotional Research Consortium (SERC) freshman study defined sexting as "sending nude pictures of yourself to a peer." However you define it, if one judged this issue by the headlines at the start of this chapter, you might conclude it was epidemic. Stories in the press suggest that everyone seems to be doing it—sports stars, teenagers, retirees, even politicians.[8]

How Often Does Sexting Really Happen?

I began measuring rates of "lifetime" sexting (i.e., having sent a nude photo at any time during your life) among college freshman in 2010. By 2014, 39 percent admitted having sent a sext by their freshman year in college. That number rose to 46 percent in 2016 and 50 percent by 2018, and it has hovered between 50 and 51 percent each year since.[9] A 2020 study that synthesized findings from fifty studies concluded that sexting was a common behavior among emerging adults; the authors measured prevalence at 38.3 percent and reciprocal sexting at 47.7 percent.[10] These are higher percentages than you might find in some other studies, as some research may focus only on sexting during the past few months or, for example, on younger teens. Indeed, a 2018 review of thirty-nine research studies conducted on younger teens (eleven years nine months old to seventeen years old) found lower prevalence: 14.8 percent reported sending a sext and 27.4 percent reported receiving one.[11]

Given this wide variability among different ages, how informative is it, really, to measure average sexting rates in large samples of teens? It seems clear that different youths may engage in sexting at different rates. The studies cited, for example, strongly suggest that older teens sext more often than preteens and younger teens. Younger teens may be less likely to send a nude photo, but when they do, the outcomes tend to be more negative.[12] Other groups may also be more or less likely to sext. For example, LGBTQ youth seem to be both more likely to sext and more likely to engage in higher-risk types of sexting, which is probably a result of their limited access to more traditional avenues of romantic and sexual exploration.[13] According to the 2020–2022 SERC study, boys may also engage in riskier sexting; male heterosexual sexters were more likely than female heterosexual sexters to engage in extrarelationship sexting.[14]

And it's not only that different types of youth engage in sexting differently; even among a broad sample, kids appear to engage in sexting quite differently. In the SERC study, 28 percent of sexters had sent a photo "only once or twice," and only 18 percent reported that they sent a sext more often than once a month. When it comes to sexting outside of relationships, subjects were more cautious: 42 percent said they never did this, and 32 percent reporting doing this only once or twice. Given that sexting "only once or twice" might still seem pretty risky, this may sound like splitting hairs, but the point is that sexting isn't a uniform behavior. Moreover, although these percentages may all seem high, recall that at least half of even older teens don't send nude photos.

The bottom line: Sexting is by no means universal, but a significant minority of teenagers do engage in this online behavior. That said, I think that the scrutiny over the frequency of sexting is really a tempest in a teapot, and instead, a realistic focus on the social and emotional impact would be more productive. We shouldn't simply assume that sexting is associated with serious difficulties, or consequences, despite media cases that document the contrary. One important finding of the freshman study is that the majority of sexting doesn't appear to result in any significant trouble, although some types of sexting may be more problematic than others. What appears to be key is the reason *why* a teen chooses to sext.

What Motivates Sexting?

We measured a series of attitudes in the SERC study that seem to form the basis for much of the motivations behind sexting. One motivating factor appeared to be the perception that sexting is a common and relatively safe activity. More than half (52 percent) of youth viewed sexting as a safer alternative to having sex in person. Of the kids who reported receiving some type of education in school about sexting (about 60 percent), only half said it had made any impact. Slightly more than 22 percent reported that in today's dating relationships, the expectation is that you will sext, regardless of whether or not you're having sex. Nearly a third (29 percent) were concerned that if you did not sext, a partner might look around for someone else, or others would think something was wrong with you.

A decade ago, much of the focus of the research examining motivations for sexting was "pressure or coercion," which was reported by about half of sexters in the 2012 MARC freshman study. When I began studying this phenomenon, this concerned me, as I worried that teens were being pressured into sexting as a form of cyberbullying. In the intervening decade, I've begun to realize that while pressure remains very common among sexters, it is not always experienced *negatively*. On the face of it, this seems counterintuitive, but bear with me for a moment.

Like pressure when it comes to engaging in traditional sex, pressure to send a nude photo can be experienced very differently, depending on the circumstances. Females are more likely to experience pressure to sext and pressure to have sex.[15] In the SERC study, 67.4 percent of females and 39 percent of males reported experiencing pressure to sext. However, in my qualitative interviews with youth, several reported pressure that they experienced as positive and flattering, or at least, not as negative or troubling. Indeed, positive or neutral pressure was more common than negative pressure in the SERC study: 36 percent reported positive pressure, 17 percent reported negative pressure, and 16 percent reported mixed (positive and negative) pressure. Similar to our findings in earlier years, 31 percent reported feeling no pressure of any type.[16]

It seems to be the case that the motivations for sexting differ between those who experienced pressure in a negative or positive way. When asked if they felt that sexting was a safer alternative to having sex in person, 47 percent of the negative pressured sexters agreed, but 57 percent of the positive pressure sexters agreed. About half (52 percent) of the negative-pressured sexters reported feeling that sexting was fun and exciting, but 79 percent of positive-pressured sexters felt that way. The majority of negative sexters (83 percent) reported that sexting made them look at their own body more critically; "only" 54 percent of the positive sexters agreed with that statement. Interestingly, sexters who "pressured themselves" were also very likely to report feeling critical of their bodies (79 percent).

I think the takeaway from the updated research on pressure and sexting is that it remains a significant concern, but as in the case of sexual activity, pressure must be understood within its context. Clearly, feeling coerced or bullied into sexting is too frequent and a serious problem, but positive pressure within a dating relationship (while still not a desirable state of affairs) may be experienced psychologically very differently.

Which brings us to our next motivation. Dating relationships appear to be an important motivation in sexting: 30 percent of sexters reported that sexting made them feel closer to a romantic partner. Sending a sext was also much more likely to occur after a dating relationship began, instead of before. More than half of sexters (57 percent) reported dating someone before sending them a nude picture. Although only 10 percent reported first sending the picture and subsequently starting to date the recipient, 33 percent said that they never dated the person to whom they send the picture. It wasn't unusual for subjects to ask the photo's recipient to keep the picture private (35 percent). Almost half (47 percent) reported that they were confident the picture was kept private, 36 percent weren't sure, and 17 percent knew that it had been shown to others.

Other types of sexual activity were also associated with sexting behaviors. Viewing pornography, for example, was associated with sexting. While viewing pornography online was not uncommon among any group of subjects, those who did so often were more likely to send sexts, as well (67 versus 53 percent). In addition, 32 percent of those who were not sexually active engaged in sexting during high school, compared with 71 percent of those who were sexually active; interestingly, the type of sexual activity (dating versus sex with people you weren't dating) wasn't associated with sexting (both types of youth engaged in sexting at about the same rate).

Finally, what about poor mental health as a motivation for sexting? A number of media stories have suggested that youth who engage in sexting must be doing so because of problems, such as poor self-esteem or depression. That appeared to be both true and not true in the SERC study. Youth who sexted because of negative pressure were more likely to report seeking mental health care (55 percent); in contrast, youth who didn't sext because of negative pressure were very different; only 35 percent sought such care. Being a cross-sectional study, this doesn't allow us to conclude that either negative pressure sexting leads to psychological difficulties or that those with such difficulties are more likely to succumb to negative pressure. It does suggest, however, that for youth who sext without pressure or because of positively experienced pressure, sexting isn't related nearly as strongly to mental health. Other research findings agree with this conclusion.[17]

Taken together, the data suggest that it's really negative pressure or coercion in sexting that represents the most significant problem. Negative types of pressure, however, are not experienced equally among all youth. In the SERC study, 43 percent of heterosexual females and 50 percent of LGBTQ youth reported negative pressure, compared with only 4.5 percent of heterosexual males. Moreover, negative pressure can, at times, be self-produced; more than half of females and LGBTQ youth reported feeling worried that they wouldn't be liked if they didn't sext (compared with 22 percent of males). Similarly, 47 percent of females and 67 percent of LGBTQ subjects were afraid they might be called "frigid" or "uptight" if they didn't sext—again, compared with only 14 percent of heterosexual boys.

But it's also clear that not *all* social pressure to sext was experienced negatively. Teens who sexted willingly for an existing boyfriend or girlfriend experienced few negative outcomes and weren't apparently upset by the experience. But keep in mind that this study didn't track any long-term effects of sexting, and questions still remain about possible consequences years, or even decades, down the road. Given the highly publicized results for a few individuals, it's not such a stretch to envision the possibility of significant long-term costs and wonder, *What on earth were they thinking?*

What teens seem to be thinking about when they sext are their peer relationships. Although adults may worry that adolescent sexting can be solicited by predatory adults online, almost all of the subjects in the 2012 MARC freshman study who had received a nude picture (96 percent) reported that they recognized the person in the picture. Furthermore, when I asked subjects, in the abstract, why sexting occurs, the most common reasons given were because a boyfriend or girlfriend wanted the picture, because the picture could attract someone you're interested in, or because it could demonstrate trust. Sexting was much less commonly attributed to reasons such as "it's the style now" or "it's just funny" or "it's a joke." All in all, subjects seemed to involve adults only rarely in sexting problems. Complications resulting from adults finding out about a nude picture were very rare in all the subjects studied between 2012 and 2022, relative to problems resulting from peers seeing or hearing about the sexting. If subjects had received a nude picture, the recipients' most common action was simply to delete it. Predictably, no subjects said that they had shown the picture to an adult, or even told an adult about receiving it in the first place.

Unique Characteristics of Negative- Versus Positive-Pressured Sexters

In the 2012 MARC freshman studied, I examined specific types of psychological challenges to assess their relationship to risky digital behaviors. Some of these risk factors were elevated in all sexters, but they were particularly elevated in either willing or pressured sexters. Willing sexters, when compared with pressured sexters and nonsexters, showed higher rates of factors generally associated with psychological difficulties. (I was actually anticipating that pressured sexters would be higher in these factors, but the opposite turned out to be true.) Willing sexters were the highest, pressured sexters were in the middle, and nonsexters were the lowest, respectively, in reporting *depression* (67 percent, 50 percent, and 40 percent); *alcohol and substance abuse* (21 percent, 11 percent, and 8 percent); problems with controlling their *temper* (36 percent, 29 percent, and 20 percent percent); and problems making or keeping *friends* (39 percent, 29 percent, and 22 percent). Note that for most of these factors, pressured sexters still reported somewhat higher rates than their nonsexting peers.

Although willing sexters reported higher rates of these problems, the pressured sexters seemed more likely to report problems having to do with dating relationships. For example, prior dating violence was a specific risk that pressured sexters were the most likely group to report: almost half (48 percent) of pressured sexters, but only one-third of nonpressured sexters and one-fourth of nonsexters, reported prior dating violence. But this pattern didn't remain true for *all* types of previous violence; all sexters were similarly elevated in their history of family violence. The prior violence risk factor for pressured sexters seemed confined to violence in prior dating relationships. Recall also that pressured sexters were most likely to engage in sexting when a prospective date asked for a nude picture (a situation I have compared to sexual harassment).

Overall, it seems that all sexters—even those who do so willingly—are higher in general psychological risk factors. Pressured sexters stand out, however, for problems in dating relationships. These difficulties may be at least part of the reason why some teens appear to be more vulnerable when they are asked to send a nude picture to someone with whom they're not in a trusting relationship.

RISKS ASSOCIATED WITH SEXTING

In addition to a teen's willingness to sext, the psychological issues associated with choosing to sext, and their feelings about having sexted, there are other consequences to consider. Although a teenager may envision sexting as a private affair between them and the photo's recipient, when other people discover what's going on, unpleasantness may ensue. These situations appear to happen regardless of whether the discovery is made by a peer, an adult, or the long arm of the law.

The Risk of Criminal Prosecution

In the United States, until fairly recently, sending a nude photo of a minor has been treated as a case of child pornography (a felony), even if it's a self-portrait. When sexting first emerged as an issue, several high-profile cases of teens being prosecuted for child pornography were widely discussed. One result of these cases is that the possibility of criminal prosecution is sometimes emphasized to students above all else.

Does it matter what that risk really is? If there's even a 1 percent chance of prosecution, many would argue that it needs to be spelled out to students. That's reasonable, but I would still argue that probability does matter, simply because educators must have credibility to teach effectively. When adults headline risks that students feel sure are very unlikely (or even rare), they tend to sacrifice believability. In the 2020–2022 SERC study, only 5 percent of the subjects felt that kids who send nude photos of themselves to peers run any risk of getting into legal trouble. Rather, teens may suspect that adults don't like sexting because of its sexual nature and are seizing on any potential risk (even a far-fetched one) to discourage its proliferation. Rather than lose the audience, it's probably better to assign prosecution a reasonable level of emphasis, even if it's hard to know what the true risk really is. Luckily, we do have some research that can help us estimate the probability of prosecution when a minor sends a nude picture of themselves or of a peer.

Although criminal prosecution for sexting still occurs, most jurisdictions appear to be backing off on prosecuting teens who sext as if they were adult purveyors of child pornography. The Cyberbullying Research Center reviewed the current state of US laws in 2022. They found a great deal of variation from state to state. Twenty-seven states now have laws that apply specifically to adolescent sexting, and more than a dozen have laws to divert youth who do sext.[18] No one can, or should, say that sexting carries no legal risks, but implying that felonious prosecution as an adult sex offender is common may be equally disingenuous.

Discovery by Peers or Adults

Media stories tend to depict sexting episodes that involve a nude picture being seen, usually with lightning speed, by many, many others. That does happen—for example, a photo could easily be passed around to dozens or hundreds of other students—but the data don't suggest that this is typical. In the 2020–2022 SERC study, 47 percent of all sexters reported that to their knowledge, the picture was never shown to anyone apart from the intended recipient. (Another 36 percent didn't think so but weren't sure.) Those proportions don't hold true for all sexters. Those who began sexting in middle school were least likely to state that the picture was never "passed around" (33 percent). In contrast, about 9 in 10 of the sexters who began sexting later in high school said the picture was never distributed. Similarly, 25 percent of negative-pressured sexters said their nude photo was never shown to others, compared with 68 percent of positive-pressured sexters.

Some teens may regard trouble with parents or adults at school as a more probable result of sexting, but that consequence also doesn't appear to happen often. Sexters reported that their parents, or adults at school, got them into trouble because of the image only 5 percent of the time. Additionally, no significant difference has been found between negative-pressure sexters and positive-pressure sexters (5 and 4 percent, respectively). Sexters who began sexting in middle school were more likely to report problems with adults (9 percent) than those who sexted later in high school (3 percent), but in general, neither group was likely to report trouble with adults.

Do We Need to Raise a Red Flag on Sexting?

Although my findings reveal that sexting is less likely to result in a backlash than the media might have led us to believe, it's quite important to understand that some significant and common outcomes were found in the 2020–2022 SERC study. The outcomes that were most often reported by sexters were *emotional* in nature. Rather than reporting, for example, that not getting into college or getting into legal trouble was common, subjects who sent a nude photo were most likely to report certain feelings. For example, 27 percent of sexters reported feeling anxious after sending the picture, 19 percent reported embarrassment, and 11 percent reported feelings of depression. On the positive side, 26 percent report feeling more self-confident or better looking, 22 percent reported feeling closer in their relationship, and 24 percent felt sexting was a positive way to explore sexuality.

Positive- and negative-pressure sexters have some differences. Positive-pressure sexters were slightly more likely to report feeling self-confident and attractive (28 versus 24 percent), and they were much more likely to report that sexting improved their relationship (26 versus 16 percent). In contrast, negative-pressure sexters were more likely to report embarrassment than positive-pressure sexters (24 versus 11 percent), depression (16 versus 4 percent), and anxiety (26 versus 21 percent).

Regardless of positive or negative outcomes or pressure, when sexting occurs between teens, it is always a situation that calls for attention and education. Assessing the context of the sexting seems critical in determining the likelihood of trauma or other emotional outcomes. Pressure applied in the context of a relationship (i.e., with a current boyfriend or girlfriend) wasn't always experienced as a problem. What's more concerning are the subjects who did experience the pressure negatively, most commonly when the pressure came from someone the sexter wanted to date. It's troubling to think that intimate pictures might be solicited from vulnerable, eager-to-please teenagers. Although I don't by any means think the higher rates of problems among all types of sexters should be ignored, the pressured sexters seem to be dealing with an additional set of troubles. Because the nature of these troubles is most likely to be emotional sequela, counseling is often likely to be the most productive response.

SELF-CYBERBULLYING OR DIGITAL SELF-HARM

In 2010, following some perceptive conversations with teenagers, danah boyd [sic] published a blog in which she described incidents of "digital self-harm," which she described as teens "who are self-harassing by 'anonymously' writing mean questions to themselves and then publicly answering them."[19] This phenomenon was initially uncovered by the staff at a now-defunct website, Formspring, who investigated some cyberbullying and found that the alleged victims had actually posted the cruel comments against themselves. I've referred to this phenomenon more casually as *digital Munchausen* because of its resemblance to the psychiatric disorders known as Munchausen syndrome.[20] The syndrome's central identifying symptom is the patient's infliction of self-harm in a quest for sympathy, attention, and admiration for their ability to cope with their "victimization." In 2019, I studied this type of online behavior in a study of 753 freshman, where 14 percent of the subjects told us that they had falsely posted a cruel remark against themselves, or cyberbullied themselves, during high school.[21] A lower rate of 6 percent was detected in a slightly younger sample.[22] Both studies found that boys were more likely to engage in digital self-harm. The British Broadcasting Company (BBC) interviewed a teen who engaged in this behavior, and she described the posts as a reflection of the self-loathing that was going on inside her head.

Motivations for, and Success of, Digital Self-Harm

In considering why teens might engage in this kind of bizarre form of self-harm, boyd speculated on three possibilities: self-harmers might be uttering a "cry for help," they might want to appear "cool," or they may be trying to "trigger compliments." In my 2019 study, subjects were most likely to say they actually did this in an attempt to encourage others "to worry about me" or to "catch the attention of someone I liked." But overall, I wouldn't characterize self-cyberbullying as a successful strategy. More than half (61 percent) of the digital self-harmers related that the strategy didn't really work as intended. Many of those (24 percent) said that not only was the strategy unsuccessful, it actually made them feel worse afterward. The remaining 15 percent said that the self-cyberbullying worked, they received the attention they wanted, and they felt "okay" about it.[23]

Whether you call it digital self-harm or digital Munchausen, the fact that some students stage their own cyberbullying is an issue that educators should be aware of. I've noticed in the field that many adults accept printed transcripts as irrefutable proof of cyberbullying, but the existence of self-bullying suggests that we may be too innocent in this regard. Short of a confession or the utilization of digital forensics (beyond the desire or the capacity of almost all schools and parents), it may in fact be hard to know when a case of cyberbullying is "real." But this issue probably has a silver lining. Because a school's jurisdiction over an online bully is not unlimited, what this phenomenon really does is reinforce the need to focus on the targets of online abuse. When students claim to be victims of cyberbullying, they need our support and attention. That need should be front and center, regardless of whether the cyberbullying is real or manufactured. In fact, students who fabricate their own cyberbullying may need our attention most of all.

DIGITAL RISK-TAKING IN ELEMENTARY AND HIGH SCHOOL

Although adults have focused almost exclusively on cyber problems among children in middle and high school, such issues do in fact emerge during elementary school. My study of more than eleven thousand elementary school children shed light on how cyberbullying and cyber behaviors emerge before preadolescence.

Cyber Risk-Taking at the Elementary Level

When I decided to study school-age children in Massachusetts, I started with third graders for a couple of reasons.[24] First and foremost, I was conducting a study using a written survey, and children are generally comfortably literate by third grade. But also, third grade seemed like a reasonable place to begin measuring the climb into digital technology. Although, at the time, many elementary school teachers I interacted with were skeptical about the idea that their students spent any significant time interacting online, I already knew that that perception was not correct.[25] As it turns out, though, by starting with eight-year-olds, I entirely missed the rising curve into online interactivity. Eight-year-olds are actually pretty "elderly" in the realm of beginning internet users; that is to say, more than 90 percent of the third graders surveyed reported that they were *already interacting* with other children online.

Early online activity

According to data from parents, their elementary-age children primarily played games online; the second-most-common activity was homework. When exactly most children begin to play online isn't clear from this data. As an educated guess, I would say that many, if not most, children in middle-class America play preliterate games online by kindergarten or first grade. Over the years, however, using the internet for homework and for social networking has steadily increased, in addition to online game-playing.

The point is that eight-year-old students are already immersed in digital technology; this is not just an issue among middle school and high school students. The games young children play are significant because they frequently involve elements of social networking, such as chatting, information sharing, or interacting with other children online, that could spill over into school the next day. In the field, I've noticed that during the earliest school years, both genders often play games together; by fourth grade, the boys begin to peel off into the action and adventure game genre.

Cell phone ownership in elementary school

In 2018, I studied 4,584 third-, fourth-, and fifth-grade students from five US states. The statistics on cell phone use were clear: kids often get cell phones in elementary school. Altogether, 49.6 percent of students reported owning their own cell phone. Genders were similar: 49.7 percent of boys and 49.5 percent of girls reported owning their own cell phone.[26] Americans are hardly unique in this trend. Ofcom (the communications regulator in the United Kingdom) studied 503 British children ages eight to eleven in 2015 and 2016. That study found that 43 percent owned a mobile phone, and 74 percent of these young owners possessed a smartphone.[27] In Denmark, possibly one of the most "wired" nations, a similar study found that 70 percent of nine-year-olds owned their own smartphones.[28]

Younger children owning cell phones is significant because, in that age-group, cell phone ownership was associated with increased involvement in cyberbullying and bullying in my 2018 study. Across the board, cell phone owners in this elementary school sample were more likely to report experiencing some type of digital cruelty. Those in grades 3 and 4 were also significantly more likely to report being a victim of cyberbullying, while the third graders were also more likely to be bullied in school if they were cell phone owners (25.9 percent versus 18.2 percent of nonowners). *Perpetrating* cyberbullying was related to ownership in all three grades.

I found it interesting that owning a digital device would increase the risk for being involved in traditional bullying (albeit among the youngest children in the sample). Having said this, it was clear that owning a cell phone was more strongly related to cyberbullying; that was true not only for the third graders, but for the fourth and fifth graders, as well. Given what we know about the frequent interplay between bullying in school and bullying online, this makes sense.[29]

All these findings might be disregarded if adults believe that cyberbullying doesn't happen in elementary school—or doesn't happen frequently enough to warrant our attention. But research conducted in the last decade suggests otherwise. One study of 1,141 students ages six to eleven years old found that 25 percent reported being cyberbullied at least monthly.[30] Another study of 660 Midwestern American children in grades 3, 4, and 5 found that almost 18 percent reported cyberbullying victimization, and furthermore, that such victimization was related to victimization in school through traditional bullying.[31] Finally, a study of Canadian ten- to twelve-year-olds (grades 4, 5, and 6) found that 27 percent reported that they had experienced cyberbullying victimization during the preceding school year.[32] These rates are lower than those observed among teenagers but are hardly insignificant.[33]

Parents often view cell phones as safety devices, and in some ways they may be. It also appears, however, that that cyberbullying can and does happen during elementary school and that owning a cell phone at that age appears to exacerbate this risk.

Risky Digital Behaviors During High School

High school has changed dramatically for adolescents during the past five years. The global coronavirus pandemic resulted in most teens going to school remotely or in a hybrid model for months on end. Not very surprisingly, a survey of teens by the Pew Research Center found that most teenagers prefer going to school in person and missed attending school during the pandemic. Moreover, the academic and social impact of missing school was not evenly distributed across all students. Students of color and low-income students were more likely to express concern about the impact of COVID-19 on their education.[34]

Although the global coronavirus pandemic is, arguably, the single-most-significant event in the lives of all children and adolescents today, another concern that ranks highly with high schoolers during this decade is fear of school shootings. A 2018 survey by the Pew Research Center found that half of US teens fear that a shooting could happen at their school.[35] And this fear is not unreasonable: in 2010, there were fifteen school shootings in the United States. That number skyrocketed during the pandemic to three hundred in 2022.[36]

Obviously, these issues carry more weight than the use of cell phones per se; however, digital devices can still increase (and, in ways, decrease) stress levels in schools, both for students and for adults.

Before I delve into problems resulting from the proliferation of social media and cell phones in high schools, I think it's critically important to point out the positives. In the 2020–2022 SERC research, teens saw social media as both as a place for problems like cyberbullying and a place for positive connections with peers. For example, 28 percent reported cyberbullying and a very similar 25 percent reported positive interactions on Snapchat.[37] In the 2022 Pew Research Center survey, 80 percent of youth said that social media allows them be more connected to what's going on in their friends' lives, and 71 percent felt that social media was a venue through which they can be creative.[38]

Still, cell phones and social media can also be sources of stress or negativity and it's important to understand this as well.

Illicit use of cell phones

A decade or more ago, several studies emerged with the news that students were using cell phones to cheat during school. One of the first, in 2009, was a study by Common Sense Media reporting that 35 percent of students had used their phone to cheat.[39] The 2012 freshman study found that a somewhat smaller percentage, 17 percent, of teens admitted using their cell phones that way, although only 1 percent of these also reported being caught.[40] Similar proportions were found in a more recent study of youth in school.[41] More recent concerns focus on the use of artificial intelligence and its use by students in lieu of their own schoolwork. A college professor in South Carolina described catching a student writing an essay using ChatGPT (an artificial intelligence [AI] "chat bot" freely available online).[42] He pointed out that it's so simple and quick to use AI for tasks like essay-writing that teachers may ultimately need to institute impromptu assessments, instead of planned ones.

Certainly cheating is a distressing problem, both because it affects all students (those who cheat and those who don't), and because it replaces genuine learning. The National Education Association News points out, however, that hand-wringing over cheating in this manner avoids the really difficult question: namely, why do students cheat in the first place? A teacher is quoted as explaining that students may feel that sharing information online about tests is part of being a "good friend"—helping out a peer who is under a lot of academic stress, for example. It is also important to understand that cheating may be a coping mechanism for students who aren't getting the support they need.[43]

Of course, digital devices involve more serious infractions. A more disturbing finding in the 2012 freshman study was that 20 percent of subjects had taken a surreptitious picture or video of their teacher, and 6 percent had posted the photo or video. Even when the intent is relatively harmless, it is an invasion of privacy; the seriousness escalates if the teacher is being *cyberbaited*—provoked to anger and then surreptitiously recorded and exposed.[44] In an international study of nineteen thousand subjects, about 20 percent of teachers reported that they had experienced cyberbaiting.[45] More recently, teachers have reported not being cyberbaited but rather being recorded expressing social or political opinions, thoughts, or even history.[46] In a handful of states, surreptitious recording may be illegal, but generally that is not a solid protection against a video that is passed around or posted online, and teachers have to consider how to address situations in which they are recorded.[47]

But illicit use of cell phones doesn't stand alone as a problem; it's also associated with cyberbullying and bullying in school. In the 2012 freshman study, illicit cell phone users were much more likely than their peers to be cyberbullies (35 percent versus 15 percent) or bullies in school (30 percent versus 18 percent). Like gateway behaviors, taking sneaky photos or cheating with a cell phone might be viewed as a minor infraction; perhaps the same students who tend to rationalize the use of eye rolling or cruel laughter are more likely to similarly justify the inappropriate use of digital devices.

Cyberbullying of teachers and administrators

In the United Kingdom, about 7,500 teachers were surveyed in 2014 and 20 percent reported being bullied online by students or parents, most commonly on social media sites and "rating" sites like Ratemyteacher. com.[48] More than a quarter of these teachers reported having videos or photos that were taken without permission and posted online. A similar study of teachers in the Czech Republic found that 22 percent had been cyberbullied, although only 3.5 percent had been persistently attacked online (over more than one week).[49] Teachers are understandably concerned about this issue. Although most schools have policy and procedures designed to respond to student-on-student cyberbullying, many may lack any such policy in the case of students cyberbullying teachers, leaving educators feeling vulnerable.[50]

In the 2012 freshman study, I examined this issue in a more nuanced way. I found that it was fairly common for kids to discuss online why they don't like a particular teacher (39 percent), but it's questionable whether that type of discussion can truly be termed misbehavior or "bullying." It's true that grousing about teachers online is essentially a public (and thus indiscreet) grievance, but in school hallways, the grumbling is often at least partially public anyway. The relative seriousness of such comments relies more on their specific content than on their arena: defamatory postings that suggest an administrator is an alleged alcoholic or child abuser are very serious, whereas those that complain about more mundane issues, like the amount of homework a teacher assigns, really aren't. About 17 percent of subjects said they had made fun of a teacher online, and 16 percent said they discussed their teachers in a derogatory way (e.g., criticizing something specifically, such as their hairstyle or their voice).

Although it's debatable whether such behaviors are truly "cyberbullying," I did find that they were related to bullying behaviors in general. Students who made fun of teachers or administrators online were also more likely to admit to cyberbullying peers (39 percent, versus 17 percent for students who didn't make fun of adults online) and to bullying peers in person (38 percent versus 19 percent). As with early cell phone ownership and illicit cell phone use in school, commenting unfavorably about teachers online seems to be a somewhat risky digital behavior that is related to cyberbullying behaviors toward peers and sometimes to bullying behaviors in school as well.

How is digital risk-taking related to bullying and cyberbullying?
Overall, there seems to be a relationship between higher-risk digital activities and engaging in cyberbullying, and a somewhat weaker relationship with engaging in traditional bullying. It's possible that getting accustomed to exploiting technology in questionable ways (e.g., criticizing your teacher publicly online) can lead to more bullying or antisocial behaviors, especially in digital realms. Being a person who generally takes risks may also increase the odds that someone will engage in cyberbullying. A 2022 study of 725 subjects ages eleven to fifteen years old explored this relationship and found that these preteens and younger teenagers were more likely to cyberbully others if their personality scored highly on sensation seeking, but only if they also described themselves as bored or highly exposed to antisocial media.[51] A much larger 2022 study in Germany of 6,561 preteens and teenagers compared kids who engaged in cyberbullying with those who engaged in bullying in school, and it found that those who only bullied others online were uniquely likely to score highly on risk-taking behaviors.[52]

The takeaway is simple and direct: by failing to discuss digital issues like risk online during childhood, we're missing an important window of opportunity. Because a correlation exists between risky online behaviors and cyberbullying, a broader discussion of risk online (including topics like illicit cell phone use and gossiping about people online) may be an important route to take with students, and the earlier we have these discussions, the better.

PRIVACY ONLINE

Privacy online, in 2023, is a somewhat incongruous issue. To a significant extent, anyone (adults or kids) who uses social media, online shopping, online news, or other searches has relinquished a great deal of privacy to the corporations that control those entities. A study of the widespread adoption of voice-based digital assistants (such as Echo devices or Google assistants) suggested that privacy has now become a more fluid concept, one in which people do not simply reject technology because of privacy concerns but rather think about their personal privacy risks and benefits.[53] Although some effort has been made to make encrypted messaging and emailing available to the public, this effort has been limited.[54] True privacy has essentially been sacrificed on the altar of convenience, entertainment, and free communication services.

Privacy issues also took a new turn during the global coronavirus pandemic. Technology not only became a central way to study and stay at work, it also became an important tool in the battle to control viral spread. But because personal medical issues are viewed as extremely private, these efforts weren't without controversy. One study of two thousand American adults found that roughly half were in favor on online measures that might otherwise have been unacceptable, such as the use of contact-tracing apps to alert users to the possibility that they might have been exposed to someone infection with COVID-19.[55]

Challenges to Talking About Privacy

Essentially, the digital immersion that I first wrote about fifteen years ago has come to pass.[56] It's increasingly difficult to maintain the kind of privacy in 2023 that we might have taken for granted in 2005. Having said that, it's still obviously worthwhile to talk to children about maintaining some types of privacy and being careful about what they post and share. When it comes to talking about this issue with kids and adolescents two challenges come to the forefront: first, it's not clear how well kids understand *how* to be private in the digital age; and, second, they need to understand why this is even a desirable goal.

How well do kids understand the concept of privacy?

Recent research suggests that even school-age kids have some understanding of the concept of online privacy. A UK study in 2019 found that their six- to ten-year-old subjects understood potential problems like oversharing or revealing private information online, but their knowledge didn't extend to an understanding about how their digital behaviors might be tracked or how things might be marketed to them.[57]

Privacy seems to be a quite different concept for adults. A study of a sample of 354 predominantly young adults (65 percent were age thirty-five or younger) found that among these more mature subjects, privacy was a more complex issue that depended on the context of the digital use, involving factors such as perceived risk, prior experiences with a device or app, age, gender, and perceived sensitivity of the information that a user was being asked to disclose.[58]

Given the complexity of the concept of "privacy," are parents attempting to educate their kids, or at least have conversations with them about this important topic? I explored this in the 2012 freshman study. Overall, about 54 percent of teens in that survey said that their parents had talked with them about internet privacy and why it matters, and those subjects were more likely to have set their social media profiles to *private* (86 percent versus 69 percent of other subjects). (Because any online friend can disseminate any private information publicly, it's questionable how much protection setting a social networking profile to "private" provides, but doing so indicates that a subject is at least knowledgeable enough to take a basic first step.)

When I asked subjects some general questions about privacy online, most answered correctly about issues such as how easy it is to copy and redistribute photos or understood that something on social media could be seen by an unintended party. The lack of knowledge about privacy seemed to be concentrated in what I would characterize as a substantial minority, generally around 33 percent. For example, about a third of subjects seemed unclear about how easy it was to redistribute photos. A third also said it was very unlikely or only moderately possible that unintended viewers might see a photo posted somewhere else on social media. A similar proportion (32 percent) also reported that they had given out their password or login to someone else. Girls were more likely to share passwords (35 percent) in comparison to boys (23 percent).[59]

Do kids value online privacy?

In 2012, researchers conducted interviews with 42 middle school students, and concluded that they did value privacy and that they used a variety of strategies to protect their privacy online. That study found that young teens typically only hear about "stranger danger" from adults but that their perception of privacy online is much more nuanced.[60] Other researchers point out that while adults are more focused on safety, kids are more focused on how their online socializing affects how their peers view them.[61] In the 2012 freshman study, I found that while 29 percent said they were concerned about how their information might be tracked and compiled by marketers, and 37 percent thought that publishing their private information could compromise their future opportunities, a substantial minority didn't seem to see the point of online privacy as it's viewed by adults (i.e., focused on marketing, tracking, or safety). About 30 percent of subjects felt that they "didn't have any private information worth worrying about," which may be part of the "it can't happen to me" perception that is so common during adolescence.

Cyberbullying and Privacy

On the face of it, cyberbullying may not appear to be related to privacy issues online. It's hard to connect how being tracked by marketers could have anything to do with whether or not peers are cruel. But some research suggests that youth who don't consider privacy concerns may be more vulnerable to bullying online. For example, a 2020 Canadian study asked the opinions of about 1,500 college students, both in an anonymous survey and in a focus group format, about how to prevent cyberbullying. The most common answers, in both formats, focused on increasing education and awareness. Having said that, the students did also discuss the role of privacy in protecting users from cyberbullying. Issues such as not sharing passwords, not leaving devices unattended, using security settings on social media apps, and being careful about the information posted or shared were all cited as protective actions that youth can take.[62] Another study, which examined more generally the question of trust online, suggested that subjects who were highly trusting online (i.e., less careful with privacy) were more likely to be subjected to cyberbullying victimization.[63] However, the relationship between privacy, trust, and cyberbullying does appear to be a complex one that may be mediated by other variables (such as past experiences). In addition, it may also be true that youth experience (at least sometimes) a conflict between their desire to socialize online and their interest in keeping at least some information private.[64]

Perhaps, eventually, we may come to realize that risky cyber behaviors help clear the way for cyberbullying or cyberabuse to occur. For now, we can recognize that these are potentially harmful behaviors and that the use of them may indicate, to adults, a student whose use of digital technology needs a little extra attention.

Which brings us, quite neatly, to our next questions: How should we apply that attention? Likewise, how should we respond to more obvious forms of bullying and cyberbullying? In the next chapter, we'll explore the concrete side of bullying and cyberbullying prevention—what to *do*. Don't touch that dial. (If you get that reference, you've dated yourself!)

CHAPTER 6

Responding Effectively to Bullying

The "Nine-Second Response" and Other Informal and Formal Strategies

Responding to bullying might seem straightforward, but in reality, it can be a confusing task. It is, in fact, a three-step process: first, the adult or peers must see a situation as one that needs attention and possibly intervention; second, they must be able to recognize a behavior as bullying or potentially bullying; and, third, they need to know *how* to intervene. When bullying was a more physical altercation, responding was not quite so difficult; but as the behavior has become increasingly psychological and digitized, seeing, recognizing, and knowing how to respond to bullying has become much more challenging.[1]

A great deal has changed during this century. Today, we are all aware that bullying comes in many forms, including psychological (verbal, relational), physical, and digital. Even knowing this, however, and knowing that all bullying is potentially quite harmful, it seems that adults may often do an on-the-spot assessment in their head of the "seriousness" of an incident. A 2020 study of thirty-eight Dutch teachers found that they often struggled to assess situations (particularly those they were told about but did not witness), and they had difficulty estimating the seriousness of an incident.[2] A recent study of teachers in training found that their willingness to intervene in bullying situations depended (at least in part) on their perception of how serious the situation seemed to be.[3] We may still assign different levels of urgency to different types of bullying, and some evidence suggests that adults tend to rate physical bullying as more severe than psychological types of bullying, such as cyberbullying.[4] As a result, physical bullying is more likely to elicit an adult response.

So what do teachers and educators actually *see*, and how can they use that information to make an assessment about severity or the possibility of bullying happening? And what about the incidents they don't witness, but are just told about?

Whether it's something you witness or something you hear about, the odds are that you're likely to actually see or hear about *gateway behaviors*. As I noted in chapter 1, gateway behaviors are socially inappropriate behaviors used to convey contempt and dominance, such as whispering about people in front of them, laughing at others openly, eye rolling, ignoring, name calling, or encouraging peers to drop friends. Children typically bully using gateway behaviors—not physical aggression.[5] These behaviors represent an advantageous way to bully, because they usually don't break any formal school rules and can thus be used in front of adults. But they also muddy the waters: *gateway behaviors can be used in a fight, to tease, to be mean just once,* or *to bully.* Even if you become an expert at recognizing these behaviors, you won't always know *why* they're being used. You may see gateway behaviors, but you won't ever be sure if you really know the back story. Two boys laughing pointedly at a third boy might be doing it for the first time or the hundredth time; they might be in a fight or just cranky; or you might have just seen something that looks minor but is part of an ongoing bullying situation. So, if you're not sure exactly what you're seeing, what should the response be? Although it is likely that you won't know if what you're seeing is bullying, you will know that what you're seeing are gateway behaviors. And it turns out that that's okay.

RESPONDING TO GATEWAY BEHAVIORS

In the field, adults who observe such gateway behaviors may pause and attempt to do an on-the-spot motive analysis: "Maybe she only meant it as a joke, or it could very well be just a passing, minor bit of nastiness." If what the adults see is definitely bullying—an overt threat, for example—then they know that they must respond. But if what they see is an inappropriate behavior and they don't know if it's being used to bully, then they're as likely as not to decide it could be counterproductive to stir the waters. That type of decision isn't rare, apparently; subjects in my 2012 MARC freshman study reported that adults were only about half as likely to respond to bullying that emerged through gateway behaviors as they were to bullying that played out through more obvious actions (such as physical fighting).[6] But don't despair. You *can* respond, even if you're not sure exactly what you're seeing.

Your Goal

Your goal in responding to gateway behaviors, *regardless of whether they're being used to fight, tease, bully, or be mean just once,* is simple: you want the children in your school to understand that *you expect them to behave in a reasonably civilized and considerate manner at all times.* This includes, by the way, times when they're mad, when their feelings have been hurt, and even when someone is being disgusting, irritating, or annoying. Feeling disgusted, irritated, or annoyed is not a license to behave however you like.

If you see gateway behaviors (rude social actions that convey contempt), remember that it's not necessary to establish the motive of the offending students (e.g., teasing versus bullying). All you need to ascertain is the presence of an inappropriate social behavior. For the moment, forget your sensitive side and disregard the offending child's intention. If necessary, you can always revisit this later.

Respond, but Don't Necessarily Report

It's important to be aware that you won't always use formal discipline when responding to gateway behaviors. Formal discipline can be effective with more obvious types of bullying, but its application for behaviors that don't break any rules, and that may or may not be being used for bullying, is limited.[7] Furthermore, using formal discipline for teasing or every random mean comment is not only overkill but also probably impossible. What you need is a response that can be used *before* behaviors rise to a level that requires formal discipline. It has to be one that is also appropriate in the event that the child has merely gone too far with a tease, or has, in a rare spiteful mood, thrown out a single mean comment or gesture.

Although most behaviors used by bullies today may not be appropriate for a more formal response, if you repeatedly see a child doing something mean, particularly to the same target, you should of course continue to respond but you should also move to the next level. Two reports should be made: (1) you suspect that bullying is going on—this is no longer a one-time event; and (2) you are asking this student to stop being offensive and he or she is ignoring you and persisting. Both counts should be subject to formal discipline.

Having said this, it's important to understand why such minor behaviors (e.g., eye rolling or mocking someone) should elicit any type of response at all.

THE NINE-SECOND RESPONSE

An analogy I used in chapter 1 and return to here to describe the impact of gateway behaviors is to think of your school environment as a beautiful beach.

Sitting there, you would enjoy the sand in your toes, the sound of the gentle waves, and the balmy sunshine. But then imagine that the same beach is covered with garbage and litter. The sand, sun, and surf are still there, but you can't enjoy them—in fact you barely notice them; your attention is entirely focused on simply trying to avoid touching all the smelly trash around you.

Gateway behaviors are the litter of the psychological climate in a school. Individually each is a small problem; but they accumulate and begin to change how the environment feels. The only way to deal with litter is to make sure that everyone knows that it's not okay to toss your garbage on the floor, because a garbage-strewn landscape affects everyone in school. Like paper litter, the way to deal with gateway behaviors is to ensure that everyone knows it's not okay to toss around psychological garbage, because everyone has a stake in the school's landscape. If you saw a student ball up a piece of paper and toss it on the floor, you wouldn't stop to consider if they did it on purpose, or if they did it just this once. You wouldn't debate whether maybe the student was just in a bad mood, or did they litter all the time? Instead, you would simply stop and tell them to pick up the paper. You would be enforcing the social good for yourself and for all the other people who have to share and inhabit this space together.

Based on this approach, I've developed a response set for gateway behaviors that has several advantages. It's quick, it's easy to do, it makes sense to everyone, it takes the onus off the target and puts it on the entire community, and it can't be debated or argued with. It avoids the entire can-you-prove-I-did-this conundrum (brought up, sometimes, by students or their parents), and it addresses bullying behaviors while not branding the inadvertent bully (akin to our casual litterers) with a scarlet B that will follow them for life. Most important, this response will clearly convey to all the students who see it what your expectations are.

Step One: Consistently Notice Gateway Behaviors

This is the difficult part of the response, because the idea of having to respond to every snicker and rolled eye may indeed be seen as, at best, overwhelming, and at worst, simply impossible. But remember that the goal of setting expectations is not to find yourself obliged to constantly point out violations, but rather to change the students' behavior so that those violations *no longer occur*. Once children understand a clearly stated expectation for their behavior, most will comply with it (the exception being those who have too many other challenges). In other words, notice and respond consistently, and you won't have to do it for long. One high school teacher I've worked with closely pointed out to me that each fall he assumes he'll have to be tirelessly on top of things for September; but after that, the kids know the score and they mostly cease the behaviors (at least while he's present—an issue I'll discuss later).

Talking once with a group of teens, they pointed out to me that the kids always know which adults notice and respond and which don't, and they adjust their behaviors accordingly. Hearteningly, one girl who was a frequent target told me that she loved the classes where teachers never failed to respond to gateway behaviors; she described how safe she felt in such environments, not needing to keep 25 percent of her attention on the other students, waiting for the blow.

Step Two: Respond by Owning the Impact

Now the easy part: once you've noticed, responding is simple and quick. When you see a child who behaves contemptuously or rudely toward another child, simply tell the offending child that *you*—not the target—are offended and bothered by the behavior and they must stop. That's it. Clocked, this takes about five seconds, although I call it the *nine-second response* because it takes another four seconds to pull your mind together when you're not accustomed to responding. Teachers who are used to doing it tell me they can respond in three to four seconds.

The critical element is to *not* emphasize the damage being done to the target ("How do you think that made Kristin feel?"). The offending student probably knows exactly how it made Kristin feel. Putting the onus on the target can also make him or her uncomfortable and may increase the likelihood of retaliation at a later time or date. Instead, emphasize the damage to yourself and to the entire school community. In fact, if the target of the cruel remark or gesture is present, you can ask that child to simply move along—implying to any watchers that the target is really not the problem. If needed, you can always talk with the target later, but for now, you're driving home the message that the use of socially cruel behaviors affects the entire school by poisoning the school climate—and that it is not the target's job to bear the responsibilities for the hurt.

Some educators prefer to emphasize the community's norms (e.g., "We don't do that here!"), but I think a broad, conceptual argument like that is less effective than telling a child that *you*, personally, are being harmed by their behavior. The fact that you are directly affected (offended, bothered) emphasizes the message that gateway behaviors don't simply harm people in the abstract. People who use them are being truly hurtful to the school community, and social rules forbid such behaviors for very good reasons. Most children who engage in these behaviors are focused only on wounding the target and haven't particularly considered that they could be having a much broader negative impact.

Consider a situation in which you see a few girls whispering and giggling about another student who is standing a few feet away and trying hard to appear indifferent. Your response could be:

> *Excuse me, girls? I don't know what you're talking about, but it's not OK to whisper about another person in front of them. That's very inconsiderate, and it really bothers me. Please stop it immediately.*

As you speak, you can sternly shoot them The Look (as an educator, you know which one I mean). If you have a moment, it's best to pause and meaningfully watch them as they scatter or their chattering trails off.

But Does It Work?

In the 2019 freshman survey, I asked subjects about the psychological climate in their school, the programs their school used to improve the psychological climate, and the adult response to gateway behaviors. When students rated their high school climate as *positive*, they were almost eight times more likely to report that most adults in their school consistently responded to gateway behaviors (38 percent versus 5 percent response rate in moderate climates and 0 percent in least favorable climates).[8] Additionally, in schools where most adults did respond consistently to gateway behaviors, kids were far more likely to report that other social and emotional or bullying prevention programs were helpful and effective.[9] You know all that work you put in to try to make school a fun, interesting, and pleasant place? Your efforts are more likely to be recognized and appreciated, if the adults respond to gateway behaviors.

Potential Problems with the Nine-Second Response

Now, I don't imagine that that's the end of it. If you've ever daydreamed about coming up with an effective response to a challenging situation, you know as well as I do that reality is always more complex. The nine-second response is simpler in the abstract than in more intricate human interactions, but it's designed to be a flexible response. Here are some of the questions and problems that will arise, and how to deal with them.

What if the student(s) simply responds, "No, we weren't doing that."

It's quite likely that student will deny the behavior. Your pleasant response is easy—just remember your goal: to make sure they know your expectations for social behaviors:

I'm so glad to hear that, because it's really offensive to talk or laugh about somebody right in front of them. We won't have this conversation again, then!

Now this is key: under no circumstances should you engage in a "Yes, you did"/"No, we didn't" debate. If they say they didn't do it, believe them (at least appear to believe them), but underline the message anyway. Whether or not they protest, you've now taught them—and every other child within earshot—that you consider laughing and talking about someone else in front of them to be rude and unacceptable behavior. Keep it up, and generally speaking, students will stop behaving this way in front of you.

What if they say, "I wasn't talking about you, so why are you bothered?"

This statement represents a truly excellent opportunity for discussion, because you then get to explain that when people are inconsiderate, rude, or even mean (you can feign shock here), it affects everybody—not just the target. You can point out that you know they weren't whispering about you, but that doesn't matter—it still bothers everyone who sees it. That's why we call whispering in front of others "rude" and why social rules forbid it.

What if they really weren't giggling or laughing pointedly at someone else?

Although the whispering and giggling behavior is generally unmistakable, in the unlikely event that you're wrong and they weren't being inappropriate, you've done no harm. You simply express your pleasure that they weren't doing what you thought they were doing. It's fine to even (briefly) apologize for your suspicions, if you like. The students aren't being forced to take any punishment they don't deserve, and no one is being demeaned, disbelieved, or dismissed. You're not damaging a child by bringing up the mere possibility of poor behavior; *nobody* gets through childhood without being asked to stop, at least once, something that they weren't actually doing.

Although the nine-second response does require you to say "Stop doing that," and you might give them a stern look in the bargain, it should *never* turn into a lengthy argument or harangue. If they say they didn't do it, you just say that's okay—do not argue the point; it is not a dispute. I'd maintain, incidentally, that even if you *are* wrong, you're still achieving your analogical antilittering goal, because you're still using the situation as an opportunity to teach social expectations.

I see these behaviors all the time; I'm not sure I can be "offended," over and over, every day. What then?

It's easy to become accustomed to these behaviors, and it's natural that after a while, they begin to lose impact; but simply provides more evidence that rude behaviors affect everyone—the entire school—and not just the target of the abuse. Research has maintained the hypothesis, incidentally, that bystanders are affected just as much (or more) than bullies and victims by bullying behaviors.[10] The goal of the nine-second response is to remove all these pieces of debris from the psychological environment, and then everyone will benefit. I don't deny that it takes effort, and occasionally some play-acting. But remember that the idea isn't to make more work for you; rather, it's to invest some effort up front to reduce problems down the road.

Also, consider this: in our legal system, if you commit a crime, the case is not between the aggressor and the victim (e.g., *Bully vs. Target*); it's between the aggressor and the entire state or commonwealth (e.g., *Bully vs. the United States of America*). If I assault person A, I'm not only hurting them, I'm also offending the entire community, and the entire community will be the victim of the crime.

What if they don't stop doing these behaviors even after I've used the nine-second response?

First, examine your performance. Are you being convincing? When you tell a student you're offended, are you doing it with a smile on your face? Given that you're not sure the behavior is deliberate bullying, do you sound tentative? You need to believe what you're saying. This may be easier to do if you remember that you're calling them on the outward manifestation, not the intent, of their behavior. Even if a student's gateway behavior is for a non-malicious reason, such behavior is problematic for your school community.

Also, consider how long you've been using the nine-second response. Students need to see a noticeable sea change in you before they conclude that there's a new sheriff in town. And you will become more comfortable with the response as you repeat it.

What if they continue using gateway behaviors, but just not around me?

It's quite normal for children and teens to engage in forbidden behaviors when adults aren't around; this includes not just issues such as bullying, but also eating junk food, drinking, and using foul language. Internalization about social rules takes years to achieve, and in the meantime, many rules are bent when parents aren't present. Having said that, I would argue that when children engage in behavior known to be expressly against the adults' rules, it feels very different from engaging in a behavior that they believe the adults don't care about. Consider drinking beer at a friend's party. The teen whose parents have clearly forbidden drinking feels very different (probably a little guilty) than the teen whose parents have never raised the issue.

The bottom line: There's no way to control behaviors that don't happen in front of you—but you can help mold students' values, so that if they do something wrong, at least they *know* it's wrong. That's the first step in internalizing rules and developing ethics.

How will they learn anything if I just tell them to stop, without an explanation?

Remember, the goal of the nine-second response is simply to convey your expectations. That doesn't mean that *why* we should treat each other decently doesn't matter, but changing behavior does not require constantly reiterating that *why*. Generally, students understand why we should be socially civil to each other, but they may forget or they may see school as a place where the rules are suspended. The nine-second response is really a prompting tool—a reminder that the rule is still in place. Childrearing is filled with such behavior prompts (imagine how different raising children would be if you only had to tell them each rule one time!).

When you use the nine-second response, the point is not to have a sociological discussion about why societies have rules; it's to remind students that their behavior bothers or offends you as a member of the community, even though you weren't the direct target. If you can, it's a great idea to have a more extended conversation at a later time or date about why these behaviors cause problems in the entire community and to discuss how they make everybody feel that school is an unpleasant and possibly unsafe place.

Positive, Proactive Ways to Address Gateway Behaviors

Having a class discussion is a great way to examine the issue of gateway behaviors and their consequences. Begin by asking your students to identify behaviors that they consider rude or inconsiderate. Make a list on the board. If the kids don't think of common gateway behaviors, like name calling or eye rolling, you can include them on the list. Once you have a reasonable catalog, ask your students, "Why do we have rules about these behaviors? What's the purpose?" Encourage a discussion about how manners aren't just meaningless, arbitrary rules—they are guidelines based on consideration for the feelings of others, and by keeping everyone feeling okay, manners allow people to function at their highest level. The point of this class discussion is to remind children that social rules aren't pointless, and they aren't even just about kindness. Finally, you can encourage a discussion about why and how these rules are sometimes broken—sometimes by accident (such as with teasing that goes too far) and sometimes on purpose.

The Dangers of Responding Neutrally to Gateway Behaviors

I think the most useful way to consider these situations is from the student's perspective. Let's use the example of two teachers who walk past a group of three girls who are whispering and giggling and casting amused glances at a fourth girl; they may not be pointing fingers in a physical sense, but their whispering is decidedly directional. The teachers, seeing such a situation for the fourth time that day, may well feel that it's certainly not nice to whisper about someone right in front of them; but the three girls are not creating a disturbance or breaking any school rules, which effectively ties the teachers' hands. To discipline a student, their behavior needs to be disruptive or against the rules. The teachers, perhaps, view their own action (walking by) as essentially neutral; they're not stopping the situation, but they're not promoting it, either.

The difficulty is that *students* may not interpret this behavior as neutral at all, however impartial the adults intend to be. The whisperers (and any bystanders or witnesses) may see the adults' walking by not as passive distaste, but rather as *implicit permission*—if no objection is raised, then the logical conclusion is that nothing offensive has occurred. From the target's perspective, it's clear that the behavior is cruel; but the adults who walk by apparently either don't care, or perhaps even agree with the whisperers. In the 2012 freshman study, I told subjects to imagine that they were in this scenario and asked them why they thought the teachers walked by. The most common answer (34 percent) was, "The teacher doesn't see it as a problem." The next most common answers (tied at 25 percent each) were, "The teachers agree with the bullies" and "The teachers don't like me." Only 16 percent of subjects felt that the teacher probably didn't know what to do. Thus, behavior that adults believe is neutral appears to be viewed by students as indicating explicit permission and even *approval*.[11] These are definitely not the kinds of expectations we want to project.

But before we judge the teachers' actions too harshly, let's consider the situation realistically. It's unlikely that the teachers walking by truly don't care what happens to the kids in their school—most teachers enter the profession because they want to work with kids and to improve their lives. It's far more likely that they don't react because they think that the incident most likely is a one-time case of teasing or meanness. Teasing, being mean, and bullying can all involve gateway behaviors, and to definitely untangle the three, you need to know the intentions of the possible aggressors.

Bullying may be obvious to the children who are directly involved in the incident, but it's not always so obvious to onlookers. However, teachers should not have to worry about whether to take action. Inconsiderate and contemptuous behaviors—gateway behaviors—are really never okay, even if they began as a tease. So. letting children know that they're not okay is *always* appropriate. It really doesn't matter whether it's bullying or not.

Why Don't All Educators Respond to Gateway Behaviors This Way?

In many schools today, educators are trained to discipline or respond only to behaviors that are clear violations of the student code of conduct. Vigorous protests that sometimes emerge from parents and students in the face of *any* disciplinary action place educators in the position of having to constantly defend themselves, and that in turn, may inadvertently undercut the school's authority to respond effectively to gateway behaviors that are bullying. It's ironic that parents, who very much want schools to control bullying, may actually make schools less able to do so by openly challenging procedure, thus weakening their authority.

As a result, schools tend to react by enforcing the idea that responding to children's misbehaviors is appropriate only when those misbehaviors violate formal, written rules, in which case formal responses (such as discipline) are most appropriate. This perspective renders educators unable to respond to the gateway behaviors used to bully others. There's no rule about rolling your eyes, or laughing at others, or whispering about people, or staring, or laughing. These rules would be unenforceable—how could we codify what constitutes the "wrong" kind of laughter? But despite lacking a formal rule about laughing, if we want to protect children, then we must respond to laughter that is being used cruelly to abuse others.

This is not to say that formal discipline is irrelevant. Formal discipline does play an important role in a response set—but in the same way that a police department shouldn't devote all of its resources to only the most egregious and serious crimes, a school shouldn't devote all of its responses to only the most obvious cases of bullying. The difficulty is that all behaviors that are troublesome don't rise to the level of sending someone down the proverbial river. Thus, we're in a double bind: we've both removed from teachers the will (and possibly the authority) to respond to minor misbehavior and limited them to addressing more serious misbehaviors by delegating the discipline to the administrators. Although it's probably not an issue to delegate serious problems to administrators, it's most certainly an issue—and a critical one—to discourage teachers from responding to small, yet cumulative, behaviors.

Likely Arguments Against the Nine-Second Response

A great deal of my work has benefited enormously from all of the interactions I have with educators, almost on a daily basis. Part of these conversations has been a pretty thorough hashing-out of the nine-second response—what works, what doesn't, and what kinds of questions emerge. Following are the issues that come up most often for debate. Each one of them represents, in my view, a valid concern.

We need to do more about bullying than just tell them to cut it out.

That's true, but remember, we're not talking about cases where we suspect there's chronic bullying or even cases in which we know bullying is happening; we're talking about the run-of-the-mill socially cruel behaviors that may *or may not* indicate a bullying situation. Obviously, repeated behaviors by the same offenders are another matter. Remember the point raised in chapter 1: if you find yourself wondering if that use of gateway behaviors reflects a bullying situation, then it's time to have a chat with the possible target and see what's going on.

It's also worth pointing out that a response is just that—a response. It's only one part of a truly effective prevention effort, which also has to include faculty, student, and parental education, awareness, and proactive behaviors, as well as support and input from the community.

Isn't it unnecessarily harsh to tell children who may be just teasing to cut it out?

I would argue, actually, that it's much more damaging to permit children to be rude to each other entirely unfettered by society's rules. The fact is that, as educators, we are charged with some responsibility for helping children prepare for life. Allowing them to believe that they are free to behave however they like (cruelly, thoughtlessly, or not) does not prepare them to behave in an acceptable way as adults. It's not "kinder" to let kids be mean. It may, in fact, just be kicking the can down the road.

What about using mediation instead of the nine-second response?

Mediation is a critically important skill that can help students throughout their lives. There has been a definitive trend toward training students and teachers to use mediation as the best method to resolve conflict in schools.[12] Most educators express a very high level of satisfaction with programs using mediation to resolve student-on-student conflicts.[13] Mediation is an attractive option because it involves both student empowerment and restorative justice.

The very real success of this trend, however, doesn't rule out the possibility that mediation (both formal and informal, adult and peer) may not be appropriate for use with some types of conflicts—and bullying is one of them. Mediation and negotiation generally assume that two children in conflict possess relatively equal power, but as we know, bullying episodes are defined by their imbalance of power. S. Theberge and O. Karan argue that the presence of a power imbalance essentially rules out the use of mediation.[14] Grethe Nordhelle points out that, especially in unequal power situations (like bullying), all parties may not always be totally truthful or candid during mediations.[15] Other researchers have also noted that mediating between a powerful bully and his or her less-powerful victim is generally not recommended.[16] Even papers that actually recommend mediation for bullying cases typically specify that the cases can't involve noticeable power differences.[17] (And according to my definition, I would argue that if a case does *not* involve a tangible power difference, then it is probably not a bullying situation in the first place.)

In addition to the power imbalance issue, using mediation with students who bully poses other problems. Some research has noted that at least some bullies are adept at being charming or lying during a mediation. Rather than being candid and up front, bullies may work hard outside of the mediation to attain their goal of dominance over the target.[18] Mediation, which deemphasizes fault and emphasizes both parties' responsibilities, may suggest to victims that they are equally responsible for the bullying.[19] In addition, the victims' fear of retribution may make it impossible for them to participate fully. In fact, in the 2012 freshman study, retaliation following mediation was tagged by subjects as the most common problem resulting from adult efforts to address bullying. When I asked subjects to specify *how* adults make it worse when they deal with bullying, the most common answer (with 64 percent endorsement) was, "They make you sit down with the bully and talk it over, and you know you'll get it worse later on." The trepidation that misused mediation evokes in students in the research should give us all significant pause. Worst of all, it may also make mediation—a valuable and important approach to conflict resolution—a much less attractive option even in the many cases in which it is actually appropriate.

Note, however, that mediation might theoretically have some uses in bullying cases. It could be useful for bystanders and targets to take part in mediation, particularly bystanders who befriend bullies and help egg on their actions (which Massachusetts Aggression Reduction Center casually refers to as *eggers*). Eggers may be more responsive to both discipline and mediation, at least during elementary school years. They typically underestimate the destructiveness of their own enabling behaviors, even when they have been bullied.[20] Mediation could also, at least theoretically, be useful in cases in which bullying has shifted into a more equal-power fight, which we know occurs in about half of all bullying cases that gravitate online.[21] However, I can't actually recommend the use of mediation in either of these cases, because I have not been able to locate any research on either situation.

The bottom line: I'm very aware that the prospect of a bully genuinely apologizing to a target and understanding the target's perspective could be extremely powerful and potentially healing. The difficulty is that in the absence of both parties being genuinely motivated to change, it is too difficult to truly know whether a mediation would be helpful or hurtful to a victim. In an equal-power fight, both parties are typically unhappy, which offers a true incentive for change. In a bullying situation, the bully is effectively "winning" the social game and therefore has little incentive for change. Wanting things to change is a key element in successful mediation.[22] Adults may choose to disregard this danger and instead rely on their personal appraisal that the mediation was successful and that the bully felt genuine contrition and offered genuine apologies. We may *think* we can reliably judge when an apology is genuine; but if we're wrong, the consequences can be quite serious for the victim. Apart from mental health and safety issues, we are also gambling that the victim hasn't ultimately learned that telling adults about bullying was a big mistake. That risk, in combination with all of the research suggesting that mediation cannot be effective with bullying, suggests to me that using mediation *in these cases* is at best imprudent and at worst damaging. Again, I emphasize that this is in no way a criticism of the mediation process. While I strongly believe that peer mediation programs should exist in every school system, I remain concerned about their use with emotionally fragile targets who may feel pressured into a repeat victimization by well-meaning counselors and administrators.

The good news, however, is that (1) mediation is always a technique that can be revisited if the power imbalance changes in a situation, as it often does; and (2) other methods can help targets feel safer and more comfortable in school.

STEPS SCHOOL PERSONNEL CAN TAKE TO HELP A TARGET FEEL SAFER

The following steps are meant primarily for use by administrators, school counselors, and school resource officers (SROs), but they also can be helpful for teachers to know as well. Teachers are often on committees that form safety plans (which can use this type of data), and if they know what is reasonable to expect from counselors and administrators, they can help confirm that certain steps are taken in appropriate situations.

Establishing a Safety and Comfort Plan

Victims may need, or benefit from, a safety and comfort plan. The student should choose this safe person—someone the child likes and can talk to anytime—and the possibilities can include administrators, counselors, nurses, SROs, teachers, and other full-time staff who are not always occupied with other students. The child's teachers should be told that this student should be permitted to see the safe person at any time. A signal can be established (e.g., the student takes a tissue, or closes a book) so the teachers know that the child wants to see the safe person, without the student needing to announce that fact. Initially, do not be concerned if a victim appears to exploit their safe person as a way to avoid schoolwork. Focus instead on the child's sense of safety and comfort. Eventually, when the situation appears to be resolving, you can address the student who exploits the situation (if necessary).

Increasing Structured Interactions

Unstructured areas can pose particular concerns. Have a plan in advance for less structured areas, such as buses and the lunchroom (and the playground for elementary-age students). Victims should never be left to hope that they can find a safe place to eat lunch or a safe seat on the bus ride home. A seat should be reserved in advance near friends (or near friendly students).

Engaging Student Help

There's little doubt that students can be the most powerful elements in any bullying prevention or reduction plan.[23] At MARC, we've trained hundreds of students to be antibullying leaders in their own schools through a special process in which the students retain much of the control and responsibility for the programs they implement. I've even seen some bullies—those with real leadership qualities—become pretty committed antibullying activists in their own schools, and although I don't have data to back up these war stories, I have been told anecdotally that this experience has "turned them around."

Although students can achieve wonderful goals when addressing bullying in the abstract, my fieldwork experiences suggest that they might be more tentative about helping targets of bullying directly, possibly because they fear being singled out as well (by association). The good news is that students can help their peers without having to commit to either a new friendship, eating lunch, or playing with a target. In the 2012 freshman study, subjects were given a scenario in which a target has been told something mean; a second individual walks past and says, "Don't pay any attention to him." When the hypothetical comment was made by an adult, 38 percent of subjects felt it would be very effective; but when it was made by a peer, 86 percent felt it would be very effective. Even just a simple comment as a student walks past appears to be potentially very helpful. Student interventions can probably be far more effective than adult ones (see chapter 7 for a discussion about engaging bystanders and other students).

Encouraging Strengths and Resources

Although this section focuses on changing the behaviors and responses of the student who's the target of bullying, it's important to emphasize that I'm not suggesting that the only or even primary response to bullying should be to "fix" the victim. In fact, implying that students have the power to change the dynamic of the relationship may suggest that *they* are the problem, which can further harm a victim of peer abuse. Disturbingly, one report focused on a teacher who advised students by saying, "Don't be so gay," which could clearly revictimize a target of bullying, even if the adult meant it as useful advice.[24] Yet, although it's clearly important to target the bully for intervention and possibly consequences, two difficult truths are also evident.

First, despite discipline, unless all contact between the bully and the target is eliminated—unless they are not even within eyeshot of each other (very difficult, even impossible, in many school settings)—it is impossible to be 100 percent certain that the bully won't retaliate against the target, even if the retaliation is only a future promise (such as looking pointedly at the target). Second, even if total isolation from each other is possible, other students may engage in retaliatory actions. In many school settings, therefore, it's difficult to be sure that intervention with a bully means that the bully's target is now 100 percent safe.

Because of that difficulty, and because of the injury that may have already been done to the target's self-esteem, it's usually worthwhile to ask how we can help targets feel better about themselves and feel more resilient in the face of any comments or actions by other students. The essential rule of thumb is to work off existing strengths. What friends does this student have, either in school or in other settings? What outside groups are he or she involved with, such as a church group or other activities? In the 2020–2022 Social and Emotional Research Consortium (SERC) study, strong social skills were associated with students whose resiliency became stronger as they grew up.[25] Alternatively, does the student shine in musical, artistic, mechanical, or other abilities? Is the family close? Are family events and visits largely positive occasions? Sometimes an increased emphasis on areas of the victim's life that are affirmative can help make the student feel better about him- or herself and thus better able to withstand cruelty from peers. Generally speaking, adults are better than children are at shifting their focus to more positive things following an unpleasant encounter, but this is definitely a skill that children can (and will) learn. Parents who are casting around for ways to help their child who's a target of bullying may feel more productive if they can focus their efforts.

RESPONDING TO BULLYING ONLINE

Much of what I've discussed in this chapter applies mainly to traditional in-person bullying. But just as cyberbullying introduces an entirely new dimension to bullying behaviors, so too does it introduce a new set of responses. Generally speaking, these responses are less developed then the interventions commonly used for in-person bullying.

Laws May Encourage Reporting

In 2019, a researcher analyzed student reports of cyberbullying and then sifted through state cyberbullying laws, finding that the adoption of such laws predicted increases in reporting of online bullying incidents.[26] Additionally, the increase noted did not appear to be due to any increase in cyberbullying; in other words, state laws didn't increase rates of cyberbullying, but they did appear to encourage youth to report online bullying when it occurred. This is an excellent example of one important way that state laws can influence attitudes toward antisocial behavior.

A Nonlawyer's Take on the Legal Issue

Unlike traditional bullying, much cyberbullying takes place off campus, most typically in the child's home. This means that the behavior falls into a different legal category. While behavior that takes place at school is clearly under the jurisdiction of educators, behavior at home is usually viewed as being under the jurisdiction of parents.[27]

One important exception to this rule is off-campus behavior or speech that makes a "real threat" or "substantial disruption" in the school climate.[28] Exactly what a "substantial disruption" means is not clear. Different courts have used different definitions for this term. For each cyberbullying case, school administrators must decide if the cyber behavior is making, or will make, a substantial disruption before they decide to discipline a cyberbully.

Even if, however, a school decides that cyberbullying is not making a substantial disruption to the school environment, *school can still take important steps to help cope with and resolve cyberbullying incidents.*

What Schools Can Do

The fact that bullying takes place online doesn't really permit schools to wash their hands of it. They can take responsible actions *regardless* of the disruption to the school environment (or lack of it).

Emphasizing awareness and social support

According to a study that examined programs that emphasize awareness of cyberbullying and coping skills, school programs that address cyberbullying can be effective. One researcher examined several different cyberbullying programs, comparing their relative efficacy, and found that the critical element was not any one specific program. Instead, an emphasis on awareness and skill-building. In addition, the capability of the presenter (i.e., their skills in understanding cyberbullying), proved to be very important.[29]

Other research has consistently found that social and emotional support can make an important difference when it comes to reducing vulnerability to cyberbullying. One study of more than 1,400 middle and high school students found that parental support and discussion effectively reduced cyberbullying involvement, and although educators can't mandate such behaviors (obviously), they can and should encourage them.[30] An interesting qualitative study examined the roles that peers play in either supporting or undermining cyberbullying when it occurs and concluded that the roles online are remarkably similar to those in traditional bullying. Many youth who witness cyberbullying are uncomfortable, and some will defend targets; conversely, some are "assistants" who help the cyberbully. The dynamic appears to be identical to the situations that happen in school hallways.[31] We know that, in person, defenders or friends can be an invaluable resource for increasing the resiliency of targets of traditional bullying.[32] Likewise, it appears that such social support may make an important difference in cases of cyberbullying.

When to involve the police

Let's make this simple. If the behavior in question involves criminal activity, threats, significant violence, or electronic or physical stalking, I believe (as a nonlawyer) that consultations with police might be in order. However, I feel strongly that faculty should begin by consulting with the building administrator or the school's legal counsel. Involving police is a serious step that can, at times, be necessary. Because police involvement can irreparably affect the students, school, and yourself, it's important to seek the advice of others in the building or the school district before making that jump.

Other actions you can take: Communication is key

It's often worthwhile to have an educational discussion with the cyberbully and with cyber bystanders. It may be important to call out that this discussion is *not* discipline; it is education about the dangers of cyberbullying and the fact that everyone is now aware of the situation. If relevant, discuss future legal problems the child may incur if these behaviors continue. It's a good idea to involve the child's parents, who, after all, are the digital technology gatekeepers, if possible.

If you're informed about an online situation, be sure to inform potential cyberbullies and cyber bystanders about the consequences for bullying or cyberbullying while in school. If the cyberbully or cyber bystanders engage in any bullying or cyberbullying in school, follow through on consequences immediately. Inform all relevant adults—teachers, coaches, counselors, and bus drivers—about the situation between the two children. Ensure that they are aware of the potential for bullying and that they keep a very sharp eye on these children. If it were me, I would document everyone I had informed of the situation.

Follow up with parents, especially parents of victims. Do not wait for them to call you; let them know that these actions are being taken. Many parents want to know what disciplinary actions are being taken against a cyberbully, and you may need to educate them about confidentiality laws.[33] Be sure that they know you are not merely refusing to furnish information because you want to protect a bully but rather are following the law.

RESPONDING AT THE LEVEL OF FORMAL DISCIPLINE

It's a funny paradox. On the one hand, I've encouraged you to disregard the "Is it bullying?" question entirely if you witness an incident of mean behavior and to respond instead to the inappropriate conduct directly. This is true when you are faced with a student who's actively engaging in a gateway behavior. On the other hand, in more formal situations, such as when you're deciding whether bullying is actually happening, or when you're evaluating a student's overall pattern of behavior, drawing the distinction between what's bullying and what's not is *very* important.

I defined bullying as an abusive behavior that involves intent, repetition, and power imbalance. Most researchers and experts also use those three elements to define bullying. The point is that while drawing the bullying/not bullying distinction isn't important when dealing with minor behaviors *informally*, it is essential when dealing with behaviors using formal responses or formal discipline. Without a clear definition of bullying, situations in which adults should focus their energies on a child's misbehavior can deteriorate into an argument over whether or not a situation merits the "bullying" label. I'm constantly asked questions like this one, which was submitted to an email list by a social worker at a middle school:

> *My son was named a bully by the principal . . . he had taken another boy & held him up against the wall & threatened him . . . now my son had never got in trouble before & was never in a fight before . . . I agree that this was hurtful behavior, but I do not believe that he was a bully as the principal said . . . What are your thoughts on this?*

Notice that the question is not, "What's the best response that will help my child learn not to repeat his aggressive behavior?" but, "We think it's not bullying; they think it is bullying—who's right?" Thus, the attention has shifted to focus on how the adults will classify the behavior, instead of focusing on the children involved, how to help the target cope with the situation, and how to teach the bully that this type of behavior was wrong. Parents who push to have a behavior labeled as "bullying" often do so because they worry that, otherwise, the problem won't be taken seriously. It's up to school personnel to ensure that parents know that they take these behaviors very seriously—regardless of the label.

Keep the Focus on the Child's Behavior

Although I always encourage parents to focus on the behavior, rather than on the label, educators in many states are obliged to make an official determination about whether or not a child's behavior constitutes "bullying." When discussing the rationale behind this decision, a few cautionary points are in order:

1. Never use the word *bullying* itself unless you must. It's emotionally loaded, and likely to generate an emotional response. Refer to a child as a bully only when you are absolutely required to.

2. If you must label a situation as bullying, make clear the criteria used for that label and how you see the case fitting these criteria. For example:

   In this school and in this state, there are three criteria for a situation to be called bullying. The behavior has to happen more than once—we can see that this is true here. The behavior can't be an accident—I think it's obvious that Bill's throwing rocks toward a bull's-eye he had painted on Henry's car wasn't an accident. And there must be a power imbalance. This last criterion is the trickiest, but I think in this case we can agree that Bill is one of the most popular boys in school, and he had a group of friends laughing and congratulating him as he did this. Henry's a great boy too—he is more shy, though, and doesn't seem to get support from other students over this matter.

3. The parents of the bully will often disagree, and it's a good idea to let them save some face. That may permit them to focus on their child's behavior without being distracted by a debate about the word *bullying*.

   I think the critical issue isn't whether or not this is bullying, but how we as adults respond to Bill's behavior. Many kids try out these kinds of behaviors, since they're so strongly associated with popularity. Let's just focus on how we can get Bill to understand how seriously we take his behavior. I see so much great potential in him; I don't want him to get sidetracked.

4. On the other side, the parents of the target may disagree if you *don't* think the situation is bullying, in which case it's often a good idea to redirect them to the behavior in question and how safe their child feels:

   I think that whether or not this is bullying really isn't the most important thing; what's most important is making sure that Henry feels we addressed the situation and that he feels safe coming back to school. Let's focus on how we can support Henry.

Never cite confidentiality without explaining it—this point cannot be overemphasized. Many parents don't understand that federal law (and possibly state law, depending on the state) forbids administrators from discussing another parent's child in any way. To an upset parent, you may appear to be stonewalling or even protecting the other student. It's critical to point out that you don't have a choice—you understand how they feel, but you must obey the law.

WHEN SHOULD YOU *NOT* RESPOND?

I've argued that some small amount of meanness is probably, in the long run, advantageous (if unpleasant) for children—sort of like going to the dentist. If the meanness isn't significantly traumatic or damaging, then it's a training ground for dealing with all the difficult situations that life inevitably produces. Having said that, when do those situations occur, and when should adults *not* respond?

Let me begin by saying that I truly believe that there's no way to get this issue exactly right, all the time. No matter how hard we try, it's likely that, at times, children who would benefit from our intervention won't get it, and at other times, children who would benefit from working things out on their own don't get to do that, either. There's no way to be 100 percent accurate because it's always possible that only the child has all the relevant information about the situation. In addition, educators are only human, and thus they are subject to influences that have nothing to do with the situation at hand. As a result, a teacher may tell the kids to "just work it out" not because that request seems appropriate, but simply because they are too tired to deal with the situation at the end of a long day.

Still, some general guidelines may help minimize the mistakes:

- *Evaluate the balance of power*: Ask yourself if one of the kids has much less power than or is afraid of the other. If the answer is yes, then taking a closer look is a better approach than dismissing the incident.
- *Weigh the content of the dispute*: Ask yourself if the dispute appears to be relatively inconsequential. A quarrel over whether someone's mother is an alcoholic is not inconsequential, but an argument over who gets to go first on the slide can be. Is the content of the quarrel something that can be really hurtful? Is it important? If the answer is no, then encouraging the kids to work it out for themselves is probably merited.
- *Consider whether the dispute is a repeat occurrence*: Regardless of content, is this a situation or problem that is appearing repeatedly? Even if the content seems trivial, students who are engaging in problem behaviors over and over again are essentially struggling with a larger issue. That's a signal that a talk is merited.
- *Look for an obvious ulterior motive*: Be careful and be sure to read the section in chapter 2, "Don't dismiss 'tattlers' by refusing to hear them

out." An obvious ulterior motive is always a signal to take a situation more (not less) seriously, although the situation may be different from the one being reported. For example, a young child persistently telling you that so-and-so is butting into line, and they want the person punished, is a signal for a talk with the "telling" child. You may ultimately decide that so-and-so is indeed guilty, or you may find yourself uncovering something entirely different, such as a situation in which the teller is actually the guilty party.

- *Determine whether the situation has escalated*: Any situation between children that appears to be escalating should be attended to by adults. Children often don't understand how their behaviors can contribute to an escalation, including their digital behaviors. Some education is often in order.
- *Always respond to fear*: If a child is afraid, that situation always merits your close attention. Always.
- *Always offer a safety hatch*: Even if you tell kids to work something out for themselves, or tell them not to "tattle" (an approach I do not recommend), end your comment by letting the children involved know that you will listen if this is important. You may not be able to listen right now, but you will soon.
- *Even if you ask them to work it out, cue them with the process*: Rather than just saying, "You two work this out," prompt the children with the process that's needed. Ask them, "How could you two work this out for yourselves, without having to ask for help from a grown-up? Can one of you propose a solution?" If the students respond with a reason why they came to you (e.g., "He never does what he says he'll do"), then help them negotiate a compromise, but also stay put to help enforce the results. Hopefully, the extra minutes you spend with them will mean that in the future, these children will be able to work out small problems for themselves.

In this chapter I've talked about responding to bullies and their targets. But what about responding to bullying by working with bystanders? If you've picked up a newspaper in the past fifteen years, you've probably read about how bystanders are key. So let's dive in: on to chapter 7.

CHAPTER 7

Engaging Bystanders and Other Peers

A Developmental Approach to Cultivating Prosocial Behavior

Bystanders: are they the silver bullet? If only we could get bystanders to do what we want them to do: actively intervene when bullying happens; discourage bullying wherever they see it; and immediately report anything they witness to an adult. Then, perhaps, the bullying issue would abate. Or would it?

So, what's the holdup?

WHO DO WE MEAN BY *BYSTANDERS*?

The term *bystander* is vague; several peripheral peer groups are potentially important in bullying situations. Some students actually witness episodes; others may not be physically present, but may become aware of incidents. I call these groups *witnesses* (they can be either *allies* or *nonallies*) and *aware peers*. Other peers may encourage bullying by befriending and supporting bullies, even if they may not know about specific bullying instances. I refer to these peers as *bully-friends*. Rather than assuming that the same prevention approach should be taken with each of these groups, I think it's more interesting to study them first and see whether any key differences emerge. The fact is, however, most research doesn't differentiate among these groups. So, in the rest of this chapter, I refer more generically to *bystanders*.

In my studies of students in grades 3–12 and the 2012 Massachusetts Aggression Reduction Center (MARC) freshman study, I *was* able to draw some comparisons among witnesses, aware peers, and bully-friends, and I cite those findings (and others) where applicable.

ARE BYSTANDERS ALWAYS PRESENT OR AWARE OF BULLYING?

A variety of studies have suggested that most bullying incidents are done in the presence of bystanders. One Canadian study of found that peers were bystanders (i.e., *witnesses*) in 85 percent of bullying instances.[1] This study, however, examined only twenty-seven children in one elementary school and was conducted more than twenty years ago. The researchers (Atlas and Pepler) used a clever tactic: they observed bullying episodes directly in a school and were thus able to watch, and literally to count, the number of instances in which peers were present or observing. Using a similar approach, O'Connell, Pepler, and Craig recorded playground bullying episodes in two Toronto schools and found that more than half of the incidents (53 percent) involved bystanders or witnesses.[2] (The authors speculate, reasonably, that the lower percentage in the second study may have been due to the difficulty, on a video, of observing more subtle bullying, such as the use of comments or psychological tactics.)

Despite these findings, concluding that the vast majority of bullying episodes involve witnesses is problematic. First, the research that leads to these conclusions is more than twenty years old. How does cyberbullying or digital behaviors weave into this narrative? Perhaps, for example, if a bully is targeting someone online, then in school, all they need to do to intimidate their victim is to look at them or do something similarly unobtrusive and unnoticeable.

The second problem, which is closely related to the first, is that even if the bullying is happening only in school, any researchers observing the kids would probably be able to note only the more obvious cases of bullying behaviors. As O'Connell and colleagues hypothesized, less noticeable actions may not be counted by adult observation. For example, it's not too hard to imagine how a chronic victim of bullying by a group of girls might feel if two of the girls pass by, snicker, and roll their eyes, even if they never stop and openly engage with the victim. But would an observer see this and know it was bullying? That was be exceptionally difficult to determine without knowing the backstory.

Because so many acts of bullying are accomplished through gateway behaviors (which are usually subtle), it's easy to speculate that researchers who are looking for obvious incidents (e.g., one child surrounded by a several kids who are taunting them) could miss these more subtle behaviors that underscore a bullying dynamic. And even if they don't miss these behaviors, it would be quite difficult to know if they were looking at bullying, fighting, or just one-time cruelty.

Note, however, that other pieces of data suggest that working with bystanders is a potentially useful strategy. First, it's clearly pretty common for children and teenagers to witness bullying. One study found that 88 percent of students had witnessed bullying; another estimated this at 68 percent.[3] The Youth Voice Project (YVP), found that 54 percent of students were exposed to verbal bullying.[4] (The YVP is a unique piece of research conducted by Stan Davis and Charisse Nixon, who asked thirteen thousand children how different adult and peer strategies affected the outcomes of bullying situations.) In my 2012 MARC freshman study, 70 percent reported that they had seen bullying or cyberbullying.[5] And these witnesses aren't only in person; a study of cyberbullying found that a similar proportion of students (88 percent) reported that they had witnessed peer cruelty online (although, importantly, only 12 percent said they saw it "frequently").[6] More recent research agrees that most, if not all, children see some type of unkindness between peers: a 2022 study of almost six hundred elementary school children in Turkey also found that virtually every child had witnessed some behavior that was potentially bullying.[7] Among older adolescents, the proportion who report actually witnessing bullying incidents is somewhat lower. In one study of more than 7,500 Irish teens, "only" 31 percent reported witnessing bullying.[8] In all of these studies, it seems probable that even more students were *aware peers*, or kids who knew bullying was going on, without having actually witnessed these incidents.

A fundamental difficulty is that although these two types of statistics are often cited together, the percentage of students who *see* bullying isn't the same as the percentage of bullying incidents that includes observers. For example, it could easily be the case that a single bullying incident is observed by multiple bystanders, which would inflate the percentage who saw bullying but wouldn't change the proportion of incidents with witnesses. In short, these numbers tell us that lots of kids see bullying and cyberbullying, but only the direct observation studies have actually suggested that a high proportion of incidents have witnesses.

Once again, digital communication complicates the issue. The direct-observation methodology may be, in many ways, the best method for measuring the proportion of in-school incidents with bystanders, but cyberbullying can rarely (if ever) be directly observed by researchers. If researchers hang around a school, this chance is good that they'll witness some bullying; but observing bullying online is a much bigger area to cover. To ensure that they witnessed cyberbullying, researchers would have to cultivate hundreds of online contacts ("friends") and hang around social networking sites for potentially a long time. Researchers still would probably miss cyberbullying from other sources, such as through text messaging. This reality necessitated the use of a different method to measure the presence of bystanders online and in school. Thus, in my 2012 study, I simply asked victims directly if other kids knew that they were being targeted (*aware peers*), and if other kids actually saw the bullying or cyberbullying happen (*witnesses*). Predictably, the incidents in which kids were aware of bullying and cyberbullying were greater than the incidents with direct witnesses. For in-school bullying victims, 37 percent of the victims said witnesses were present, but 42 percent that aware peers were present. In contrast, 23 percent said they had witnesses online, but 30 percent said that other kids knew about the cyberbullying.

Measuring bully-friends also reminds us that bullies are not socially isolated in schools; 25 percent of elementary students reported that they were friends with kids who were bullies. An additional 18 percent said that they had been, at some point, friends with bullies. A high proportion of victims also were friends with their bullies at one point or another before the bullying (40 percent in elementary school and 46 percent in middle or high school). Although I wouldn't expect a victim to actively support their bully (even if the person is a friend), one could argue that by befriending a bully, they inadvertently supported an environment that promotes or tolerates bullying.

Going by the numbers, these results might suggest that friends of bullies, those who know about bullying at the school, and direct witnesses are all fairly common. In turn, and consistent with the gist of Atlas and Pepler's study, that finding suggests that many bullying incidents are either seen or talked about between peers, in person or online (but especially in person). Sixty-one percent of bystanders in the 2012 freshman study talked with peers about bullying they saw (in school or online), yet only 15 percent said that they reported it to an adult at school. Similarly, in the 2020–2022 Social and Emotional Research Consortium (SERC) study, 83 percent of the bullied kids said they talked with peers, and either discussed a strategy or experienced some emotional relief by doing so.[9] Students, not adults, have the best idea of what's happening at school, and although some targets undoubtedly feel humiliated that other people know what's happening, perhaps we can use this peer awareness to help address these situations.

WHY BYSTANDERS MATTER

Bullying is widely described as a "whole-school" process.[10] Bystanders are fundamentally involved, both as facilitators and as preventers. If bullies are seeking power and status, then it is desirable to have others witness or know about the bullying activities.[11] This motivation to have witnesses is a key difference between peer abuse and other types of interpersonal abuse, and it has important implications for prevention. Adult-perpetrated child and spouse abuse are typically hidden behaviors in which secrecy is key (legal reasons and social norms may call for such secrecy). Peer abuse (bullying and cyberbullying) *are* often kept secret from the adults, but in the child-only world, peers are encouraged to observe this behavior. One result is that we have a tool in combating bullying that we don't have against concealed types of abuse. Peers who know about bullying and cyberbullying represent a distinct opportunity to prevent these problems, but we don't pursue their help only because they may help the target of bullying. Whether or not they realize it, bystanders are direct stakeholders in the school climate, and they in turn affect that environment, as well.

Bystanders Can Cause or Exacerbate Bullying

The presence of witnesses is often seen as a key reason that bullying occurs. Konstantina and Pilios-Dimitris felt that the presence of bystanders is one of the primary reasons for bullying, because witnesses confer social prestige upon the bully, and more recent research has confirmed that this is an important motivation.[12] O'Connell's study found that (averaged across all episodes) more than half of bystanders actively supported bullying by watching it and thus (perhaps unintentionally) reinforcing the bullies' behavior.[13] O'Connell, Pepler, and Craig's study of recorded playground bullying episodes went a step further: they found it wasn't simply that a witness could be the reason for bullying, but rather that more witnesses actually exacerbated an episode. On average, four children witnessed each bullying episode that they recorded, and the more witnesses there were, the longer the episode lasted. In spite of the data, my field experiences have suggested that many students believe that "just watching" is neutral and has no impact on bullying incidences, but the findings of these studies suggest otherwise. Like adults who observe (see chapter 5), perhaps bystanders can't really take a neutral stance—if they watch and do nothing, they may be reinforcing the bully's behavior.[14] One lesson to bystanders could be, "No, you're not being neutral when you watch bullying," along with a discussion of the many possible ways witnesses can respond, including simply removing yourself from the scene. That may often feel uncomfortably like abandoning the victim, but if this removal is combined with other tactics (e.g., getting friends or adults to help), it might be a good solution. Indeed, one international study found that leaving the scene, combined with a secondary goal like getting a teacher, was actually the preferred strategy.[15]

Bystanders Are Affected by the Bullying They See

Several studies have found that bystanders are psychologically affected by observing bullying. Callaghan et al.'s 2019 study of more than 7,500 Irish youth found that bullying bystanders were more likely to report psychological and somatic symptoms, and they had lower life satisfaction than those who weren't bystanders.[16] Carney, Jacob, and Hazler studied the impact of bullying on bystanders in 2011.[17] They found that bullying was a psychological trauma that resulted in psychological and physiological changes in both the victims and bystanders. The level of anxiety, trust in relationships, and physiological indicators of stress (cortisol levels) were all related to exposure to bullying (as either a victim or a witness).

Rivers completed an important study examining the impact of bullying on bystanders in 2009.[18] In that study of more than two thousand children in the United Kingdom, significant mental effects were found among those who observed bullying, including (among other symptoms) anxiety, hostility, phobias, depression, somatic complaints, and obsessive-compulsive behaviors. Importantly, these effects were observed even in observers or bystanders *who were not themselves victims of bullying or other forms of violence.* How does seeing bullying affect those who were prior victims versus those who weren't? Rivers theorized that among bystanders who were prior victims, psychological revictimization may be an important cause of trauma. However, even those bystanders who weren't prior victims might feel significant tension between their belief that they *ought* to confront a bully and their failure to do so. Such tension (termed *dissonance* by psychologists) could account for bystander hostility toward targets. It's presumably more comfortable for bystanders to decide that a victim deserves the bullying than to conclude that they are personally failing as bystanders by not actively confronting the bully. In contrast, in Callaghan et al.'s study, bystanders who focused on helping targets experienced significantly less psychological trauma.[19] This finding raises the possibility that programs and adults should consider advising youth to be *up*standers by helping targets rather than emphasizing to witnesses that they should assertively confront the bully.

Bystanders Can Be Powerful Allies for Targets

Bystanders have power—no doubt about it—but they don't often see what another student's bullying situation has to do with them. Unfortunately, slogans used to encourage students to intervene in bullying episodes don't always convey the key role they might play. For example, the slogan "Tell an adult" may mistakenly give children the impression that other students are not really part of the equation when it comes to peer abuse. It highlights the role of adults and thus fails to emphasize the responsibility that *all* people (including children) have to be solicitous of one another.

Bystanders may also not understand their responsibility with regard to bullying if they don't realize how much bullying affects the entire school. *All* community members suffer when bullying happens in their midst, so all community members have a stake in the problem and thus a motivation to stop or reduce bullying. Children in any school need to understand and think about how bullying any child affects them personally. Although many kids I encounter in the field don't always recognize how bullying affects the school in general, they do perceive that witnessing or knowing about bullying affects them personally. I've yet to hear a child say that bullying in their school doesn't affect them at all or that they couldn't care less if it happens, as long as they're not personally targeted.

WHAT SHOULD BYSTANDERS DO?

In this discussion of what bystanders should do, I don't address long-term strategies, such as changing the school climate or getting parents more involved. Rather, I suggest immediate strategies that we can encourage students to engage in when they see bullying or cyberbullying, or soon afterward. These actions include telling an adult, telling a bully to stop, helping a target escape a bad situation, or fostering peer support.

The emphasis on telling adults is visible, so I'll start there. A lot of the following discussion, however, focuses on the kinds of responses that students *actually* use (based on my data and others' work).

Action 1: Reporting to Adults

In the field, I often run across two different beliefs that surprise me. First is the assertion that children must be encouraged to report to adults, without any acknowledgment that an enormous amount of data indicates that children are far more comfortable (usually) reporting to peers. The second belief that surprises me is the implicit assumption that reporting to adults is, in fact, an effective way to stop a bullying situation. Because my goal is to retain credibility with students and adults, I think it's important to consider both of these assumptions.

They may report—just not to you

Children do report, or they don't, depending on how you define *reporting*. A number of studies have found that despite encouragement, many students don't report bullying to adults. Overall, about a third to a half of bullied youth appear to report the incidents to an educator.

A 2019 review examining twenty-three articles focusing on bullying and harassment of Asian America youth found that only about one in three victims notified an adult after a bullying incident.[20] Other research yields some good information about how and why students do or don't report to grown-ups. A 2019 study of 1,266 elementary and middle school students in Scandinavia found that many victims of bullying (45 percent) do not report to anyone and of those who do report, about half talk with parents and half to an adult at school. This study found age and gender differences: younger students and girls were more likely to report to adults. Also, having peer support, being a target of a bullying for a longer period of time, and believing that your teacher doesn't tolerate bullying all increased the probability that a student would report to an educator.[21] Another study suggested that, at least sometimes, the characteristics of the victim influence whether or not they report to adults. In a 2022 study of Australian preteens and teenagers, 45 percent did not seek help from adults. This study found that those targets with mental health challenges, weaker social skills, and less social support were less likely to report. In addition, those who used digital technology more often, were similarly less likely to report.[22]

Of course, students have more than one way to report. If a student sees or experiences bullying and doesn't tell *anyone*, then they're not reporting. But most subjects report that they frequently *do* discuss the bullying with a friend or sibling. Under the "tell an adult" strategy, this isn't considered reporting. But I would argue that talking to friends about a distressing situation is most definitely reporting—and reporting in a potentially productive way. My 2012 MARC freshman study found that subjects knew how to help friends who came to them to talk about a bullying situation. Almost two-thirds said they would talk about the situation with their friend and try to make them feel better; 41 percent said they would discuss, or help their friend act on, the possibility of telling an adult; and 27 percent said they would help their friend report cyberbullying to the relevant website. Friends can help friends frame or reframe situations; they can point out inconsistencies or ask questions that help the reporter better understand the incident. Friends can also offer emotional support and can help plan and carry out strategies, if any, that should be taken. Last but definitely not least, as children grow, they seek out peers more and more for reporting purposes; this is not pathological but is developmentally normal and even adaptive.

This tendency to increasingly shift reporting from adults to peers throughout the school years was documented very clearly in my study of twenty-one thousand schoolchildren in 2011. Elementary students preferentially reported to parents and teachers; but by middle and high school, the students had placed teachers near the bottom of the list, and peers had assumed their developmentally appropriate place at the top. Older students continued to report the more serious incidents to parents, but after elementary school, single-incident or minor social cruelties were reported much less often to parents. Reporting to teachers simply declined, and reporting to peers increased, as children grew.[23]

In the 2012 freshman study, the largest group of students who reported were those who reported *only* to peers (41 percent). The remaining 60 percent were equally split between 20 percent who only reported to adults, 20 percent who said they didn't report to anyone, and 20 percent who said they reported to *everyone*—adults *and* peers. These proportions are similar to what other research has found.[24] Combining these groups, we can see that 37 percent of students reported to adults (school adults and/or parents), but 60 percent reported to peers, revealing a preference that really shouldn't surprise anyone reading this book. Some gender differences shouldn't be too surprising either; for example, the shift from telling adults to telling peers is a more marked preference among the female subjects. Together, 66 percent of girls told peers versus just 45 percent of boys. Similar proportions told adults, but boys were more likely to prefer reporting to no one.

We could look at this data and regard the reduction in reporting to adults over the span of childhood as representing a failure, but I would argue that it is not a failure for children to shift some emotional needs to their peers during adolescence. Rather, I contend that it represents a normal trajectory and that we as educators have been less than successful in encouraging children to report to us precisely because we've been rowing upstream, instead of working *with* the inevitable juggernaut of cognitive and social growth. Note that teens are not choosing to report to insignificant acquaintances; in the 2012 freshman study, both boys and girls who reported to peers overwhelmingly chose to confide in their "closest friends" rather than "other kids" (85 percent versus 15 percent). If we look at the data from the perspective of normal adolescent development, it may be easier to see why we should expect that so many teenage students will report to peers rather than to adults.

Of course, we should be crystal clear about this: nothing is wrong with encouraging your students to report bullying to adults. The problem is that, realistically, they have a range of choices (educator, parents, friends, siblings), but the message "tell an adult" implies they have only one choice (educator). How many programs discuss with children the emotional benefits of talking about their situation with anyone they're close to—friends, siblings, *or* adults? It's somewhat contradictory that we don't encourage children to discuss their difficulties with their friends, even though this is precisely the tactic that most individuals ultimately learn to use in life. The fact that we may be omitting this obvious resource could make adults appear to be clueless and, therefore, even less attractive as confidants. If we truly want students to talk with adults, we have to be a credible alternative. But there are two sides to this coin. If we want to be realistic about encouraging victims to go to their friends for help, then we also should consider asking students to think in advance about *how* they would help friends who approach them for assistance with a bullying situation.

Aside from of the fact that kids may prefer to report to peers, our emphasis on adult reporting poses another problem. The "tell an adult" plea is predicated on an important assumption: that reporting to the powers that be will make the situation *better* for the victim. But does it?

Does reporting work?

Data from the 2012 freshman study suggest that reporting works, in the sense that students who reported felt that adults responded positively. Adults most often told reporters that they would deal with the situation; they made the reporter "feel better" and told him or her "not to worry." Negative reactions, like telling the student to "mind your own business," were rare. But in many other respects, reporting cannot always be viewed as a satisfactory solution to bullying. When my youngest was in kindergarten, he described a playground scene in which another little boy was (slightly) mean to a girl.

"She should go tell the teacher," was my (reflexive) advice.

"Mom," he said soberly, "that's not good advice. If you're always telling the teacher about every little thing, no one will play with you."

He had made a serious point. We often fall back on "tell an adult," and although we say this with the best intentions, its usefulness as advice is probably more limited than we'd like to admit.

The literature on reporting effectiveness is decidedly mixed. For example, a 2004 study of more than twenty-seven hundred children in the Netherlands reported that most adult intervention was not effective.[25] A 2019 longitudinal study followed middle schoolers over two years and compared their experiences with bullying and reporting to adults at school at two different times. Students who reported to staffers at Time 1 were more likely to be victimized again by Time 2—not a desirable outcome.[26] The 2020–2022 SERC study found that most adult actions, like "trying to defuse a bullying situation" or "punishing the bully," were rated as effective by fewer than 10 percent of bullying victims. In a large study of Toronto schools, students reported that teachers' actions following reporting were largely ineffective, although the teachers felt that they were responding well.[27]

Other studies suggest that under certain circumstances and with certain groups of children, adult interventions may be helpful. A study found that the effectiveness of adult advice depended on the age of the children—namely, younger teens found adults' advice to be more effective than older teens did.[28] A study of 5,774 adolescents in Peru found that bullying victimization was associated with negative life satisfaction, but that relationship was mitigated most strongly by adult support at home, and secondarily, adult support at school also had a significant protective effect.[29] Finally, a 2020 study of 2,627 preteens and teenagers sampled from the YVP found that support-seeking strategies were, overall, the most effective coping strategies when being bullied; however, strategies did differ by age, gender, and type of victimization. Telling an adult at school was most effective for younger students but was not very effective in physical bullying episodes.[30] Finally, in another study of 1,406 middle and high school students, teacher failure to intervene in traditional bullying was associated with increased involvement in cyberbullying.[31]

One possible explanation for some of the variability lies in the expectations that we place on reporting. What is reporting supposed to accomplish? Should it resolve the bullying situation (perhaps immediately), or is reporting a more useful way to help targets cope emotionally? The YVP found that adult responses that emphasized alliance and emotional support were experienced by victims as the most helpful. These included "listened to me," "checked in with me afterwards to see if the behavior stopped," and "gave me advice." Strategies that were more focused on resolving the situation (punishing the bully, mediating, increasing adult supervision, and promising to talk with the other kids) were sometimes helpful, but sometimes were also harmful. Subjects in my 2012 freshman study similarly ranked talking and being supportive as the most helpful action adults can take (64 percent endorsed this). About half felt that having adults check in with them frequently was helpful, and a similar proportion said that speaking with other teachers (so more people are watching out) helped. These studies suggest that you can't just ask if reporting was effective, because different people might define that concept differently. To accurately measure efficacy in reporting outcomes, we need to explain what we mean by *effective*.

Using imprecise terms like the word *effective* isn't the only possible reason for mixed outcomes about reporting. Another possibility is that some studies ask about abstract situations, whereas others ask about situations that subjects have actually experienced. These two approaches can yield different results. For example, in the 2012 freshman study, I asked about both the effectiveness of reporting in the abstract (e.g., "If this were to happen, should kids report it to an adult?") and whether subjects found it effective to report bullying they had actually seen or experienced. For abstract situations, most subjects endorsed some kind of reporting. Subjects who were willing to report in real life were the most positive about reporting, either because it would make the reporter feel better to talk about the situation, or because it would help resolve the situation. Kids who reported to no one, in contrast, were the most negative: 22 percent believed that kids should learn to cope with bullying on their own, and 7 percent felt that reporting would make the situation worse. Except for the nonreporters, these beliefs were rarely endorsed. In the abstract, therefore, most saw reporting to adults as a good idea.

But when I asked subjects about real situations that involved their own personal reporting, a somewhat less positive picture emerged. This part of the study asked subjects if their reporting had "worked" for them and offered four possible answers:

- It definitely worked.
- It worked somewhat.
- I didn't see an impact, but I believe the adult was working behind the scenes.
- It didn't have any effect.

Most kids said that reporting had an impact, but only about 26 percent responded that it "definitely" worked. The highest proportion (38 percent) felt that reporting made "a little bit" of a difference. This result suggests a generally positive, albeit tepid, endorsement. (We'd rather hear, of course, that reporting is unquestionably successful most of the time.) The kids who told *only* adults (not peers) were the most positive about the outcomes. Girls were more likely than boys to give the adults credit, even if obvious evidence of impact wasn't present; in fact, that was the top answer for girls. Perhaps adults are more likely to follow up with girls and to reassure them that even if they see no obvious signs, action is being taken (this is a step I *always* recommend, because not following up often leads reporters to conclude that you've forgotten about or are ignoring the report). Overall, boys were more lukewarm, but girls weren't vastly more enthusiastic. Only the girls who reported just to adults were likely to feel that reporting made a difference.

This study, combined with the YVP, suggests that when you ask subjects in the abstract, they are more enthusiastic about telling adults; but when you ask them about their personal experiences with reporting, they are less positive and are more mixed in their responses. This difference could be due to subjects feeling pressured to supply the "correct" answer—namely, that students should report to adults. That kind of pressure would be experienced more in abstract situations, but should be less common when subjects are discussing what really happened to them. It's also possible that in real life, the effectiveness of reporting to adults is truly mixed or that (as noted above) subjects differ on how they define "successful" reporting. My takeaway from these studies is that we really don't understand why reporting to adults seems so checkered as a strategy, and this is an area where we need more research. The situation isn't dire—neither my studies nor the YVP were extremely negative about reporting—they just weren't extremely positive, either.

Does reporting result in peer retaliation?

A final issue with reporting is a fear many students express—that even if reporting to adults does help, retaliation or attacks from peers could negate any positive effect. Shaw's study did find that reporting in grades 6 or 7 was associated with repeated victimization in grades 7 and 8 (one of the few studies to explore this using a longitudinal model).[32] I explored this finding by asking subjects first if they were concerned before they reported about how their peers might respond, and then, after reporting, whether they experienced any problems with their peers. In general, about 22 percent of students told me they were initially very worried about peer reaction, and another 33 percent were "somewhat" worried. The good news is that most subjects apparently worried unnecessarily. Although overall 55 percent were worried about peer reaction to their reporting, only 27 percent reported any negative reactions from peers, and 70 percent of these reactions were characterized as mild rather than significant.

The one exception to this trend was the segment of students who reported only to adults and not to peers. They were the least worried about peer responses (only 39 percent were worried) but had the highest rate of actual trouble from peers following the reporting (39 percent reported having trouble, which was mostly mild). Therefore, it would appear that reporting is most likely to lead to retaliation if the student reports only to adults and does not also discuss the situation with his or her peers. It seems likely that students who report only to adults may have other social problems with their peers, which probably magnifies any negative peer responses.

The bottom line: We can probably make reporting a more successful experience for students by framing it as an action that can either make you feel better, help resolve or stop the situation, or both. I think adults should emphasize strategies that have been identified as helpful in my research and in the YVP, as well as in Nixon's more recent research (strategies that build alliance and support).[33] The fact that students are more likely to endorse reporting in the abstract reminds us that we should probably give less credence, in general, to situations in which students may feel pressure to give a "right" answer.

Action 2: Saying "Stop"

The runner-up for favorite adult-endorsed tactic is a simple one: encourage students to be more active as bystanders—that is, to confront bullies when they see an incident and to tell them to stop. This approach to "say no" is attractively straightforward and assertive (in a way that many of us wish we were) and in many ways is an intuitively commonsense response. It's true that adults who are appropriately assertive often have better life skills and do better in myriad situations. Still, general research on the utility of being assertive in the face of bullying suggests that it's a complex issue, in which a standardized one-size-fits-all approach is unlikely to work. Most of the research on the success of confronting abusive behaviors has been done in the context of psychotherapy, in which case it's been repeatedly found that direct confrontation, even by highly skilled adult therapists, is ineffective in changing abusive behaviors.[34] In the 2020–2022 SERC study of 2,427 youth, only 29 percent of targets said that confronting their bully helped the situation.[35] Yet in my fieldwork, I've encountered a number of adults who feel deeply committed to encouraging young children to use this tactic.

Despite its broad appeal, I see two major problems with this approach. First, it recommends an exceptionally difficult course of action. We know from many studies that victims of bullying lack assertiveness.[36] Victims who rate themselves as shyer than any other subjects, and victims with weaker social skills who attempt to assert themselves, have been observed to be unsuccessful at this strategy and to continue to be victimized.[37] Yet, it's these very students—those who are among the least likely to be assertive—who are being asked to be exceptionally brave. It's frankly difficult to see how simply encouraging children to be more assertive in the face of peer abuse would be effective.

Second, confrontation may either be ineffective or may backfire and actually *increase* bullying against the bystander, the victim, or both. A Canadian study did find that about half the time, the immediate incident ceased when an assertive peer stepped in to confront the bully.[38] That's encouraging, but other research has pointed out that the approach appears to fail as often as it works. A more recent study by Stiller et al. found that saying "stop" was effective only about 15 percent of the time, although it was rated as sometimes helpful another 50 percent of the time.[39] Studies of children's opinions have been somewhat less positive. A survey of 285 middle schoolers in the United States found that pledges, rules, and telling bullies "No bullying!" (a version of "stop") were rated as among the least effective methods.[40] The YVP found that a peer's confronting a bully and telling him or her to stop was, at best, a checkered approach. Almost three-quarters of the time (73 percent) it had no real impact, or even made things worse for the victim in the long run.[41]

Despite these findings, I think failing to be effective 100 percent of the time really isn't a strong argument against using this method. If being assertive toward a bully stops even a small percentage of incidents, isn't it worth trying? The real gamble isn't just that confrontation is difficult to achieve and only questionably effective; it's the risk that confrontation may actually *increase* bullying. Although being assertive may stop a bullying incident in the moment, in the long term, it may worsen the situation (for either the confronter or the victim). Witnesses often perceive confrontation to be a risky strategy, because it can result in their becoming a victim. This does appear to pose a real risk. Witnesses who confront bullies can be socially (and sometimes physically) targeted; this has been noted as being particularly true for girls.[42] But it's not only witnesses who can suffer as a result of direct confrontation; victims can find their situation worsened, too. In one longitudinal study, teens who tried to avoid victimization by being assertive actually ended up being more victimized than their peers.[43] Even when the victim isn't the one doing the confronting, bullies may become more aggressive against the victim in the long run, even if it causes the immediate incident to stop.[44] The YVP, which has compared the differential impact of several specific short-term and long-term strategies, found that a peer's telling a bully to "stop" helped the victim's situation 27 percent of the time, but also made it *worse* 30 percent of the time.[45] Taken together with the proportion of incidents in which confrontation had no impact, we can see that 73 percent of the time, telling a bully to "stop" may be either ineffective or detrimental for the victim.

This doesn't mean that we should throw out the baby with the bathwater. It's entirely possible, especially in light of the variably effective use of assertion in general, that some children or some situations can use the "stop" approach successfully. Perhaps encouraging more assertive children to use their social skills to support targets might be more productive as a strategy. Unfortunately, we don't yet understand all the nuances in which assertiveness might work, including *for which children* or *in which situations*. For example, perhaps schools with trained faculty, or children with strong social skills, can use the tactic successfully. Perhaps saying "stop" works when it's used in conjunction with other strategies (e.g., saying "stop" and then helping the target leave). Unfortunately, at this point, this is all just conjecture.

In light of this research, does the evidence justify investing time, money, and effort in programs that center on training students to engage in active confrontation of bullies? Additionally, even if we decide the answer is no, should we encourage children who feel able to assertively confront bullies (i.e., students who don't require an investment in training) to do so? Standing up for a peer can make a child feel powerful and kind, and it can both reinforce positive social norms in the children who witness it and make targets feel much better.

Research-based, effective programs do include the "stop" method, but these programs also combine this method with a variety of other actions, such as teacher training, positive reinforcement of prosocial behaviors, and active student involvement.[46] Thus, it is difficult to tease apart the effectiveness of these different specific approaches. All we truly know is that there *is* evidence of effectiveness for whole-school programs that include, but are not limited to, a "stop" strategy, with the following caveats:

- Assertiveness is not a panacea; it doesn't always work.
- The "stop" strategy harms victims as often as it helps them, although we don't know why, where, or how.
- The YVP's comparison of different strategies makes the "stop" strategy appear decidedly weaker than other strategies.
- Focusing support strategies on targets, instead of on aggressive children, may be a more reliably effective strategy.

In light of these four facts, adopting programs whose core is the "stop" strategy appears unwarranted and possibly even unwise. Of course, future programs using new approaches might be able to utilize this technique. It does have the potential to be effective, but I don't think we know enough yet to harness that potential.

None of this should be taken as a contention that children should meekly accept powerlessness and helplessness in the face of peer abuse. Because students often feel at a loss when faced with difficult social situations, we ultimately want them to learn that they actually have a variety of possible responses at their disposal. Perhaps, however, instead of focusing only on tactics that are more risky and less reliable, it would be more productive to consider positive strategies that have evidence of broad effectiveness. These strategies are discussed in the next sections.

Action 3: Refusing to Be the Bully's Audience or Admirer

In MARC's fieldwork, discussions with children often tend to coalesce around the concept that simply *not watching* (e.g., walking away, not providing the bully with an audience) can be a low-risk strategy that's easy to employ. The difficulty is that walking away or ignoring doesn't feel empowering; in fact, it often feels like an abandonment of the situation. But we've found that that feeling may begin to change following a discussion and some recognition that the presence of more witnesses likely means that the bully will persist for a longer time.[47] Indeed, I typically encounter much more resistance to this idea from adults than I do from children. The kids may be right to think that by refusing to watch, they could ultimately benefit the target.

Note, however, that *used by itself*, ignoring the situation was definitely not an effective strategy (at least during middle school), according to both the YVP and the 2012 freshman survey, in which only 35 percent of subjects felt that ignoring the situation was a good tactic. Similarly, in the 2020–2022 SERC study, only 37 percent felt that ignoring the bully either helped the situation or made the target feel better. With that in mind, in MARC, we train children to pair "not being the audience" with other strategies (e.g., conferring with an adult, getting other peers to help, helping a target feel better).

Action 4: Peer Friendliness and Peer Alliance

Apart from simply *not* watching an incident unfold, or telling an adult, research has demonstrated that other options can be reasonably effective—that is, these strategies may not always stop bullying in its tracks, but they are significantly more likely to make the situation better than to make it worse. One such possibility is friendly actions by peers.

Victims of bullying suffer particularly from a lack of social support from peers.[48] Friendly actions by peers, therefore, can be particularly powerful. In the 2012 freshman study, 85 percent of subjects said that a friendly remark by a peer would be extremely helpful in a bullying situation, but only 29 of subjects felt that a friendly remark by an adult would be similarly helpful. In the YVP, the most helpful action by peers ("spent time with me") was effective 54 percent of the time; the most effective action by adults ("listened to me") was slightly less likely to be effective at 43 percent of the time.

An interesting study examining two Italian middle schools found not only that friendly actions by peers were among the most effective interventions but also that their major impact was to make helpers and victims *feel* better.[49] Anecdotally, many kids have told us that when they are feeling bad about themselves socially, after being bullied, nothing makes them feel as good as a peer who reaches out to them. The YVP found that from the victim's perspective, the most helpful strategies by peers were those that were *emotionally* supportive. These included, in order of helpfulness, the following:

- Spent time with me
- Talked to me
- Helped me get away (from the situation)
- Gave me advice
- Called me
- Helped me tell an adult
- Made a distraction
- Told an adult

These are arranged in order of impact; the top of the list catalogs the most effective (and least potentially harmful) tactics. This list is interesting both for what's on it and for what's *not* on it. As Davis and Nixon wrote: "It is notable that the peer actions reported as most helpful are also the safest for peers as well, *and represent acts of alliance rather than of confrontation* [original emphasis]. Even the relatively silent and thus totally safe action of calling a student at home to give support was reported to be helpful much more often than it was unhelpful. Consistent with our data about teachers, these data suggest that students feel that giving advice is most helpful when the peer is giving encouragement."[50] Although the YVP focused on in-school bullying, it's likely that its findings pertain to cyberbullying as well. There's no plausible reason to suppose that socially supportive actions wouldn't similarly help children who are suffering through their peers' digital cruelties.

The broad conclusion that I take from all of the data is that we may be misplacing our efforts by focusing intently on "fixing" bullying and cyberbullying situations. What targets experience as the most consistently helpful actions aren't efforts to assertively stop bullying, but rather, actions by adults and peers that help a victim cope emotionally, usually through talking, connecting, and providing social support. This feels counterintuitive. Why wouldn't stopping the situation always be best? Perhaps, it would be best if it could be done successfully, but clearly adults cannot always stop bullying. Taking the emotionally supportive route can feel frustratingly slow or even inert in a society that reveres action, but I don't think the consistency of these findings can be ignored. No rule dictates an all-or-nothing approach. In rallying peers to do their part, we can emphasize both creating emotional connections and actively helping victims.

Early in this chapter, I pointed out that fellow students are a key part of the idea of the whole-school approach to bullying prevention. Of course, another group forms a critical part of that community, but it's one we haven't yet examined. In the next chapter, we turn to the role that parents can play in the bullying dynamic. Perhaps, I've saved the best for last.

CHAPTER 8

Working with Parents

Shared Goals, Different Perspectives

Most parents and educators work in tandem on issues such as bullying and cyberbullying—they are both invested in putting a stop to them—but you don't need to be Sigmund Freud to pick up on an occasional undercurrent of tension. Bullying is one of the top mental health concerns for parents, especially parents in lower-income brackets.[1] Schools are held responsible for the actions of children (including bullying, and sometimes cyberbullying, behaviors), even though there's no doubt that outside influences can substantially determine those actions. Despite the impossibility of constant monitoring, and the reality of the child-only world, schools are pressured to guarantee that bullying behaviors stop. In contrast, parents may suffer from a lack of information because of confidentiality laws, and in the face of what may feel like inaction or indifference, they may be concerned enough to take inappropriate actions or even threaten more extreme actions in defense of their children.[2] Parents of accused bullies can deny the severity of their children's behaviors, deny the actions altogether, or insist that appropriate (but lengthy) investigations be undertaken. The need to stop bullying can run headlong into realities that sometimes prevent that very goal. That is the tension that we need to think about.

Let's begin by examining a study I conducted of 1,940 parents of children of all ages across the state of Massachusetts.[3] I used the data to examine some key questions: How do parents feel about their child's school's response to reported bullying incidents? How much do their children tell them, and how much do they, in turn, tell schools? Most important, how can we help parents understand their role in these issues? How can we understand, and help parents get through, at least some of the denial? And how can we actively promote a more cooperative environment?

HOW MUCH DO PARENTS KNOW?

Approximately one-third of the Massachusetts schools that surveyed students and faculty also wanted to survey parents. Schools were given a secure link to an online questionnaire, which they then forwarded to parents on their mailing lists. Only 3 percent of respondents were screened out because they didn't have children in the local schools. No other identifying or demographic information was gathered on the respondents, because that request might have caused parents to feel concerned that their answers were not completely anonymous. Additionally, of course, I wanted to encourage parents to complete the survey by keeping it succinct.

Overall, the sample was fairly equitably distributed across the grades: 916 of the respondents had a child in elementary school, 789 had a child in grades 6 through 8 (middle school), and 823 had a child in high school. A number of parents had children at more than one level (which is why the numbers add up to more than 1,940). Contrary to my expectations, the sample wasn't solely—or even mostly—composed of parents whose children were victims of bullying (see more details on that later in the chapter).

When considering what parents hear from their children, and what they in turn expect from schools, it can be tempting to throw in the towel and accept the fact that parents are always likely to overestimate the ability of schools to fix bullying. However, some of the tensions between schools and parents arise from real differences in what parents and children (and thus schools, which is where most of these episodes take place) know about bullying incidents. So, understanding what parents know about the bullying experienced by their children is the place we have to start. Comparing data from parents with that obtained directly from students can provide clues about constructive ways to approach this difficulty. What really struck me in looking at all of the surveys was that it appears likely that parents and educators actually are seeing *different pools of information*, and it's that difference that may lead to some problems.

Parents Do Not Hear About All Bullying Incidents from Their Older Children

A 2021 study that conducted open-ended interviews with fifty parents found that most parents are confident that their child not only will report, but also will report fully (i.e., will not omit any facts or information).[4] Yet, as I noted in chapter 7, the data from students and parents suggest that K–8 children usually report many kinds of incidents to their parents, but older children are much choosier about what they report. Consider this survey data: for the younger grades, a similar proportion of children said that they were victims and had reported incidents to their parents. For example, among K–5 students, about 45 percent of parents had received a child's report, and a similar number of children (38 percent) stated that they were victims on the survey of students in grades 3–12. I observed a comparable situation for the students in grades 6 to 8; about 52 percent of those surveyed said they were victims, and 44 percent of parents were aware of those victimizations. These numbers aren't identical, but they're in the same ballpark.

For the older children, however, some real differences emerged. On the student survey, 50 percent or more of the children said that at some point during high school they were targets either in school, online, or both. In contrast, only 30 percent of high school parents were aware that their children were bullied. This suggests that high school victims are only selectively reporting to their parents. Parents may be doing better in helping teens with cyberbullying, comparatively. A 2022 Pew Research Center Survey found that 66 percent of teens reported that their parents were doing a good or excellent job helping them address online harassment.[5]

As I've pointed out in past chapters, I don't think this represents a failure of parenting, but rather a natural outgrowth of teens' social development. Indeed, a second nugget of information is reassuring in that regard. In addition, this information begins to shed light on the differences between what parents and educators see and hear.

Kids Report the More Serious Incidents to Their Parents, Particularly as They Grow Older

At every grade level, more of the incidents reported to parents were just one-time events; but parents appear to disproportionately hear about the more serious problems as their children grow older. For example, the elementary parents knew about almost three times as many one-time problems as they knew about ongoing, repeated bullying situations. As the kids grew up, I observed that they were less and less likely to report these one-time problems; however, they remained likely to reveal repeated bullying. Perhaps, as they get older, these children are simply less inclined to report the more commonplace, insignificant, or transient cruelties. Other pieces of data lead me to the same conclusion. Just as older kids are more likely to continue to report *repeated* bullying, they're also more likely to report *physical* bullying, which is often perceived as more serious than psychological bullying. (This is not to imply that psychological bullying is unimportant, but being physically threatened can certainly increase the urgency of a problem.[6])

In all age-groups, parents do appear to hear reports that are skewed toward physical bullying. More than half (52 percent) of elementary parents characterized the bullying of their children as at least partly physical; and about a third of the middle school and high school parents (30 percent and 33 percent, respectively) said their child had reported being physically bullied. In contrast, when high school students report bullying, only about 10 percent of all their reports concern physical bullying. If we assume that the lion's share of the physical attacks are reported to parents, then an extrapolation of these numbers would suggest that about three-quarters of the psychological bullying that happens to high schoolers is not being reported to parents. This is one factor that skews parents' perception of the kind of bullying that goes on, and their perception of the responses of schools, which are dealing with many more incidents on many different levels (I go into more detail about this later).

Parents Often Don't Report to Schools

Another piece of data that dovetails with these findings is that parents frequently do not report to schools, at least when children are adolescents. Parents who believed that their child was a victim of bullying were much more likely to report to school authorities if their child was in elementary or middle school. Rates of parental reporting dip precipitously as the child enters high school. A 2019 study of 1,117 parents of students in middle and high school found that only 23 percent contacted the school about the bullying their child reported to them. It was much more common for parents of these slightly older students to talk and discuss the situation, and to consider strategies for resolving the bullying, directly with their child. About 5 percent reported that they felt that their child could or should handle the situation themselves, without assistance from adults. If parents believed the school had effectively trained the staff to deal with bullying situations, they were more likely to contact the school.[7]

To sum up, during elementary school, students appear to tell their parents about many of the incidents that happen to them—both small and significant—and their parents, in turn, frequently report these issues to the school. But as children get older, students tend to focus more and more on telling parents primarily about the more serious incidents of cruelty. Furthermore, high school parents appear to be less willing to report bullying to the schools, which probably means that when they *do* report, the incident is quite serious (or they *believe* it's serious, which is admittedly something quite different). When a high school parent reports a problem, therefore, that issue has already made it through two filters:

first, the student would have considered it serious enough to report it to his or her parents; and, second, the parents would have considered it serious enough to report to the school. Parents go to the ensuing meeting at the high school already certain that the problem is very serious; educators, in contrast, may walk into that same meeting with the idea of exploring the problem to determine how serious it is. Those two agendas can certainly clash.

HOW DO PARENTS VIEW THEIR CHILDREN'S SCHOOL ON THE ISSUE OF BULLYING AND CYBERBULLYING?

Parents—and communities—tend to form impressions about their school's interest in reducing bullying and cyberbullying. I won't say that these impressions are always wrong, as I frequently find myself taking the temperature, so to speak, in a school where I'm working. But impressions aren't always correct, either. Right or wrong, parents' sense of a school's commitment matters because it can determine whether they approach a bullying problem with an olive branch or a baseball bat.

Do Parents Know if Their School Works on Bullying Prevention?

Consider the following problem: overall, too many parents remain unaware of the antibullying efforts at their child's school. According to my survey, parents at the middle school level were the most likely to be aware of the bullying- and cyberbullying-prevention efforts at their child's school, probably because bullying and cyberbullying provoke more anxiety at that age. Parents at every level, however, should know that their child's school is actively working on prevention (particularly in a state like Massachusetts, where every school is mandated to be doing exactly that). It's striking that between one-third (33 percent) and one-half (47 percent) of parents said they didn't know about any such efforts at their child's school. Making parents aware of these efforts is the first step in communicating to them that, yes, their local school does care about this issue. Additionally, as I pointed out, if parents view the school's faculty as well-trained in bullying prevention, they are more likely to contact the school in the event of a bullying incident.[8]

Parents' Views of the Schools' Response to Their Reporting

When surveying parents about their child's possible bullying victimization, I was well aware that parents sometimes overuse the term *bullying* to describe a wide assortment of social problems. As a way of taking this into account, parents were given the option of reporting their child's victimization as either a one-time incident of cruelty or as a repeated targeting. These two choices were used to tease apart the single-incident cases from those that more closely resembled true bullying (intentionality, repeated occurrence, and power imbalance). Parents who reported that their child had been exposed to *repeated* bullying were subsequently asked a series of questions about the school's response to the situation:

- How satisfied do you feel with the school's response to this report?
- Did the school do a good job of communicating and "checking in" with you?
- Did the school make your child feel better and safer about attending school?

I realize that the tenor of these questions implies that the onus is entirely on the *school* to resolve the bullying situation—but keep in mind that the goal of asking these questions was in fact to see how successful parents viewed the school's actions in these situations. The good news is that parents of elementary school children were more positive overall than parents of older children: they were more satisfied with the school's response to their child's bullying situation, they were more likely to feel that the school did a good job of "checking in" with them, and they were more likely to feel that the school made their child feel safer about attending. The bad news is that even the elementary school parents were not very positive, and the parents of older children (particularly middle school parents) were mostly negative about their school's reaction to bullying. Clearly, there's plenty of work to be done.

PROBLEMS BETWEEN SCHOOLS AND PARENTS

All of this can be very important in helping us understand the perspective that parents take and the problems that arise between parents and schools. We've all heard plenty of stories about parents overreacting to bullying; but I've also heard many stories from parents who feel that their distress and their child's situation simply aren't being taken seriously by the school. Looking at the data from students and parents, I'm left with the strong impression that parents and educators approach these conversations from two fundamentally different perspectives. Educators see the whole gamut of misbehaviors, and they see all of them on a regular basis; what happens, therefore, rarely feels like a crisis to them. Their perspective is shaped by the entire group of students they see daily. Conversely, parents have only the one child (or perhaps a few), and they see only those problems that get through their child's "seriousness" filter. They hear about problems so rarely, and the nature of the problems they're told about tends to be so significant, that they may well regard any problem their child brings to them as potentially very serious. If they then decide to approach the school, they've undoubtedly decided that it's very serious indeed.

So, when you and a parent sit down, you're not at the same starting point; that parent is already halfway around the track. This doesn't mean that you necessarily need to change the content of what you have to say (e.g., "I don't think this is a critical issue for Jennifer"), but appreciating where they're coming from can help you adjust your approach:

> *I realize how serious this is—that's why you're here today. I absolutely see how a situation like this can be serious; but I'm seeing some behaviors that are leading me to sense that Jennifer's actually coping really well with it on her own. Let me tell you some details about what I see, and then I would really like to hear what you think about that, and learn what you're seeing at home that's leading you to feel concerned.*

The idea, ultimately, is to let parents know that you understand that, from their perspective, the issue is indeed serious, that you want to hear specifically why they think this is so, and that you want to share why you either agree or don't agree. The clue is to listen to what parents say: because their data have likely gone through two "seriousness" filters, the situation *could* in fact be more grave than you perceived it at first. Remember a few facts: first, specific behaviors (e.g., gateway behaviors) can seem minor but can be an indication of a much more serious situation; and, second, if students are truly being traumatized, they are more likely to report it first to their parents rather than to any educator.[9]

Parents May Insist That a Situation Is Bullying, Even When It Doesn't Meet Legal or Policy Criteria

Bullying is a word that almost universally evokes anxiety; conversely, it may also reveal anxiety. Parents who are anxious to have their child's situation resolved may insist that a situation is bullying in an attempt to get educators' attention, sympathy, and (they hope) ruthless action. It's also possible that they simply lack knowledge about what constitutes bullying (or, like many, are working from their own personal definition). Regardless, I rarely find that it's fruitful to debate whether or not a situation is truly bullying. The rule of thumb is to respond to the anxiety, rather than to the content, in the parent's appraisal of the situation. Reassure parents that you're taking the situation *very* seriously indeed and focus the conversation back on the problem at hand—the actual situation—rather than on what label should be used.

> *I want you to know that I am very committed to resolving this situation and to making Kevin feel safe here at school. What I'd like to do now is focus not so much on labeling the problem; instead, let's focus on what we need to do today to make sure that he feels okay about coming to school tomorrow. Do you think he would find it helpful if I had a talk with him, one-on-one, first thing in the morning, to let him know that he can always come see me anytime he feels threatened? Do you think that would be a helpful first step?*

Tip: Parents who insist that something is bullying likely feel anxious enough about the situation that they are not apt to accept any suggestion that the incident is not bullying. They may worry that "not bullying" means that no follow-up or action is needed. If they call a situation "bullying," then it needs your attention—regardless of whether or not it's actually bullying.

Parents May Not Believe Their Child Is Involved in Bullying

Certainly, a rare pathological type of parent would deny their child's misbehavior regardless of the circumstances; however, for most parents, only a small amount of denial is commonplace. I categorize parental denial into three types: type I parents simply don't see the bullying; type II parents see the behavior but believe the teacher or the class is the real problem; and type III parents think the behavior is normal.

Type I denial

In type I denial, parents simply do not see the behavior you're referring to and don't believe it's happening. The more general and vague the information you give them, the more likely they are to pursue this course of denial. The solution, therefore, is to be as specific as possible when reporting a misbehavior. Ideally, a list of exactly when, where, and what took place is best; it's hard to maintain that a child has done nothing in the face of such specifics. So the conversation shouldn't be about how "Meredith is bullying someone in her class" but about how "on Tuesday morning, the teacher in Meredith's homeroom reported to me that Meredith had, with other students, pointed at a disabled student and laughed aloud, mocking her inability to pronounce certain letters."

Tip: Avoid, if possible, the dreaded "B" word. Its use often simply throws gasoline on the fire. Use it only if you must (e.g., if the problem behavior, because it is classified as bullying, has triggered a response required by your school's bullying procedures).

Type II denial

In type II denial, the parents essentially accept that there's a problem, but they decide that the genesis of the problem is the teacher or the class, and not their child. These parents usually focus on how the teacher has "picked on" or singled out their child for criticism; or how their child is bored by the class and so is acting out; or how the teacher has neglected their son or daughter. Sometimes parents deflect blame onto another student, rather than onto a teacher; they may suggest that the other student is the "ringleader" or that their children were only tangentially involved.

Sometimes type II denial can be a response to a controversial educational or awareness program. For example, an Australian bullying prevention program called *Safe Schools* addresses homophobic bullying and the disproportionate victimization of LGBTQ youth in schools. In a 2020 study of parents, many were concerned that the topic of the program might harm their child and maintained that bullying was in fact quite rare.[10] Thus, a program's content can easily become the focus of a conversation about a child's bullying behaviors.

Responding to type II denial is really about gathering your data before this discussion ever takes place. If children are engaging in abusive behavior, they likely are doing it in more than one place—so you need to have a conversation with the other teachers who teach and supervise that child. What are they seeing? If they are observing similar issues, then the response to a type II denial is to point out (gently) that this isn't happening only in your class or only during one program's implementation; rather, you're simply the one who's bringing it to the parents' attention. If other teachers truly see no indication of what you're describing, then more work is needed before you approach the parents. Why is this child acting out only in your class? Perhaps he or she is taking advantage of a specific situation—for example, maybe your class is the only place in school that provides access to a preferred target (although that is unlikely). Or perhaps a challenging psychological dynamic exists between you and this student. (Unpleasant to consider but, realistically, this is a possibility that should never be dismissed out of hand. Teachers are, after all, human beings.)

Tip: Type II denials often come from parents who are anxious and unhappy about the idea that their child may be a bully, and they may need to save face while they digest the evidence they're presented with. It is smart strategy—not capitulation—to adopt the tactful attitude that many children engage in these behaviors from time to time ("Yes, we do need to respond firmly; but between us adults, this isn't the end of the world"). The more judgmental and disapproving you appear, the more parents will dig in their heels. If you can get past this type of denial at the first offense, then if the child repeats the problem behavior, the parent will be much more likely to accept that this is now a serious problem that requires professional help.

Type III denial

Type III denial is quite common, and it emerges from the fact that parents have one (or a few) kids at home, and you have a thousand (or several hundred) at school. In type III denial, parents do see and acknowledge the behavior you're referring to, but they mistake it for normality—they just don't have the comparison group that you have. Sure, they see their son acting out, but isn't that what all boys do? You know, because you have a comparison group of hundreds of boys, that, no, that's not what all boys do. Lacking that context, it's hard for a parent to know what's normal and what's not.

In 2021, several researchers at the University of Amsterdam conducted a study with 38 elementary school teachers, designed to examine how teachers dealt with difficult bullying situations.[11] They often described situations in which the parents were in type III denial, such as one in which the parents saw nothing wrong with their child frequently swearing at other students. Teachers described parents who simply didn't take reports of bullying behaviors seriously.

Tip: You will need to tell parents in type III denial that you find it useful to hear that they see the same things you see. You also want to assure them that there are ways to deal with these behaviors and that (again) many children will try them out. The important thing is to respond appropriately. Sometimes parents need to hear that it's harder to recognize a challenge when you don't have hundreds of other kids to compare and that working in a school full of children provides a useful perspective. Although I think it's fine to draw general comparisons (e.g., "You're right, Tom is a very active boy, but I have twenty-four other students who can sit through a lesson without throwing spitballs at another student; that's why I'm concerned"), you should never draw specific comparisons to another student.

Tip: When you talk to parents about these difficult topics, always be sure to "sandwich" what you say between positive comments, as we'll discuss next.

Parents May Demand More Information Than You Can Legally Disclose

When parents of both supposed targets and bullies hear about or report incidents, they often want to know the identity of the other children involved. This raises the sensitive issue of confidentiality. When educators respond to information requests by saying "That's confidential," they may be misinterpreted as stonewalling, avoiding a conversation, or even protecting the bully. The problem, I think, is a communication issue.

Educators know what *confidentiality* means, so they refer to it as anyone might speak of any familiar rule—without explanation. Unfortunately, parents often don't know the meaning as understood in schools, and so they may think that your lack of a detailed explanation suggests a different agenda. To avoid this problem, make sure that whenever you cite confidentiality, you do it with a brief explanation:

> *I completely understand why you want to know this; I would want to know also, in your shoes. But federal [and state, if applicable] law forbids me from talking to anyone about another parent's child. No matter how much I sympathize, I would be breaking the law if I gave you that information, and I just can't do that.*

Repeat this explanation as often as needed, even to the same parent, and ensure that you continue to do so gently. You also can download, print, and distribute to parents my free brochure, "That's Confidential."[12]

Parents May Demand That the Other Child Be Disciplined

Just as information about the other child cannot be disclosed, actions taken in regard to a child who bullies (or is perceived to bully) can't be discussed specifically with the parents of the target. In a 2021 Dutch study, parents often came into meetings expecting or wanting specific sanctions to be taken with a child who was accused of victimizing their child.[13] This is understandable, of course, given that it can be distressing to see a child who is being bullied suffer. However, one approach that can be productive is to review with the parents the specific steps that your school takes in all bullying cases.

This is a problem area, however: not all schools have a series of specific steps they take in bullying cases. Yet, many states now require such policies in schools.[14] In the event your school hasn't developed a policy yet, you'll need to consider doing so, because it's useful to be able to discuss what happens in the abstract, especially when confidentiality laws forbid you from discussing what happens on a personal level to other children. Then, if a parent demands that another child be expelled, your answer could focus on two points: first, although you can't discuss that child's situation specifically, you can describe the steps that are taken in all bullying situations and that also will be taken in this situation; and, second, you want to focus on the target, and what steps you and the parents can take to make sure he or she feels safe at school.

On a side note: policy isn't always just words on paper; it can also help encourage effective responding to bullying incidents. A 2021 study of almost nine thousand educators from 156 schools in the United States in found that having and training staff on a bullying prevention and response policy significantly increased the odds that educators would intervene in bullying instances.[15]

> **Tip:** Visual aids help a lot. They provide a physical focus during what can be a difficult moment and can even help calm down parents. Have a printed handout that reviews the steps taken in all bullying cases and include even those steps that you may consider obvious (e.g., "interview the target"). Review this information with the parents, and ask for their help with any step as appropriate (e.g., in gathering information from their child). Anecdotally, several schools founded by religious orders have told me that a brief prayer with the parents of a victim can help reduce the emotional level of a meeting, but that option is obviously not available to public schools.

Parents May Not Understand the Limits of What Schools Can Do

Although cyberbullying has made everyone much more conscious of the limits of school jurisdiction, some of the psychological "leftovers" of earlier decades may lead parents to believe that schools can intervene in problem behavior no matter where it happens. The tricky part is that while it's a good idea for parents to let the school know what's going on in off-campus or online bullying cases, parents can't always expect the school to take disciplinary action against the offender.

The jurisdiction that schools have in disciplining off-campus offenders is actually a heated, divisive legal issue. Because I am not a lawyer, I'm not going to address it here. Schools can, and should, take other steps, even when bullying takes place off campus. Notably, children who are targets of off-campus bullying or cyberbullying may well need the support of school personnel, and regardless of your legal obligation to respond to the offender, your humane obligation toward the target means that that support should be forthcoming.

Tip: Never simply wash your hands of a situation or tell an upset parent, "There's nothing I can do." Always emphasize what you *can* do, and you can always say that you're ready to support a child who's a victim.

Tip: Cyberbullying sometimes targets teachers, counselors, or administrators. Try not to overreact if a child says something mean about you on the internet. Just as they are in the hallways, children are interested in discussing their feelings toward their teachers when communicating online; it's usually not anything truly personal, even when they mention you by name. Casual comments (even mean ones) about your appearance, your teaching style, your intelligence, and so forth should probably be utilized as a teachable moment (or ignored), rather than responded to vehemently. (For the curious reader, yes, my students have said very unflattering things about me online.) Obviously you have to protect yourself from serious libel or slander. But I believe that part of the new digital reality is that we all need to grow a thick skin about casual online comments, because so many of us will be the subject of kids' posts. If you feel up to it, there's nothing wrong with using such comments as a learning opportunity to discuss the public nature of social networking sites (assuming, of course, that you viewed them legitimately) and to explain to students how easy it is for unintended audiences to see the posts intended only for their peers.

Parents May Not Make the Effort to Understand the Facts About Bullying or Cyberbullying

Parents often list bullying as one of their primary concerns today, and you, as an educator, may hear from parents incessantly about this problem. Your school, like many others, may have taken the time and trouble to hold educational evenings about bullying and cyberbullying, or more generally about children's social relationships and screen use. These evening programs are one of the few things (in my opinion) that have been greatly improved by the global coronavirus pandemic. Before the pandemic, I regularly made evening visits to schools to present to parents. Audience turnout varied widely, but I always saw how hard educators worked to try to get as many parents there as possible. Since 2020, most of the events are still held in the evenings, but they're now online. Instead of having to find a babysitter, rush to finish dinner early, and leave the house after an exhausting day, parents can now simply tune in online while they're cooking at home or relaxing after a long day at work. Being a parent, I sympathize with how difficult it can be to get out of the house at night, and I think the advent of online parent programs is a wonderful thing, and much, much larger audiences regularly attend. Still, I think it's a wise idea to offer parents several different ways to educate themselves about bullying and cyberbullying.

1. *Use multiple methods to communicate*: Don't just offer parent education evenings; use a variety of methods to disseminate the information. Post a dedicated page about bullying on your school's website, and make it easy to find. Send out a paper flyer telling parents about that page, and post the flyer around your town or neighborhood. Start a committee and invite parents to serve alongside educators and local police. Partner with your local cable access channel to produce a show or two about bullying and cyberbullying, and explain what parents can do about these issues. Invite students and parents to be on the show. Write articles for the local newspaper. Email a survey for parents (you can get a free one from the Massachusetts Aggression Reduction Center, MARC).[16] Approach your local district attorney's office or your school's counseling office and ask for their help and ideas. (If this sounds like a lot of work, consider how many phone calls all of this readily available information might eliminate.)

2. *Make evening presentations noteworthy*: If you do put on an evening program, make it count—it is usually more effective to put on one noteworthy evening rather than several less enticing evenings. When I say *noteworthy*, I mean that you should try to have a speaker who is either relatively high up in the school hierarchy (e.g., the superintendent) or not from the school system but who is recognized and will draw parents in. Look for local authors of relevant works, and offer to help sell their books at the event. Partner with the other schools in your system; a districtwide event is often seen as more important than one for just one school. Engage parents; ask for their feedback and ideas before the evening. Promote the evening as you

traditionally might, but also ensure that information online is easy to find. I think every event involving parents should be featured on the school's home page as well. Offer students extra credit if they attend the evening with their parents. Ask speakers if they are willing to record the event, particularly if it's online, and then you can offer a recording of the event online, where you will be certain to reach even more parents.

3. *Offer information and resources*: You can list these on the web page that you devote to bullying and cyberbullying. Think about these resources in advance and print lists of helpful websites that you can give to parents. This does take some effort, but it really demonstrates your interest in being effective.

PARENTAL ATTITUDES THAT CAN HINDER EFFECTIVE RESPONSES TO BULLYING SITUATIONS

As a parent—of kids who, I hasten to point out, are now young adults but were most definitely *not* always perfectly behaved—I'm loathe to begin pointing fingers at mothers and fathers who are doing their utmost to keep up with their children's digital technology use. As I discussed in chapter 4, parents often struggle with a persistent sense of anxiety when it comes to technology and the accompanying belief that, being less knowledgeable than their children, they aren't in a position to supervise or teach them about cyber issues. It's not that today's parents don't use technology—they do, of course—but they may feel unable to keep up with the rapid pace of change that characterizes so much of youth technology use. If parents do too little to monitor their offspring's digital behaviors, they're criticized as being neglectful. If they do too much, they're criticized as being "helicopter parents" or "spies." It's no wonder so many parents have the sense that they can't win. For the record, only 15 percent of youth in the 2020–2022 Social and Emotional Research Consortium (SERC) study characterized their parents as loving but too involved (helicopter parents); 64 percent said their parents were warm and loving but also had firm rules, and the remaining 21 percent said their parents were not warm and were very strict, or were not very involved.[17]

Still, I think parents can adopt attitudes that, while understandable, may contribute to their children's misbehaviors. Listening for, and being prepared to address, these attitudes can help parents see the connection between their child's cyber behaviors and their behaviors in school (and in life).

Nice Kids Wouldn't Do That

Parents can be misled by their own preconceptions of who could, or who would, bully someone else. Adults often retain a ready-made profile of who might be a bully: a seriously maladjusted misfit, someone without friends, and someone with lots of academic and emotional problems. With that profile in mind, they may reject any implication that their own child might have done something bad to someone else. Because adults tend to expect online behaviors to align closely with offline behaviors, they regard the volunteer work and good grades their children achieve as evidence that their kids could not possibly have done anything cruel online. But we know that some children who misbehave online *do not bully in person.* Can it be that otherwise "nice" kids might cyberbully?

As noted in chapter 4, the factors that affect electronic communications can result in cyberbullying or cyberfighting that otherwise might not occur. The lack of tone in electronic writing (especially short tweets or text messages) can result in misunderstandings that sprout, in turn, into full-blown conflicts and bullying. The lack of nonverbal feedback cues (e.g., facial expressions) can result in digital writers blithely pursuing what they believe is only mild criticism, without realizing that it's actually having a hurtful impact—a phenomenon I've termed *negligent cyberbullying.* Digital environments can feel deceptively private and confidential. Factors like these mean that it's far from impossible that an essentially well-behaved child could express feelings, with unexpectedly severe consequences, from a place of perceived safety. Relying on the offline personality, therefore, to predict any propensity to get into online trouble, is probably a shaky proposition. The truth is that misbehaving online is an understandable mistake that *any* child can make.

If I'm a Good Parent, My Children Will Never Lie to Me

In the field, I often have parents approach me with essentially the same problem: the school has contacted them about a bullying incident their child has allegedly engaged in, but the child denies everything. As a result, the parent simply can't believe it. This sometimes happens even in the face of pretty strong evidence (e.g., they may have found evidence of their child's cyberbullying on their home computer). If you peruse the internet, you can find many blogs written by parents who are "shocked" and "stunned" when they discover their child in a lie. Parents seem unaware that surveys of teens pretty consistently demonstrate that lying to parents is normal, not abnormal. Self-reported data from one study of 120 teenagers (average age about sixteen years old) found that almost all of the teens

(98 percent) reported that they had lied to their parents.[18] Another study of forty-three thousand teens found that 83 percent reported lying to their parents.[19] In the 2012 MARC freshman study found that 77 percent of the students who were facing discipline in a school situation lied to their parents about their role in the incident. Adults tend to believe that they can reliably tell when a child or teen is lying, which probably contributes to their perception that they haven't been lied to.[20] (This conviction, by the way, is a normal holdover from parenting toddlers; during toddlerhood, a lying child is ridiculously transparent. "I didn't eat any ice cream," a three-year-old may insist, with ice cream all over his or her face. Because they were once so obvious, it's easy to forget that they may not be that way anymore.)

The difficulty, of course, is that refusing to accept any child's normal propensity to lie (especially to save their skin) can make parents part of the problem instead of part of the solution.

PARENTAL ATTITUDES THAT CAN HINDER RESPONSES TO CYBERBULLYING PREVENTION

A major part of dealing with cyberbullying situations is prevention and education about how to use digital technology. This doesn't mean that teachers and parents have to become computer experts; but it does mean that they have to talk with youth about what's going on with them online. Sometimes, however, I've noticed that the adoption of certain perspectives can prevent positive conversations of this sort. Let's go through them briefly.

Teens Have an Unhealthy Addiction to Cell Phones

Many teens seem unable to function without cell phones in hand. Their reluctance to put them down, even for a moment, causes specters of addiction to haunt parents (and teachers). In the 2012 freshman study, subjects readily acknowledged that cell phones interfered with daily life; they estimated that cell phones intruded on social situations 57 percent of the time and on school or work 59 percent of the time. In the 2020–2022 SERC study, 32 percent of subjects reported that they were constantly "connected," unless they were sleeping. Despite this high level of use, many subjects report that they do take breaks from their devices. More than half of the subjects in the SERC study agreed that they often use technology but denied being *constantly connected* (defined as being notified within five 5 minutes of emails, messages, social media posts, or other communications). In the 2012 freshman study, many of the subjects expressed anxiety when asked how they would feel if they could not check or handle their cell phone for *one hour*. About 28 percent of boys and 35 percent of girls reported that they would feel anxious and worried if that were the case; 29 percent said it would be boring for the hour. The good news is that despite those high levels of anxiety, 42 percent said they could handle an hour of not being connected without having any significant feelings, one way or the other.

Today, intense use of technology by teens is complicated by the fact that adults are also frequent users of social media and screens. In the SERC study, 45 percent of kids reported that their parents were often or sometimes distracted by their own technology when their kids wanted their attention. In 2023, putting down the device is an issue for families, not just for youth. In trying to conceptualize this discomfort with being disconnected, I often use driving without a seat belt as a good analogy. If you're accustomed to driving your car with your seat belt buckled, then you may find that it feels peculiar not to use one, so much so that even if you're only moving your car from one parking space to another, a mere thirty feet away, you still want to buckle up. Perhaps by the same token, a generation of children (and some of their parents) who have grown up with constant connectivity find it uncomfortable to be untethered from each other, even if only for a single hour.

Children Can Be Supervised Online

A Pew Research Center survey of teens and their parents in 2010 found that parents are reporting increased supervision of their children online—77 percent of parents reported that they had reviewed where their children go online and what they see, and 41 percent had "friended" their child on a social networking site.[21] More than half of the subjects in the 2020–2022 SERC study reported that their parents checked their cell phones during middle school.[22] I think that parents' efforts to watch what children do online, however, is to a great extent being thwarted by the rapid proliferation of internet-enabled mobile devices. Almost all (95 percent) teens have a cell phone, according to 2019 research by the Pew Research Center.[23]

The proliferation of personal devices, with small screens and constant access, makes it very challenging for parents to control, for example, the hours in a day a child or adolescent uses screens. During the global coronavirus pandemic, 72 percent of parents reported that their kids' screen time use was higher than before 2020.[24] Following each and every device is potentially such a daunting task that it's not surprising that many kids report being able to surf the web without parents looking over their shoulder, either literally or virtually. In the 2012 freshman study, subjects were asked to rate, on a scale of one to ten, how much they felt their parents *intended* to supervise them online versus how much they were actually supervised. They reported that their parents intended to supervise them, on average, a 3.45 out of 10; not terribly high, but higher than their estimate of *actual* supervision, which rated, on average, 2.75. Almost 40 percent of subjects said that their parents exercised literally zero supervision. This wasn't necessarily due to parental ineptness with digital devices, either; on the same scale, students rated their most knowledgeable parent a 6.05 out of 10 on technological know-how. The low rating seems more likely to be due to the impossibility of supervising every possible internet-connected device, as well as the Pew Research Center's finding that 85 percent of kids use the internet outside their homes.[25]

As the number of connected devices increases, and the availability of internet access everywhere grows, the ability of adults to literally follow children around the internet may well decrease or disappear altogether. We may already be at that point; but at least we will always have the ability to help them use the best safety device of all—the one between their ears.

TIPS FOR PREVENTING PROBLEMS

Ultimately, we want to help parents overcome any problem perspectives or denial, and to appreciate what they hear and what they know about their own children. So working with parents is not just about reactions; it's also about taking steps to prevent parents from feeling that you are criticizing them, ignoring them, picking on their children, or taking the other child's "side," or from having to face other tribulations. Following are two basic tips to help parents see that you're on their side. These techniques can go far in convincing parents that you're not attacking them when you discuss their children's shortcomings.

The first technique is the positive phone call. If, at the beginning of each school year, you spend a few moments leaving each household a message just to let them know that things are going well so far and that you are really enjoying teaching their child, and would welcome any questions or concerns they have, you will buy yourself a lot of capital for those less-pleasant phone calls when something does go wrong. (A letter or email is a good second choice.)

The second technique is to always "sandwich" your concerns between two comments about the student's potential, abilities, or just general wonderfulness. There's a big difference between hearing, "I'm calling because we're having a problem with Joey," and "I wanted to touch base with you about Joey. He has so much potential and is such a terrific boy; I am concerned that we're seeing some behaviors that could get in the way of his success. I really don't want to see that happen to such a smart student." Generally speaking, even cynical parents who are sure that "every" teacher says agreeable things about "every" student may feel much more positive about that teacher, and often that school.

CONCLUSION

Moving the Field Forward

Sometimes I think that the biggest obstacle facing the field of bullying and cyberbullying is the sheer volume of variable-quality information. Sifting through all of this data in an attempt to get to the bottom line is a real challenge. In the case of cyberbullying, we can add on the stress of trying to address an issue that evolves with exceptional rapidity. I know very well that many educators are overwhelmed by, and may even avoid, the subjects of bullying and cyberbullying. In the interest of making the topics reemerge as both refreshingly interesting and accessible, I haven't presented a truly exhaustive analysis; instead, I've tried to highlight the main issues and make better sense of what happens with children in the day-to-day world.

It might interest you to know, by the way, that in the 2020–2022 Social and Emotional Research Consortium (SERC) study, 74 percent of subjects felt that bullying and cyberbullying need to be talked about *more* often. Sometimes that's hard to believe, especially if you work with teenagers; but regardless of the pinpoint accuracy of the number, I do think a majority of kids continue to think and worry about these issues.

Understanding bullying and cyberbullying involves both learning new topics and reminding ourselves about the underlying issues and techniques that have always been germane, but are sometimes forgotten in the cascade of anxiety and information overload that accompanies a constantly publicized social problem. Many of the messages and prevention efforts we already know about bullying remain the cornerstones of our efforts to reduce it. The *goal* in bullying prevention is still equable, civilized, self-controlled behavior among children, even when angry or irritated (actually, especially when angry or irritated). The *tools* are still knowledge and awareness about the impact of cruel behaviors on others, ways to intervene and help, and healthy and successful relationships, and also, today, a good grasp of how digital communications are different from more traditional forms of social interaction. The *mechanisms* remain clear and effective education, an eye trained on the different developmental needs of children, the emotional connections we make with our students, and our common sense.

I've now spent almost two decades training faculty and staff at K–12 schools, and these principles seem to translate into a few key ideas that are helpful, going forward. First, improve your school's climate by responding consistently to gateway behaviors. Many faculty say things like, "I can't believe I was ignoring gateway behaviors," after a training, and that's understandable. But we know now that choosing not to simply ignore or tolerate social cruelty does make a difference. Second, recognize that most children learn resiliency, and that they do so by having social skills and successful social relationships with peers. It's the support of peers that can make the difference between an incident a child can tolerate, and one that devastates him or her. Third, the role of bias as an engine in cruelty between children has only strengthened its grip since the first edition of this book was published in 2013. I think many of us had hoped this problem was in the rearview mirror; if so, we were wrong. Finally, rather than focusing on the minutiae of digital life (e.g., which app someone is using), it's more productive to discuss how digital interactions are affecting children psychologically: Are they feeling anxious? Abandoned? Restless? Sleep deprived? Digital technology is about bullying, but it's also about mental health.

Bullying is, without a doubt, still a major focus; but it *has* changed. The major changes are the shift from physical to predominantly psychological bullying, and the ways that cyberbullying and cyber behaviors interact with the social lives of children today. These changes, in turn, mean that adults have to change their prevention efforts. For example, the shift to psychological bullying means that similar types of behaviors are utilized by bullies and by those who aren't attacking seriously (e.g., teasing). This may mean we need to focus less on bullying per se and more on preventing all types of cruel, mean, or thoughtless behaviors. As always, the consistency of the adult response is key in guiding the development of social behaviors in children, but the response itself may need to take a new tack at times. We have to take care not to dismiss behaviors that don't meet the technical definition of bullying, and to emphasize that a behavior doesn't have to be bullying for it to matter. It's always been true that being mean or cruel is never justified. It hurts if someone else was mean first, and other people can make you feel annoyed, disgusted, or even mad, but none of these are a license to do whatever you like. That doesn't mean we should teach children to disregard how they feel about someone. But it does mean that we should make an important distinction between constructive and appropriate responses to interpersonal difficulties and responses that are both destructive and likely to worsen a tense situation.

Cyberbullying represents, I think, a different kind of problem. This new taxonomy may be helpful in understanding how likely it is that a digital incident really affects a child. When an online incident is minor (i.e., it is not interpreted by the target as deliberate cruelty), it's not likely to have much of an effect—unless that target is also being bullied at school, in which case it will affect them. In contrast, cyberbullying that is severe (whether one time or, especially, repeated) is consistently associated with problems like depression, anxiety, and substance abuse. When it comes to digital incidents, it seems to be more important to assess severity and repetition as well as a child's general situation (e.g., are they also being bullied at school). That assessment may be much more helpful in understanding exactly what they're going through.

Bullying and cyberbullying are different, but they still often coexist and closely interact (especially in older children). This is even more true today than it was in 2013. It can be difficult to accept new realities, especially those that gallop at lightning speed across our landscape (as the digital revolution has). The very rapidity of these transformations challenges us emotionally and intellectually, but it's the old techniques—being connected to, and communicating with, our students—that can mitigate our anxieties and even our ignorance. Sometimes adults take pleasure in demeaning electronic communications, rather than listening to their students and learning alongside them about how to coexist with digital life in a healthy way. Children (and adults, for that matter) need to learn to control their devices, and not permit their devices to control them. Technological advances have brought us great benefits, but of course these advances have costs as well—and communicating face-to-face is always best in some circumstance. Although it may be hard to believe, I've never talked with a group of kids who failed to perceive this.

Adapting commonsense education to new types of risk has certainly been done before. What can be challenging is teasing apart the different types of risk associated with new issues, like cyberbullying. One way of conceptualizing different types of risk is to separate what I call horizontal and vertical risks. I define *horizontal risk* as simply the likelihood that a bad thing will happen. *Vertical risk*, in contrast, is the seriousness of the hazardous outcome if it does occur. When people are feeling anxious about a situation, they tend to consider both horizontal and vertical risks. And in the case of bullying, the anxiety is often truly terrible. Parents can worry that bullying will cause their child to commit suicide (horizontal), which would be the worst outcome they might ever deal with (vertical). But when "experts" address risk, they may ignore vertical risk. So a blog or an editorial in the newspaper might discuss only the fact that bullying seems to lead to suicide very rarely. It's good to hear that horizontal risk is low, but it doesn't address the anxiety around vertical risk (i.e., "It may be rare, but if it does happen to me, it will be completely devastating"). In educational efforts, it's important to acknowledge high vertical risk to avoid appearing indifferent; but for a very rare event, it's still wise to emphasize the low horizontal risk.

In spite of all of our efforts to be sensible about risk and trauma, when it comes to children, it's easy for common sense to curtsy to anxiety. Too often, we allow our nervousness about our effectiveness as caregivers to sideline our collective understanding that some negative social experimentation is simply part of childhood development. In the wake of the global coronavirus pandemic, as we try to help children recover psychologically, we may all be feeling less effective than ever. It's important to remember that *any* child or teen (even a typically kind one) might make the mistake of "trying on" cruelty as a social lever, but we perpetuate and legitimize the adults' anxiety through finger-pointing at parents or schools. We need to stop looking for someone to blame and acknowledge our common burden, successes, and failures, as adults who raise children. The fact is that children are *supposed* to try out different roles and different behaviors. Sure, some of these roles and behaviors will land them in trouble. That's just part of life.

Our anxieties also tend to attach themselves to impossible expectations. Every person reading this book hid some things from their parents. Knowing that, it never fails to astonish me when adults today insist that a child hides *absolutely nothing* from them. Children, remember, live partly in a world of their own. You, as an adult (even an adult who is very important to them), don't get access to that world. Rather than sensibly accepting that all children will at times be avoidant or deceitful, we attach far too much drama to their misconduct.

Not all parents are educated about developmental differences in children, but I think it benefits all educators to be. A focus on developmental issues has always been an important part of bullying prevention, and it remains so today. How do bullying and cyberbullying change as children grow and develop? Who is most affected by, and vulnerable to, bullying and who is more resilient? Keeping a focus on vulnerability and resiliency can help empower targets to live successfully with the meanness that is an inevitable part of life, which can help children vulnerable to aggression develop better coping mechanisms. A developmental focus can also help us assess what children need at different ages to develop the social skills necessary to avoid and cope with antisocial peers. For example, both the Association for Childhood Education International and the American Academy of Pediatrics have come out with official positions expressing concern over the reduction of play in the lives of many young children and the (possibly associated) reduction in social, cognitive, and academic skills.[1] Although there is some controversy in the field of early childhood education over the value of "academic" versus "play-based" preschool and kindergarten, the consensus among researchers and practitioners seems to be that enriched, educational play is the best method for young children to learn.[2] Because we know that play is associated with social skills, particularly with the kind of social skills that children use to cope with challenging social situations, it has been hypothesized that the reduction in children's play may be a contributing factor to the increase in bullying and cyberbullying. Although some play situations are outside of education's purview, others are not, notably playtime in preschool and kindergarten.

WRAP-UP: THE FINAL CHALLENGE

Could I condense this entire book into one bullet list (a *short* bullet list)? Yes, the following ten bullets say it all.

- What we call bullying has changed; it's now more often played out as psychological, rather than physical, attacks.
- What we call cyberbullying is often simply cruel or thoughtless digital behavior, but it may be experienced as bullying by the recipient. When the target interprets it as deliberately cruel, it's more damaging.
- What happens online and what occurs offline are inextricably linked, especially among teens.
- Kids start online interactions very young—early in elementary school. The older they get, the more bullying migrates online.
- It's critical to recognize the beginning level of abusive behaviors—gateway behaviors—and stop them when you see them.
- Teach your students how digital interactions lack a lot of social information and explain how that can lead to problems with others if they're not careful.

- Encourage the development of social skills, friendships, and friendly actions among peers. That's the best way to increase resiliency.
- Throw parents a bone. Most are trying their best. It's not easy, especially in the wake of a global pandemic.
- Don't minimize the concerns of kids who seek you out. Ask about their situation. Connect with them. Connect with them. Connect with them. *Working with children is never just about the academic content.*
- Consult the Massachusetts Aggression Reduction Center website, which has quite a few free downloads. Use them! (www.MARCcenter. org or www.elizabethenglander.com)

Fundamentally, I think that bullying prevention is like exercise: anything you do is better than doing nothing, and collective efforts can particularly pay off. You won't do everything perfectly, but who ever has? You won't know everything, either, but children can learn very well from adults who are willing to learn alongside them. Maybe bullying prevention is really about learning to be more accepting of others, and more skeptical of ourselves. Take a deep breath, and take the first step.

APPENDIX A

The Research
Discussed in This Book

For reference sake, I have provided a few details about the sources of the data that I discuss in the book. With some exceptions, all findings that are presented are differences that reached statistical significance at or very near the $p < 0.05$ standard (through chi square, regression, analysis of variance [ANOVA] or multivariate analysis of variance [MANOVA]). For fluency's sake, and because this is not intended as a book for fellow researchers, I did not specify statistical details (e.g., $X^2 = 456.77, p < 0.000$). When differences did not reach statistical significance, but were interesting nonetheless, I used the word "slightly" (as in, "Boys were slightly more likely to like the color blue."). Many other researchers' findings are cited, too, of course.

ANNUAL STUDY OF COLLEGE FRESHMAN
AT BRIDGEWATER STATE UNIVERSITY

Each year between 2010 and 2018, my students and I anonymously surveyed hundreds of college freshman at Bridgewater State University, most of whom were enrolled in the introductory course in psychology. Beginning in 2019, after the founding of the Social and Emotional Research Consortium (SERC), that Consortium began to annually study freshmen in three states: Massachusetts, Virginia, and Colorado. Data gathered as part of SERC is gathered by research programs headed by Dr. Katalin Parti (Virginia Tech University), Dr. Cheryl Sanders (Metropolitan State University of Denver), and myself. In this book I'll be sharing findings from the 2010–2012 Massachusetts surveys of 1,234 students, Massachusetts surveys in 2017, and the three-state SERC study of 2,427 youth between 2020 and 2022. These students come from a variety of backgrounds: in the SERC study, slightly more than half identified as Caucasian, another quarter identified as Hispanic, and 8 percent as Black. Many subjects came from working-class to middle-class families. Both survey samples are clearly varied but also probably not statistically representative of teens across the country. However, these surveys have as a significant asset very detailed information, with more than three hundred variables studied, and we ask questions not only about bullying and cyberbullying, but also about family life, relationships with teachers, peers, friends, and others, social behaviors, substance abuse, and digital behaviors. It is a retrospective study (meaning that they have to remember past conditions), although eighteen-year-olds don't have to recall back very far to remember high school. Most of the data collected are about high school, but some questions ask students about earlier events in their childhood.

WAVES OF CHILDREN IN GRADES 3–12

Beginning in 2011, we started anonymously surveying children in grades 3 through 12 across the states of Massachusetts and New Hampshire. Unlike the Freshman Study, these data were collected only from within Massachusetts and New Hampshire, from a variety of social classes and from both urban, suburban, and rural areas. Wave 1 was measured between March 2011 and June 2011. During those months, we surveyed more than twenty-one thousand children: approximately seven thousand at each academic level (elementary, middle, and high school). This survey was broader but also shallower: it examined fewer variables but gave me a great way to assess how bullying and cyberbullying develop and change between elementary school and high school. Wave 2, in 2015–2016, included both children from our region and children surveyed in South Korea. Finally, Wave 3, which was conducted between 2017 and 2019, included children in grades 3 through 5 from five states: Massachusetts, Virginia, Oregon, New York, and New Jersey.

SURVEYS OF ADULTS

Between September 2010 and June 2011, 3,715 teachers and administrators and 1,941 parents were anonymously surveyed. Unlike parents, who took the survey only if they were personally motivated to do so (and thus were an almost certainly biased sample), faculty were generally asked to complete the survey because their schools were participating in the survey system on students. Neither sample was nationally representative, but faculty data are probably a closer match to the population in general, whereas data collected from the parent survey suggest that parents who were most concerned about bullying—often because their child had been a target—predominated (not surprisingly) in the parent results.

In addition, this book references a study conducted with educators in November 2021, at the height of the global coronavirus pandemic, during which problem behaviors with children were felt to be at their peak. In that study, 188 educators were surveyed from fifteen states, and from schools whose response to the pandemic varied from remaining entirely open to shifting to a 100 percent remote model. Most schools adopted a hybrid model. Classroom teachers, administrators, and school counselors were all surveyed about the types of social problems they observed in students, including fighting, bullying, and social skills deficits.

ANECDOTAL DATA FROM CHILDREN AT THE SCHOOLS IN WHICH MARC WORKED

Because graduate and undergraduate students usually deliver programming to the children in these schools, students often relate interesting and informative anecdotes and personal stories. In addition, between 2020 and 2022, I met with several groups of students to ask questions about social relationships and the impact of the pandemic. This type of qualitative data cannot definitely answer questions, but it can raise issues that help inform the direction of the research we conduct.

APPENDIX B

The Massachusetts Aggression
Reduction Center

The Massachusetts Aggression Reduction Center (MARC) is a partnership
between higher education educators and researchers and K–12 educators,
guidance counselors, administrators, law enforcement, and public servants
in the legal sector (e.g., the district attorney's office). The ultimate purpose
of such a partnership is to:

- provide free or low-cost prevention programs throughout K–12
  communities (faculty, guidance counselors, administrators, parents,
  and students) about the causes of aggression, bullying, cyberbullying,
  and cyber behaviors in children;
- conduct research and disseminate current research findings in that
  area in a speedy and comprehensive manner; and
- provide K–12 faculty and personnel, law enforcement, physicians,
  attorneys, and other stakeholders with the knowledge and
  understanding to cope with aggression, bullying, and safety issues in
  schools, including effective responses and behavior techniques.

In 2019, before the global coronavirus pandemic, MARC programs were
used in twenty-four US states. By 2021, all fifty states had schools using
these programs.

In 2018, MARC was a founding member of the Social and Emotional
Research Consortium (SERC), along with Dr. Katalin Parti at Virginia Tech
University and Dr. Cheryl Sanders at the Metropolitan State University of
Denver. SERC is a research group that gathers data in tandem at these three
universities. The purpose of this Consortium is to promote diverse
sampling, ensure larger pools of research subjects, and increase research
opportunities and publication rates for other researchers.

STUDENT OPPORTUNITIES IN MARC

Undergraduate and graduate students at Bridgewater State University in the fields of psychology, sociology, education, social work, and related areas of study, can apply to become student associates in MARC. Students can become involved in research, training students at local area schools, giving assemblies, and participating many other activities of the Center. Students do not provide training and programs for faculty, parents, or administrators, but beyond that, each student freely chooses the areas they would like to become involved in.

University students are powerful role models to younger students in a way that many other adults (such as parents and teachers) cannot be. Adolescents, who may turn a deaf ear to parents and teachers, tend to respond to college students because they are considered high-status individuals.

GOALS OF THE STUDENT TRAINING

A MARC student undergoes training and thereafter provides that training to younger peers. These university students, who receive course credits for their work in MARC, help high school and middle school students:

- learn how to *recognize* and *label* the problems they see, and how to use small group discussion to more precisely identify what they consider to be the most pressing problems in their own high school or middle school; and
- brainstorm and problem solve about how they can lead an engagement in their specific school culture to work against violence and bullying.

The power of this method lies in the fact that it is the teenagers who both *identify their schools' challenges* and come up with *their own ideas about how to address these issues*. Neither the problems nor the solutions are defined or imposed by adults. We utilize a unique training method that shows students how to transform free-floating ideas into concrete plans.

Student training is designed to help the school successfully launch a student-initiated program, or programs, designed to reduce violence and bullying or accompanying problems (as an example, such a program might work to reduce gossiping or cyberbullying). MARC gets the ball rolling, but it is up to the school to provide some format for their student group to continue its activities.

Student Training Format

The length of student trainings are generally between one hour and thirty minutes and three hours. Trainings may include an hour or so of educational pedagogy.

MARC facilitators are training teenagers to become "peer helpers." Peer helping is a model wherein teens are trained to become educators and counselors for their peers, and Benard pointed out that while peers can destroy a child's sense of safety, they are also among the most powerful providers of support.[1] Benard's 1990 study found that peer helping was a valid intervention strategy resulting in reduced at-risk behaviors. The MARC program aims to teach teenagers how to identify what they consider to be the "problems" and to coach teenagers in coming up with their own ideas for improving their school climate. In 2005, the Innovation Center released a review of peer helping programs that identified important characteristics that made such programs successful. These were, among others:

- being "youth-run and led";
- raising awareness in young people without taking too much power from them;
- "meeting young people where they are";
- "when young people have full ownership, they step up to the tasks"; and
- "teen trainers are more effective than adult trainers."[2]

Because MARC seeks to supplement and not replace other types of bullying prevention programs, the program opted to develop student programming for teenagers based on the peer-helping model. This approach is particularly attractive for an academic center, which has a ready pool of college students to serve as high-status peer models for high school and middle school children.

Student Training Procedure

The actual student training follows a six-step procedure:

1. The MARC supervisor begins by orienting everyone to what will happen. S/he discusses what training is and explains that they are available to hear what the students are seeing happen in their school and to think about ways to work on it.
2. A short slideshow presentation is given to get the students thinking and focused. Remote polling may be used during the presentation to engage the students and to assist the facilitators by revealing facts or issues of interest in the school.

3. If we have data from the student group, we will share it with them.

4. Next the high school and middle school students are divided into small discussion groups of approximately three to seven students each. Each small group sits down with one or two facilitators. One student is asked to take notes.

5. All students go through a process in which they transition between small groups and the larger group. During this process, the students learn how to produce original insights and ideas and to transform them into concrete, useable plans.

6. Students usually have many ideas. Although facilitators are careful not to dismiss any of them, they do guide them toward practical or realistic goals. The critical point is that the students must feel that they have thought up these programs and that they will be the ones to implement them.

Notes

Introduction

1. Elizabeth Englander, "Cell Phone Ownership and Cyberbullying in 8–11 Year Olds: New Research," *Pediatrics* 142, no. 1 MeetingAbstract (2018): 724, https://doi.org/10.1542/peds.142.1MA8.724.
2. "Survey Shows Parents Alarmed as Kids' Screen Time Skyrockets During COVID-19 Crisis," ParentsTogether Foundation, April 23, 2020, https://parents-together.org/survey-shows-parents-alarmed-as-kids-screen-time-skyrockets-during-covid-19-crisis/.
3. "COVID-19 Data Explorer," *Our World in Data*, 19, accessed December 18, 2022, https://ourworldindata.org/explorers/coronavirus-data-explorer.
4. Elizabeth Englander, *Crisis in the Classroom: Educators' Experiences and Attitudes During the Coronavirus Pandemic* (Massachusetts Aggression Reduction Center, Bridgewater State University, Bridgewater, MA, December 1, 2021), https://www.marccenter.org/crisis.
5. Justin Patchin, "Bullying During the COVID-19 Pandemic," Cyberbullying Research Center, September 29, 2021, https://cyberbullying.org/bullying-during-the-covid-19-pandemic; Ojasvi Jain et al., "Has the COVID-19 Pandemic Affected the Susceptibility to Cyberbullying in India?," *Computers in Human Behavior Reports* 2 (August 2020): 100029, https://doi.org/10.1016/j.chbr.2020.100029; So Young Shin and Yeon-Jun Choi, "Comparison of Cyberbullying Before and After the COVID-19 Pandemic in Korea," *International Journal of Environmental Research and Public Health* 18, no. 19 (2021): 10085, https://doi.org/10.3390/ijerph181910085.
6. Elizabeth Englander, "Bullying, Cyberbullying, Anxiety, and Depression in a Sample of Youth During the Coronavirus Pandemic," *Pediatric Reports* 13, no. 3 (2021): 546–51, https://doi.org/10.3390/pediatric13030064; Jordan Bate and Norka Malberg, "Containing the Anxieties of Children, Parents and Families from a Distance During the Coronavirus Pandemic," *Journal of Contemporary Psychotherapy* 50, no. 4 (2020): 285–94, https://doi.org/10.1007/s10879-020-09466-4; Marla Garcia de Avila et al., "Children's Anxiety and Factors Related to the COVID-19 Pandemic: An Exploratory Study Using the Children's Anxiety Questionnaire and the Numerical Rating Scale," *International Journal of Environmental Research and Public Health* 17, no. 16 (2020): 5757, https://doi.org/10.3390/ijerph17165757.
7. Englander, "Bullying, Cyberbullying, Anxiety, and Depression."
8. Meghan McCoy, Elizabeth Englander, and Alex Trahnstrom, "Bias Based Bullying: New Data, and Educational Approaches with Youth" (International

Bullying Prevention Association Annual Conference, Nashville, TN, November 5–7, 2017).

9. Jay Mcfarland, KSLNewsRadio, "JayMac: Fining the Parent Won't Stop School Bullying (and Might Make Things Worse)," KSLNewsRadio, June 11, 2019, https://kslnewsradio.com/1906712/jaymac-fining-the-parent-wont-stop-school-bullying-and-might-make-things-worse/.

10. "Utah District to Be Sued by Family of Bullied 5th Grader Who Died by Suicide," K–12 Dive, accessed December 17, 2022, https://www.k12dive.com/news/utah-district-lawsuit-bullying-suicide/636115/.

11. "Illinois' Strong Anti-Bullying Law Was Ignored at Latin School, According to Parents of Teen Who Took His Life," WBEZ Chicago, April 29, 2022, https://www.wbez.org/stories/illinois-strong-anti-bullying-law-ignored-at-latin-school-according-to-parents-of-teen-who-took-his-life/c006b46d-aebf-4c40-b45c-b3bdbde51b17.

12. Elizabeth Englander, *Bullying and Cyberbullying: What Every Educator Needs to Know* (Cambridge, MA: Harvard Education Press, 2013).

13. Stephen Hackwell, "Teachers Tell Bullied Kids: Don't Be So Gay," Echo, November 2, 2011, http://www.echo-news.co.uk/news/local_news/9337363.Teachers_tell_bullied_kids__Don_t_be_so_gay/?action=complain&cid=9788420.

14. John Medina, "Kids Lie Every 90 Minutes–And That's a Good Thing," *Huffington Post*, January 15, 2011, http://www.huffingtonpost.com/john-medina-phd/kids-lie-every-90-minutes_b_807775.html.

15. Englander, "Bullying, Cyberbullying, Anxiety, and Depression"; A. Ahuja, "LGBT Adolescents in America: Depression, Discrimination and Suicide," *European Psychiatry* 33 (2016): S70, https://doi.org/10.1016/j.eurpsy.2016.01.981.

16. Timothy D. Baker and John H. Hoover, "The Relationship Between Bullying and Suicide in a Sample of 53,000 Young Minnesotans," *International Journal for Talent Development and Creativity* 1, no. 2 (2013): 85–95.

17. Englander, *Bullying and Cyberbullying*.

18. David Finkelhor, Heather A. Turner, and Sherry Hamby, "Let's Prevent Peer Victimization, Not Just Bullying," *Child Abuse & Neglect* 36, no. 4 (April 2012): 271–74, https://doi.org/10.1016/j.chiabu.2011.12.001.

19. Whitney K. Jeter and Laura A. Brannon, "Moving Beyond 'Sticks and Stones': Chronic Psychological Trauma Predicts Posttraumatic Stress Symptoms," *Journal of Trauma and Dissociation* 15, no. 5 (2014): 548–56, https://doi.org/10.1080/15299732.2014.907596.

20. Dan Olweus, *Bullying at School: What We Know and What We Can Do* (Malden, MA: Wiley-Blackwell, 1993).

21. Edward Donnerstein, "Section V: Need for Longitudinal Research," in *Cyberbullying: Current and Future Research and Directions: A White Paper Submitted to the Institute of Child Development and Digital Media* (Institute of Child Development and Digital Media, Jericho, NY, 2015).

22. Elizabeth Englander et al., "Defining Cyberbullying," *Pediatrics* 140, Suppl. 2 (2017): S148–51, https://doi.org/10.1542/peds.2016-1758U.

23. Helen Cowie and Ragnar Olafsson, "The Role of Peer Support in Helping the Victims of Bullying in a School with High Levels of Aggression," *School*

Psychology International 21, no. 1 (2000): 79–95, https://doi.org/10.1177/0143034300211006.

24. *At the Table: Making the Case for Youth in Decision-Making* (University of Wisconsin-Madison, Innovation Center for Community and Youth Development and National 4-H Council, Madison, WI, 2003), https://www.youthpower.org/sites/default/files/YouthPower/resources/Youth_in_Decision_Making-At_The_Table-Report.pdf.

25. Stan Davis and Charisse Nixon, *Youth Voice Project: Student Insights Into Bullying and Peer Mistreatment* (Champaign, IL: Research Press, 2013).

26. Katerina Sinclair et al., "Cyber and Bias-Based Harassment: Associations with Academic, Substance Use, and Mental Health Problems," *Journal of Adolescent Health* Short Communication (February 2012), https://doi.org/10.1016/j.jadohealth.2011.09.009; Jochem Tolsma et al., "Who Is Bullying Whom in Ethnically Diverse Primary Schools? Exploring Links Between Bullying, Ethnicity, and Ethnic Diversity in Dutch Primary Schools," *Social Networks* 35, no. 1 (2013): 51–61, https://doi.org/10.1016/j.socnet.2012.12.002.

27. Federal Bureau of Investigation, "FBI Releases 2017 Hate Crime Statistics," press release, November 13, 2018, https://www.fbi.gov/news/pressrel/press-releases/fbi-releases-2017-hate-crime-statistics.

28. For the sake of readability, and because this isn't a book for fellow researchers, the research findings I cite in the chapters don't include statistical or methodological details. Those can be found in appendix A. All differences I cite in this book are statistically significant, with a few exceptions. Findings that approach significance but don't achieve the $p < 0.05$ standard are worded as "slightly different" or something similar.

Chapter 1

1. "Special Edition School Bullying," Education.com, accessed May 10, 2012, http://www.education.com/special-edition/bullying/schoolbullying/.

2. Dan Olweus, *Aggression in the Schools: Bullies and Whipping Boys* (Oxford, UK: Hemisphere, 1978), http://psycnet.apa.org/psycinfo/1979-32242-000.

3. T. Parker-Pope, "Web of Popularity, Achieved by Bullying," NYTimes.com, 2011, http://well.blogs.nytimes.com/2011/02/14/web-of-popularity-weaved-by-bullying/.

4. "Aggression in the Schools: Bullies and Whipping BOYS, DanOlweus. Washington, Hemisphere Publ. Corp., 1978. No. of Pages: Xiii 4 + 218," *European Journal of Social Psychology* 10, no. 1 (1980): 101, https://doi.org/10.1002/ejsp.2420100124.

5. Elizabeth Englander, *25 Myths About Bullying and Cyberbullying* (Newark, NJ: Wiley, 2020), https://books.google.com/books?id=S7fRDwAAQBAJ.

6. Stan Davis and Charisse Nixon, *Youth Voice Project: Student Insights Into Bullying and Peer Mistreatment* (Champaign, IL: Research Press, 2013).

7. US Department of Education, "Bullying: Peer Abuse in Schools," LD Online, 1998, http://www.ldonline.org/article/6171/.

8. Englander, *25 Myths About Bullying and Cyberbullying*.

9. Elizabeth Englander, "Preliminary Report: Bullying and Cyberbullying in Massachusetts 2011–12" (workshop, PCP Interventions, Freehold, NJ, December 5, 2011).

10. Surilena Hasan and Jessica Jessica, "Non-Exposure Parenting Increases Risk of Bullying Behavior in Junior High School Students," *Universa Medicina* 35, no. 1 (2016): 56–64; Jeter and Brannon, "Moving Beyond 'Sticks and Stones': Chronic Psychological Trauma Predicts Posttraumatic Stress Symptoms," *Journal of Trauma and Dissociation* 15, no. 5 (2014): 548–56, https://doi.org/10.1080/15299732.2014.907596.

11. Davis and Nixon, *Youth Voice Project*.

12. Elizabeth Englander, "Bullying, Cyberbullying, Anxiety, and Depression in a Sample of Youth During the Coronavirus Pandemic," *Pediatric Reports* 13, no. 3 (2021): 546–51.

13. Gaby Hinsliff, "Why Have We All Become so Casually Cruel?," *Guardian*, July 3, 2010, http://www.guardian.co.uk/commentisfree/2010/jul/04/steven-gerrard-twitter-facebook.

14. Maria Wiertsema et al., "Bullying Perpetration and Social Status in the Peer Group: A Meta-Analysis," *Journal of Adolescence* 95 (2022): 34–55, https://doi.org/10.1002/jad.12109.

15. Englander, "Preliminary Report."

16. Chad A. Rose and Dorothy L. Espelage, "Risk and Protective Factors Associated with the Bullying Involvement of Students with Emotional and Behavioral Disorders," *Behavioral Disorders* 37, no. 3 (2012): 133–48, https://doi.org/10.1177/019874291203700302.

17. Grace Hwang Lynch, "Survey: Bullying of Marginalized Students on the Rise," *School Library Journal*, March 13, 2017, http://www.slj.com/2017/03/diversity/survey-bullying-of-marginalized-students-on-the-rise/; Englander, "Bullying, Cyberbullying, Anxiety, and Depression."

18. Englander, "Bullying, Cyberbullying, Anxiety, and Depression."

19. US Department of Education, "Bullying: Peer Abuse in Schools."

20. Depending on your location, the issue of repetition may be legally moot. In some states, no repetition is required in the legal definition of bullying. Most researchers and psychologists, however, do recognize that repetitively cruel behavior is psychologically distinct from one-time events, and thus likely to be experienced very differently by the target.

21. Yuanyuan Xiao et al., "Childhood Maltreatment with School Bullying Behaviors in Chinese Adolescents: A Cross-Sectional Study," *Journal of Affective Disorders* 281 (2021): 941–48, https://doi.org/10.1016/j.jad.2020.11.022.

22. Davis and Nixon, *Youth Voice Project*.

23. Kris Varjas et al., "High School Students' Perceptions of Motivations for Cyberbullying: An Exploratory Study," *Western Journal of Emergency Medicine* 11, no. 3 (August 2010): 269–73.

24. Lin Wang and Steven Sek-yum Ngai, "The Effects of Anonymity, Invisibility, Asynchrony, and Moral Disengagement on Cyberbullying Perpetration Among School-Aged Children in China," *Children and Youth Services Review* 119 (2020): 105613, https://doi.org/10.1016/j.childyouth.2020.105613.

25. Lydia Laninga-Wijnen et al., "The Norms of Popular Peers Moderate Friendship Dynamics of Adolescent Aggression," Child Development, October 2016, https://doi.org/10.1111/cdev.12650.
26. Wang and Ngai, "The Effects of Anonymity, Invisibility, Asynchrony, and Moral Disengagement."
27. Elizabeth Englander, "Freshman Study 2011: Bullying and Cyberbullying," Research Reports from the Massachusetts Aggression Reduction Center (Bridgewater State University, June 2011), http://webhost.bridgew.edu/marc/research.html.
28. Dan Olweus, *Bullying at School : What We Know and What We Can Do* (Oxford; Cambridge, USA: Blackwell, 1993).
29. Elizabeth Englander, "Risk Stratification in Adolescent Cyberbullying and Sexting," *Journal of the American Academy of Child and Adolescent Psychiatry* 61, no. 10 (2022): S329–30, https://doi.org/10.1016/j.jaac.2022.07.748.
30. Samuel Hughes, "Alone Together," *Pennsylvania Gazette*, May 2, 2010, 1–4.
31. Rhonda Clements, "An Investigation of the Status of Outdoor Play," *Contemporary Issues in Early Childhood* 5 (2004): 68–80.
32. Robin S. DeWeese et al., "Active Commuting to School: A Longitudinal Analysis Examining Persistence of Behavior over Time in Four New Jersey Cities," *Preventive Medicine Reports* 26 (2022): 101718, https://doi.org/10.1016/j.pmedr.2022.101718.
33. Mariana Brussoni et al., "What Is the Relationship Between Risky Outdoor Play and Health in Children? A Systematic Review," *International Journal of Environmental Research and Public Health* 12, no. 6 (2015): 6423–54, https://doi.org/10.3390/ijerph120606423.
34. W. Bösche, "Violent Content Enhances Video Game Performance," *Journal of Media Psychology: Theories, Methods, and Applications* 21, no. 4 (2009): 145–50, https://doi.org/10.1027/1864-1105.21.4.145.

Chapter 2

1. "Safe and Caring Schools Targets Bullying," Safe and Caring Schools, Petersen Argo, Inc., n.d., http://www.safeandcaringschools.com.
2. Ashley Psychology Center, n.d., https://ashleypsychology.com.
3. Anushka Asthana, "Bullying Is Exaggerated, Says Childhood Expert," *Guardian*, October 28, 2007, https://www.theguardian.com/uk/2007/oct/28/schools.pupilbehaviour.
4. Steven Woloshin and Lisa Schwartz, "Giving Legs to Restless Legs: A Case Study of How the Media Helps Make People Sick," *PLoS Medicine* 3, no. 4 (2006): e170, https://doi.org/10.1371/journal.pmed.0030170.
5. Tracy Evian Waasdorp et al., "Ten-Year Trends in Bullying and Related Attitudes Among 4th- to 12th-Graders," *Pediatrics* 139, no. 6 (2017): e20162615, https://doi.org/10.1542/peds.2016-2615.
6. Justin Patchin, "School Bullying Rates Increase by 35% from 2016 to 2019," *Cyberbullying Research Center* (blog), May 19, 2019 (accessed January 3, 2023), https://cyberbullying.org/school-bullying-rates-increase-by-35-from-2016-to-2019.

7. Elizabeth Englander, "Bullying, Cyberbullying, Anxiety, and Depression in a Sample of Youth During the Coronavirus Pandemic," *Pediatric Reports* 13, no. 3 (2021): 546–51.
8. Tuhin Biswas et al., "Global Variation in the Prevalence of Bullying Victimisation Amongst Adolescents: Role of Peer and Parental Supports," *EClinicalMedicine* 20 (2020): 100276, https://doi.org/10.1016/j.eclinm.2020.100276.
9. Linda Beckman, Lisa Hellström, and Laura Kobyletzki, "Cyber Bullying Among Children with Neurodevelopmental Disorders: A Systematic Review," *Scandinavian Journal of Psychology* 61, no. 1 (2020): 54–67, https://doi.org/10.1111/sjop.12525.
10. Beckman, Hellström, and Kobyletzki, "Cyber Bullying Among Children with Neurodevelopmental Disorders."
11. Tracy Vaillancourt et al., "School Bullying Before and During COVID-19: Results from a Population-Based Randomized Design," *Aggressive Behavior* 47, no. 5 (2021): 557–69, https://doi.org/10.1002/ab.21986.
12. Elizabeth Englander, "Cyberbullying: New Research and Findings" (2012 National Cyber Crime Conference, Norwood, MA, April 30, 2012).
13. Elizabeth Englander, *Study of 21,000 Children in Grades 3–12 in Massachusetts* (Massachusetts Aggression Reduction Center, Bridgewater State University, Bridgewater, MA, June 2011), https://vc.bridgew.edu/marc_reports/.
14. Elizabeth Englander et al., "Defining Cyberbullying," *Pediatrics* 140 (Nov. 2017): S148–51, doi:10.1542/peds.2016-1758U.
15. Sameer Hinduja and Justin W. Patchin, *Cyberbullying: Identification, Prevention, and Response* (Cyberbullying Research Center, 2021), https://cyberbullying.org/Cyberbullying-Identification-Prevention-Response-2021.pdf.
16. Harris Interactive, *Teens and Cyberbullying Research Study* (Washington, DC: National Crime Prevention Council, 2007), http://archive.ncpc.org/resources/files/pdf/bullying/Teens%20and%20Cyberbullying%20Research%20Study.pdf.
17. Elizabeth Englander, "Spinning Our Wheels: Improving Our Ability to Respond to Bullying and Cyberbullying," *Child and Adolescent Psychiatric Clinics of North America* 21, no. 1 (January 2012): 43–55, https://doi.org/10.1016/j.chc.2011.08.013.
18. Sevda Arslan et al., "Cyberbullying Among Primary School Students in Turkey: Self-Reported Prevalence and Associations with Home and School Life," *Cyberpsychology, Behavior, and Social Networking* 15, no. 10 (2012): 527–33, https://doi.org/10.1089/cyber.2012.0207.
19. Englander, "Study of 21,000 Children in Grades 3–12"; Englander, "Bullying, Cyberbullying, Anxiety, and Depression."
20. Elizabeth Englander, "Cell Phone Ownership and Cyberbullying in 8–11 Year Olds: New Research," *Pediatrics* 142, no. 1 (2018): 724.
21. Gellan K. Ahmed et al., "Prevalence of School Bullying and Its Relationship with Attention Deficit-Hyperactivity Disorder and Conduct Disorder: A Cross-Sectional Study," *Egyptian Journal of Neurology, Psychiatry and Neurosurgery* 58, no. 1 (2022): 60, https://doi.org/10.1186/s41983-022-00494-6.
22. Englander, *25 Myths About Bullying and Cyberbullying* (Newark, NJ: Wiley, 2020).
23. Ilona Markkanen, Raili Välimaa, and Lasse Kannas, "Forms of Bullying and Associations Between School Perceptions and Being Bullied Among Finnish

Secondary School Students Aged 13 and 15," *International Journal of Bullying Prevention* 3, no. 1 (2021): 24–33, https://doi.org/10.1007/s42380-019-00058-y.

24. Englander, "Bullying, Cyberbullying, Anxiety, and Depression."

25. Glenn E. Richardson et al., "The Resiliency Model," *Health Education* 21, no. 6 (1990): 33–39, https://doi.org/10.1080/00970050.1990.10614589.

26. Marilyn Langevin, "Helping Children Deal with Teasing and Bullying" (International Stuttering Awareness Day Online Conference, Minnesota State University, Mankato, MN, October 22, 2001), http://www.mnsu.edu/comdis/isad4/papers/langevin.html.

27. Lucy Bowes et al., "Families Promote Emotional and Behavioural Resilience to Bullying: Evidence of an Environmental Effect," *Journal of Child Psychology and Psychiatry* 51, no. 7 (2010): 809–17, https://doi.org/10.1111/j.1469-7610.2010.02216.x.

28. Ann Wolbert Burgess, Christina Garbarino, and Mary Carlson, "Pathological Teasing and Bullying Turned Deadly: Shooters and Suicide," *Victims and Offenders* 1, no. 1 (2006): 1–14, https://doi.org/10.1080/15564880500498705; Clayton Cook et al., "Predictors of Bullying and Victimization in Childhood and Adolescence: A Meta-Analytic Investigation," *School Psychology Quarterly* 25, no. 2 (2010): 65–83, https://doi.org/10.1037/a0020149; Anat Brunstein Klomek et al., "Bullying, Depression, and Suicidality in Adolescents," *Journal of the American Academy of Child and Adolescent Psychiatry* 46, no. 1 (2007): 40–49, https://doi.org/10.1097/01.chi.0000242237.84925.18; Wendy Craig, "The Relationship Among Bullying, Victimization, Depression, Anxiety, and Aggression in Elementary School Children," *Personality and Individual Differences* 24, no. 1 (1998): 123–30, https://doi.org/10.1016/S0191-8869(97)00145-1.

29. Harris Interactive, "Teens and Cyberbullying Research Study" (National Crime Prevention Council, February 28, 2007), https://studylib.net/doc/8869510/teens-and-cyberbullying-research-study.

30. Sara Jaffee and Robert Gallop, "Social, Emotional, and Academic Competence Among Children Who Have Had Contact with Child Protective Services: Prevalence and Stability Estimates," *Journal of the American Academy of Child and Adolescent Psychiatry* 46, no. 6 (2007): 757–65, https://doi.org/10.1097/chi.0b013e318040b247.

31. Robert Faris and Diane Felmlee, *Social Networks and Aggression at the Wheatley School* (Davis: University of California, Davis, 2011).

32. Natalie Spadafora et al., "Do Little Annoyances Relate to Bullying? The Links Between Personality, Attitudes Towards Classroom Incivility, and Bullying," *Educational and Developmental Psychologist* 37, no. 1 (2020): 30–38, https://doi.org/10.1017/edp.2019.20; Englander, *25 Myths About Bullying and Cyberbullying.*

33. Katerina Sinclair et al., "Cyber and Bias-Based Harassment," *Journal of Adolescent Health* 50, no. 5 (2012): 521–23; Kelly Lynn Mulvey et al., "Understanding Experiences with Bullying and Bias-Based Bullying: What Matters and for Whom?," *Psychology of Violence* 8, no. 6 (2018): 702–11, https://doi.org/10.1037/vio0000206.

34. Lisa Rosenthal et al., "Weight- and Race-Based Bullying: Health Associations Among Urban Adolescents," *Journal of Health Psychology* 20, no. 4 (2015): 401–12, https://doi.org/10.1177/1359105313502567.
35. In-school bullying: r = 0.749, $p < 0.000$; online bullying: r = 0.76, $p < 0.000$.
36. Ernest V. Hodges et al., "The Power of Friendship: Protection Against an Escalating Cycle of Peer Victimization," *Developmental Psychology* 35, no. 1 (1999): 94–101; Michael J. Boulton et al., "Concurrent and Longitudinal Links Between Friendship and Peer Victimization: Implications for Befriending Interventions," *Journal of Adolescence* 22, no. 4 (1999): 461–66, https://doi.org/10.1006/jado.1999.0240.
37. Richard Armitage, "Bullying in Children: Impact on Child Health," *BMJ Paediatrics Open* 5, no. 1 (2021): e000939, https://doi.org/10.1136/bmjpo-2020-000939.
38. Karen Sugden et al., "Serotonin Transporter Gene Moderates the Development of Emotional Problems Among Children Following Bullying Victimization," *Journal of the American Academy of Child and Adolescent Psychiatry* 49, no. 8 (2010): 830–40, https://doi.org/10.1016/j.jaac.2010.01.024.
39. Manuel Gámez-Guadix et al., "Longitudinal and Reciprocal Relations of Cyberbullying with Depression, Substance Use, and Problematic Internet Use Among Adolescents," *Journal of Adolescent Health* 53, no. 4 (2013): 446–52, https://doi.org/10.1016/j.jadohealth.2013.03.030; Amir Ahuja, "LGBT Adolescents in America," *European Psychiatry* 33, Suppl. 1 (2016): S70, https://doi.org/10.1016/j.eurpsy.2016.01.981.
40. Reeve S. Kennedy et al., "Childhood Sexual Abuse and Exposure to Peer Bullying Victimization," *Journal of Interpersonal Violence* 37, no. 19–20 (2022): NP18589–613, https://doi.org/10.1177/08862605211037420.
41. Terri Messman, "Child Sexual Abuse and Its Relationship to Revictimization in Adult Women: A Review," *Clinical Psychology Review* 16, no. 5 (1996): 397–420, https://doi.org/10.1016/0272-7358(96)00019-0.
42. $X^2 = 29.7$, $p < 0.003$.
43. Stan Davis and Charisse Nixon, *Youth Voice Project: Student Insights Into Bullying and Peer Mistreatment* (Champaign, IL: Research Press, 2013).
44. Davis and Nixon, *Youth Voice Project.*
45. Elizabeth Englander, "New Findings in Bullying and Cyberbullying Research" (keynote, Wellness Conference for Brevard County, Satellite Beach, FL, September 10, 2012).
46. Sherri Oden and Steven R. Asher, "Coaching Children in Social Skills for Friendship Making," *Child Development* 48, no. 2 (1977): 495–506.
47. Tessa A. M. Lansu, "How Popularity Goal and Popularity Status Are Related to Observed and Peer-Nominated Aggressive and Prosocial Behaviors in Elementary School Students," *Journal of Experimental Child Psychology* 227 (2023): 105590, https://doi.org/10.1016/j.jecp.2022.105590.
48. Elizabeth Englander, "New Data and Findings: Cyberbullying, Bullying, and Youth" (School Administrators: New Resources; Virtual: Free Spirit Press, 2022).
49. Dan Olweus, *Aggression in the Schools: Bullies and Whipping Boys* (Washington, DC: Hemisphere, 1978).
50. University of New Hampshire, "Why Do Some Children Bully Others? Bullies and Their Victims" (Family Development Fact Sheet, University of New

Hampshire Cooperative Extension, 2002), https://s3.amazonaws.com/assets.cce.
cornell.edu/attachments/9461/NH-Why-Do-Some-Children-Bully-26s07gn.
pdf?1434850940.

51. Faris and Felmlee, *Social Networks and Aggression at the Wheatley School.*
52. Elizabeth Englander, "Bullying, Cyberbullying and Socio-Emotional Learning in
    2023 and Beyond" (IV Global StopCyberbullying Telesummit, Virtual, October
    3–31, 2022), https://cyberbullying.pt/.
53. Elizabeth Englander, "Cognitive and Perceptual Factors in Digital
    Communications" (The Science of Character: Teaching Self-Regulation,
    Resilience, Empathy and Anti-Bullying Skills in Children and Teens,
    Massachusetts Institute of Technology, Cambridge, MA, November 15, 2015).
54. Englander, "New Data and Findings: Cyberbullying, Bullying, and Youth."
55. Linda Beckman, *Traditional Bullying and Cyberbullying Among Swedish Adolescents :
    Gender Differences and Associations with Mental Health* (Sweden: Karlstad
    University, Faculty of Health, Science and Technology, 2013), http://www.diva-
    portal.org/smash/record.jsf?pid=diva2:639930.
56. Englander, "New Findings in Bullying and Cyberbullying Research."

Chapter 3

1. Sélim Benjamin Guessoum et al., "Adolescent Psychiatric Disorders During the
   COVID-19 Pandemic and Lockdown," *Psychiatry Research* 291 (2020): 113264,
   https://doi.org/10.1016/j.psychres.2020.113264; Elizabeth Englander, "Bullying,
   Cyberbullying, Anxiety, and Depression in a Sample of Youth During the
   Coronavirus Pandemic," *Pediatric Reports* 13, no. 3 (2021): 546–51.
2. Elizabeth Englander, *Crisis in the Classroom: Educators' Experiences and Attitudes
   During the Coronavirus Pandemic* (Massachusetts Aggression Reduction Center,
   Bridgewater State University, Bridgewater, MA, December 1, 2021), https://www.
   marccenter.org/_files/ugd/c3a603_67ebd58855fe40f480595e8c46b17e92.pdf.
3. David Finkelhor, "Trends in Adverse Childhood Experiences (ACEs) in the
   United States," *Child Abuse and Neglect* 108 (2020): 104641, https://doi.
   org/10.1016/j.chiabu.2020.104641.
4. Englander, *Crisis in the Classroom.*
5. Dan Olweus, *Aggression in the Schools: Bullies and Whipping Boys* (Washington,
   DC: Hemisphere, 1978).
6. Olweus, *Agression in the Schools.*
7. John H. F. Chan, "Systemic Patterns in Bullying and Victimization," *School
   Psychology International* 27, no. 3 (2006): 352–69, https://doi.org/10.1177/
   0143034306067289.
8. Keith Nissen, "US TV Viewing Behavior Largely Unchanged despite Proliferation
   of Smart TVs," S&P Global, June 8, 2022 (accessed January 6, 2023), https://www
   .spglobal.com/marketintelligence/en/news-insights/research/us-tv-viewing-behavior-
   largely-unchanged-despite-proliferation-of-smart-tvs.
9. Dade Hayes, "Average US Household Now Has 7 Screens, Report Finds," Fierce
   Video, May 31, 2017, https://www.fiercevideo.com/cable/average-u-s-household-
   now-has-seven-screens-reportlinker-finds.
10. Brian Stelter, "Young People Are Watching, but Less Often on TV," *New York
    Times*, February 8, 2012, http://www.nytimes.com/2012/02/09/business/

media/young-people-are-watching-but-less-often-on-tv.html?_r=2&hpw=
&pagewanted=all.

11. Elizabeth Englander and Amy Muldowney, "Just Turn the Darn Thing Off: Understanding Cyberbullying," in *Proceedings of Persistently Safe Schools: The 2007 National Conference on Safe Schools*, ed. D. L. White, B. C. Glenn, and A. Wimes (Washington, DC: Hamilton Fish Institute, George Washington University, 2007), 83–92.

12. "Daily Media Use Among Children and Teens Up Dramatically From Five Years Ago - Kaiser Family Foundation," Kaiser Family Foundation, January 20, 2010, http://www.kff.org/entmedia/entmedia012010nr.cfm.

13. "Number of TV Households in the US 2022," Statista, accessed January 6, 2023, https://www.statista.com/statistics/243789/number-of-tv-households-in-the-us/.

14. Elizabeth Englander, "Bullying, Cyberbullying and Socio-Emotional Learning in 2023 and Beyond" (IV Global StopCyberbullying Telesummit, Virtual, October 3–31, 2022), https://cyberbullying.pt/.

15. Anne Niccoli, "Paper or Tablet? Reading Recall and Comprehension," *EduCause Review*, September 28, 2015, https://er.educause.edu/articles/2015/9/paper-or-tablet-reading-recall-and-comprehension.

16. Bi Ying Hu et al., "Relationship Between Screen Time and Chinese Children's Cognitive and Social Development," *Journal of Research in Childhood Education* 34, no. 2 (2020): 183–207, https://doi.org/10.1080/02568543.2019.1702600.

17. Englander, *Crisis in the Classroom*.

18. Mark Rumfola, "Cyber-Bullying: Bullying in the 21st Century" (master's thesis, State University of New York, Brockport, 2008), http://digitalcommons.brockport.edu/cgi/viewcontent.cgi?article=1092&context=edc_theses.

19. Elizabeth Englander, *Freshman Study 2011: Bullying and Cyberbullying* (Massachusetts Aggression Reduction Center, Bridgewater State University, Bridgewater, MA, June 2011), https://vc.bridgew.edu/marc_reports/.

20. Elizabeth Englander, "A New Way to Look at Cyber-Data" (International Bullying Prevention Association Annual Conference, Nashville, TN, November 12, 2013).

21. "The Trevor Project | For Young LGBTQ Lives," The Trevor Project, accessed January 6, 2023, https://www.thetrevorproject.org/.

22. Scott Fahlman, "Smiley Lore :-)," accessed July 4, 2012, http://www.cs.cmu.edu/~sef/sefSmiley.htm.

23. Elizabeth Englander, "Cell Phone Ownership and Cyberbullying in 8–11 Year Olds: New Research," *Pediatrics* 142, no. 1 (2018): 724.

24. Teresa Correa, Amber Willard Hinsley, and Homero Gil de Zúñiga, "Who Interacts on the Web? The Intersection of Users' Personality and Social Media Use," *Computers in Human Behavior* 26, no. 2 (2010): 247–53, https://doi.org/10.1016/j.chb.2009.09.003.

25. Regina M. Milteer et al., "The Importance of Play in Promoting Healthy Child Development and Maintaining Strong Parent-Child Bond: Focus on Children in Poverty," *Pediatrics* 129, no. 1 (2011): e204–13, https://doi.org/10.1542/peds.2011-2953.

26. Milteer et al., "The Importance of Play."
27. Joan Almon and Edward Miller, *The Crisis in Early Education: A Research-Based Case for More Play and Less Pressure* (Ithaca, NY: The Alliance for Childhood, 2011), https://static1.squarespace.com/static/5d24bb215f3e850001630a72/t/5d3874c610096100016f3521/1563980998460/Crisis+in+Early+Ed+-+A+Research+Based+Case+for+More+Play.pdf.
28. Robin Marantz Henig, "Taking Play Seriously," *New York Times*, Children and Youth, February 17, 2008, http://www.whywaldorfworks.org/03_NewsEvents/documents/TakingPlaySeriously.pdf.
29. Milteer et al., "The Importance of Play."
30. Henig, "Taking Play Seriously."
31. Karin Hellfeldt, Laura López-Romero, and Henrik Andershed, "Cyberbullying and Psychological Well-Being in Young Adolescence: The Potential Protective Mediation Effects of Social Support from Family, Friends, and Teachers," *International Journal of Environmental Research and Public Health* 17, no. 1 (2019): 45, https://doi.org/10.3390/ijerph17010045.
32. Scott Caplan, "A Social Skill Account of Problematic Internet Use," *Journal of Communication* 55, no. 4 (2005): 721–36, https://doi.org/10.1111/j.1460-2466.2005.tb03019.x.
33. Englander, *Crisis in the Classroom*.
34. Roy Pea et al., "Media Use, Face-to-Face Communication, Media Multitasking, and Social Well-Being Among 8- to 12-Year-Old Girls," *Developmental Psychology* 48, no. 2 (2012): 327–36, https://doi.org/10.1037/a0027030.
35. H. Foot, A. Chapman, and J. Smith, "Friendship and Social Responsiveness in Boys and Girls," *Journal of Personality and Social Psychology* 35, no. 6 (1977): 401–11, https://doi.org/10.1037/0022-3514.35.6.401.
36. Edward Powers and Gordon Bultena, "Sex Differences in Intimate Friendships of Old Age," *Journal of Marriage and the Family* 38, no. 4 (1976): 739, https://doi.org/10.2307/350693.
37. Elizabeth Englander, "New Data and Findings: Cyberbullying, Bullying, and Youth" (School Administrators: New Resources; Virtual: Free Spirit Press, 2022).
38. Elizabeth Englander, *Study of 21,000 Children in Grades 3–12 in Massachusetts* (Massachusetts Aggression Reduction Center, Bridgewater State University, Bridgewater, MA, June 2011), https://vc.bridgew.edu/marc_reports/.
39. 2010 Tracking Survey, "Internet and American Life Project" (Pew Research Center, September 13, 2010).
40. Michael Shermer, "Patternicity: Finding Meaningful Patterns in Meaningless Noise," *Scientific American*, December 2008.
41. Tracy Vaillancourt, Shelley Hymel, and Patricia McDougall, "Bullying Is Power," *Journal of Applied School Psychology* 19, no. 2 (2003): 157–76, https://doi.org/10.1300/J008v19n02_10.
42. Marina Camodeca and Frits Goossens, "Aggression, Social Cognitions, Anger and Sadness in Bullies and Victims," *Journal of Child Psychology and Psychiatry* 46, no. 2 (2005): 186–97, https://doi.org/10.1111/j.1469-7610.2004.00347.x.

43. Donald Dutton et al., "Intimacy-Anger and Insecure Attachment as Precursors of Abuse in Intimate Relationships," *Journal of Applied Social Psychology* 24, no. 15 (1994): 1367–86, https://doi.org/10.1111/j.1559-1816.1994.tb01554.x.
44. Felicity W. K. Harper, "The Role of Shame, Anger, and Affect Regulation in Men's Perpetration of Psychological Abuse in Dating Relationships," *Journal of Interpersonal Violence* 20, no. 12 (2005): 1648–62, https://doi.org/10.1177/088626050 5278717.
45. Ágnes Zsila et al., "Gender Differences in the Association Between Cyberbullying Victimization and Perpetration: The Role of Anger Rumination and Traditional Bullying Experiences," *International Journal of Mental Health and Addiction* 17, no. 5 (2019): 1252–67, https://doi.org/10.1007/s11469-018-9893-9.
46. Kenneth Dodge et al., "Peer Rejection and Social Information-Processing Factors in the Development of Aggressive Behavior Problems in Children," *Child Development* 74, no. 2 (2003): 374–93, https://doi.org/10.1111/1467-8624.7402004.
47. Kenneth Dodge et al., "Hostile Attributional Biases in Severely Aggressive Adolescents," *Journal of Abnormal Psychology* 99, no. 4 (1990): 385–92, https://doi.org/10.1037/0021-843X.99.4.385.
48. Englander, "Bullying, Cyberbullying and Socio-Emotional Learning."
49. E. W. Gondolf, "The Case Against Anger Control Treatment Programs for Batterers," *Response to the Victimization of Women and Children* 9, no. 3 (1986): 2–5.
50. D. Dietrich et al., "Some Factors Influencing Abusers' Justification of Their Child Abuse," *Child Abuse and Neglect* 14, no. 3 (1990): 337–45, https://doi.org/10.1016/0145-2134(90)90005-E.
51. Oommen Mammen, David Kolko, and Paul Pilkonis, "Negative Affect and Parental Aggression in Child Physical Abuse," *Child Abuse and Neglect* 26, no. 4 (2002): 407–24, https://doi.org/10.1016/S0145-2134(02)00316-2.
52. M. B. Eberly and R. Montemayor, "Adolescent Affection and Helpfulness Toward Parents: A 2-Year Follow-Up," *Journal of Early Adolescence* 19, no. 2 (1999): 226–48, https://doi.org/10.1177/0272431699019002005.eb.
53. Brian Barber, Joseph Olsen, and Shobha Shagle, "Associations Between Parental Psychological and Behavioral Control and Youth Internalized and Externalized Behaviors," *Child Development* 65, no. 4 (1994): 1120–36, https://doi.org/10.1111/j.1467-8624.1994.tb00807.x.va.

Chapter 4

1. "Angus Council Anti-Bullying Policy" (Angus Council, Angus, UK, updated March 2015), https://www.angus.gov.uk/sites/angus-cms/files/Anti_Bullying_Policy.pdf.
2. Charlotte Dodds, "How Is Cyberbullying Different from 'Traditional' Bullying?," Cybersmile Foundation, September 4, 2014, https://www.cybersmile.org/blog/how-is-cyberbullying-different-from-traditional-bullying.
3. Cisco, *Cisco Connected: World Technology Report* (San Jose, CA: Cisco, September 21, 2011), http://www.cisco.com/en/US/solutions/ns341/ns525/ns537/ns705/ns1120/CCWTR-Chapter1-Press-Deck.pdf.

4. McAfee, "A Look Beyond Their Lock Screens: The Mobile Activity of Tweens and Teens," *McAfee Blog* (blog), February 24, 2022, https://www.mcafee.com/blogs/family-safety/a-look-beyond-their-lock-screens-the-mobile-activity-of-tweens-and-teens/.

5. Elizabeth Englander, "Preliminary Report: Bullying and Cyberbullying in Massachusetts 2011–12" (workshop, PCP Interventions, Freehold, NJ, December 5, 2011).

6. Elizabeth Englander, "Cell Phone Ownership and Cyberbullying in 8–11 Year Olds: New Research," *Pediatrics* 142 (2018): 724, https://doi.org/10.1542/peds.142.1MA8.724.

7. Elizabeth K. Englander, "Achieving a Consensus on the Effects of Digital Media on Youth Mental Health," *2020 Virtual Meeting* (presentation, American Academy of Child and Adolescent Psychiatry, Virtual Meeting, October 23, 2020).

8. Englander, "Achieving a Consensus on the Effects of Digital Media."

9. Elizabeth K. Englander, "Sexting in LGBT Youth," *2020 Virtual Meeting* (presentation, American Academy of Child and Adolescent Psychiatry, Virtual Meeting, October 20, 2020).

10. Elizabeth Englander, "New Data and Findings: Cyberbullying, Bullying, and Youth" (School Administrators: New Resources; Virtual: Free Spirit Press, 2022).

11. Michele L. Ybarra, M. Diener-West, and P. Leaf, "Examining the Overlap in Internet Harassment and School Bullying: Implications for School Intervention," *Journal of Adolescent Health* 41, no. 6 (2007): S42–50, https://doi.org/10.1016/j.jadohealth.2007.09.004.

12. Juan Manuel Rodríguez-Álvarez et al., "Relationship Between Socio-Emotional Competencies and the Overlap of Bullying and Cyberbullying Behaviors in Primary School Students," *European Journal of Investigation in Health, Psychology and Education* 11, no. 3 (2021): 686–96, https://doi.org/10.3390/ejihpe11030049.

13. Larry Magid, "Time to Take the 'Cyber' out of Cyberbullying," *CNET News*, February 3, 2011, http://news.cnet.com/8301-19518_3-20030511-238.html.

14. Dan Olweus, *Aggression in the Schools: Bullies and Whipping Boys* (Washington, DC: Hemisphere, 1978).

15. Kevin C. Runions and Michal Bak, "Online Moral Disengagement, Cyberbullying, and Cyber-Aggression," *Cyberpsychology, Behavior, and Social Networking* 18, no. 7 (2015): 400–405, https://doi.org/10.1089/cyber.2014.0670.

16. Englander, "Achieving a Consensus on the Effects of Digital Media."

17. Zack Whittaker, "Nine out of Ten Teenagers Experience Bullying and Cruelty on Facebook, Twitter," *Zdnet* (blog), November 8, 2011, http://www.zdnet.com/blog/igeneration/nine-out-of-ten-teenagers-experience-bullying-and-cruelty-on-facebook-twitter/13321?tag=content;siu-container.

18. Christopher P. Barlett, "Anonymously Hurting Others Online: The Effect of Anonymity on Cyberbullying Frequency," *Psychology of Popular Media Culture* 4, no. 2 (2015): 70–79, https://doi.org/10.1037/a0034335.

19. Englander, "New Findings in Bullying and Cyberbullying Research" (keynote, Wellness Conference for Brevard County, Satellite Beach, FL, September 10, 2012).

20. Charles Naquin, Terri Kurtzberg, and Liuba Belkin, "The Finer Points of Lying Online: E-Mail Versus Pen and Paper," *Journal of Applied Psychology* 95, no. 2 (2010): 387–94, https://doi.org/10.1037/a0018627.
21. Elizabeth Englander, *Freshman Study 2011: Bullying and Cyberbullying* (Massachusetts Aggression Reduction Center, Bridgewater State University, Bridgewater, MA, June 2011), https://vc.bridgew.edu/marc_reports/.
22. E. Frank Stephenson, "Is This Exam Hazardous to Your Grandmother's Health?," *Atlantic Economic Journal* 31, no. 4 (2003): 384, https://doi.org/10.1007/BF02298496.
23. Andreas B. Eder, Vanessa Mitschke, and Mario Gollwitzer, "What Stops Revenge Taking? Effects of Observed Emotional Reactions on Revenge Seeking," *Aggressive Behavior* 46, no. 4 (2020): 305–16, https://doi.org/10.1002/ab.21890.
24. Elizabeth Englander, "Bullying and Cyberbullying in Teens: Clinical Factors" (presentation, 59th Annual Meeting, American Academy of Child and Adolescent Psychiatry, San Francisco, CA, October 22, 2012), https://aacap.confex.com/aacap/2012/webprogram/Session8538.html.
25. Ronald Slaby and Nancy Guerra, "Cognitive Mediators of Aggression in Adolescent Offenders: I. Assessment," *Developmental Psychology* 24, no. 4 (1988): 580–88.
26. T. Ito, N. Miller, and V. Pollock, "Alcohol and Aggression: A Meta-Analysis on the Moderating Effects of Inhibitory Cues, Triggering Events, and Self-Focused Attention," *Psychological Bulletin* 120, no. 1 (1996): 60–82, https://doi.org/10.1037/0033-2909.120.1.60.
27. Englander, "Achieving a Consensus on the Effects of Digital Media."
28. S. Murphy, J. Monahan, and R. B. Zajonc, "Additivity of Nonconscious Affect: Combined Effects of Priming and Exposure," *Journal of Personality and Social Psychology* 69, no. 4 (1995): 589–602, https://doi.org/10.1037/0022-3514.69.4.589.
29. Englander, "Bullying and Cyberbullying in Teens: Clinical Factors."
30. Jephtah Abu, "Conflict De-Escalation Techniques to Use in Your Online Community," Commsor, June 16, 2022, https://www.commsor.com/post/conflict-de-escalation-techniques-to-use-in-your-online-community.
31. Englander, "New Findings in Bullying and Cyberbullying Research."
32. 2010 Tracking Survey, "Internet and American Life Project" (Pew Research Center, September 13, 2010).
33. Dodds, "How Is Cyberbullying Different from 'Traditional' Bullying?"
34. American Psychiatric Association et al., *Diagnostic and Statistical Manual of Mental Disorders (DSM)* (Washington, DC: American Psychiatric Association, 1994), 143–47.
35. Dorothy L. Espelage, Mrinalini A. Rao, and Rhonda G. Craven, "Theories of Cyberbullying," *Principles of Cyberbullying Research: Definitions, Measures, and Methodology*, ed. Sheri Bauman, Donna Cross, and Jenny Walker (New York: Routledge, 2013), 49.
36. M. Sapacz, G. Rockman, and J. Clark, "Are We Addicted to Our Cell Phones?," *Computers in Human Behavior* 57 (2016): 153–59, https://doi.org/10.1016/j.chb.2015.12.004.
37. Charisse L. Nixon, "Current Perspectives: The Impact of Cyberbullying on Adolescent Health," *Adolescent Health, Medicine and Therapeutics* 5 (2014): 143–58, https://doi.org/10.2147/AHMT.S36456.

38. R. Ortega et al., "The Emotional Impact on Victims of Traditional Bullying and Cyberbullying: A Study of Spanish Adolescents," *Zeitschrift Für Psychologie/ Journal of Psychology* 217, no. 4 (2009): 197–204, https://doi.org/10.1027/0044-3409.217.4.197.o.
39. Englander, "Bullying and Cyberbullying in Teens: Clinical Factors."
40. Craig N. Hase et al., "Impacts of Traditional Bullying and Cyberbullying on the Mental Health of Middle School and High School Students," *Psychology in the Schools* 52, no. 6 (2015): 607–17, https://doi.org/10.1002/pits.21841.
41. Maite Garaigordobil and Enara Larrain, "Bullying and Cyberbullying in LGBT Adolescents: Prevalence and Effects on Mental Health," *Comunicar* 28, no. 62 (2020): 79–90, https://doi.org/10.3916/C62-2020-07.
42. "66% of the Population Suffer from Nomophobia the Fear of Being Without Their Phone," SecurEnvoy.com, February 16, 2012, http://blog.securenvoy.com/2012/02/16/66-of-the-population-suffer-from-nomophobia-the-fear-of-being-without-their-phone/.
43. Sudip Bhattacharya et al., "Nomophobia: No Mobile Phone Phobia," *Journal of Family Medicine and Primary Care* 8, no. 4 (2019): 1297–1300, https://doi.org/10.4103/jfmpc.jfmpc_71_19.
44. Elle Hunt, " 'It Just Doesn't Stop!' Do We Need a New Law to Ban Out-of-Hours Emails?," Money, *Guardian*, June 29, 2021, https://www.theguardian.com/money/2021/jun/29/it-just-doesnt-stop-do-we-need-a-new-law-to-ban-out-of-hours-emails.
45. Meira Gebel and William Antonelli, "How to Turn Off All Notifications Across Your Devices to Reclaim Your Time and Attention Span," Business Insider, 2021, https://www.businessinsider.com/guides/tech/how-to-turn-off-all-notifications-across-devices.
46. Elizabeth Englander, "Bullying, Cyberbullying, Anxiety, and Depression in a Sample of Youth During the Coronavirus Pandemic," *Pediatric Reports* 13, no. 3 (2021): 546–51.
47. Englander, "New Data and Findings: Cyberbullying, Bullying, and Youth."
48. J. Blum, "The Digital Skeptic: Teens Are Web-Addicted, but Digital Illiterates," *CantonDailyLedger.com* (blog), June 26, 2012, http://business-news.thestreet.com/cantondailyledger/story/the-digital-skeptic-teens-are-web-addicted-but-digital-illiterates/11596144.
49. Michael Shermer, "Patternicity: Finding Meaningful Patterns in Meaningless Noise," *Scientific American*, December 1, 2008, https://www.scientificamerican.com/article/patternicity-finding-meaningful-patterns/.
50. M. Lindeman and M. Saher, "Vitalism, Purpose and Superstition," *British Journal of Psychology* 98, no. 1 (2007): 33–44.

Chapter 5

1. Njeri Mbugua, "Sexting Rampant in Social Media Circles," *Star*, October 11, 2019, https://www.the-star.co.ke/sasa/lifestyle/2019-10-11-sexting-rampant-in-social-media-circles/.
2. Kayla McKiski, "Sexting May Be Less Common Among Teens Than You Think," *Ortho Atlanta*, July 26, 2019, https://www.orthoatlanta.com/health-news/sexting-may-be-less-common-by-teens-than-you-think.

3. G. Bergen, R. Shults, and R. Rudd, "Vital Signs: Alcohol-Impaired Driving Among Adults—United States, 2010," *Morbidity and Mortality Weekly Report* 69, no. 39 (2011): 1351–56.

4. Sabina Barrolaza, "Looking Back on How Schools Handled the Spanish Flu Pandemic," *Burlingame B* (blog), November 24, 2020, https://theburlingameb .org/3469/showcase/looking-back-on-how-schools-handled-the-spanish-flu-pandemic/.

5. Colleen McClain et al., "The Internet and the Pandemic," *Pew Research Center: Internet, Science and Tech* (blog), September 1, 2021, https://www.pewresearch. org/internet/2021/09/01/the-internet-and-the-pandemic/.

6. Michelle Faverio, "Share of Those 65 and Older Who Are Tech Users Has Grown in the Past Decade," *Pew Research Center* (blog), January 13, 2022, https:// www.pewresearch.org/fact-tank/2022/01/13/share-of-those-65-and-older-who-are-tech-users-has-grown-in-the-past-decade/.

7. Allen St. John, "Warning Kids About Digital Privacy Doesn't Work. Here's What Does," *Consumer Reports* (blog), 2018, https://www.consumerreports.org/privacy/ kids-and-digital-privacy-what-works-a7394637669/.

8. Kevin Diaz, "Congressman Joe Barton, Hit with 'Sexting' Revelation, Bows out of 2018 Race," *Chron*, November 30, 2017, https://www.chron.com/politics/article/ Congressman-Joe-Barton-hit-with-sexting-12395264.php.

9. Elizabeth K. Englander, "Risk Stratification in Adolescent Cyberbullying and Sexting," *Journal of the American Academy of Child and Adolescent Psychiatry* 61, no. 10 (2022): S329–30, https://doi.org/10.1016/j.jaac.2022.07.748.

10. Camille Mori et al., "The Prevalence of Sexting Behaviors Among Emerging Adults: A Meta-Analysis," *Archives of Sexual Behavior* 49, no. 4 (2020): 1103–19, https://doi.org/10.1007/s10508-020-01656-4.

11. Sheri Madigan et al., "Prevalence of Multiple Forms of Sexting Behavior Among Youth: A Systematic Review and Meta-Analysis," *JAMA Pediatrics* 172, no. 4 (2018): 327, https://doi.org/10.1001/jamapediatrics.2017.5314.

12. Katalin Parti, Cheryl E. Sanders, and Elizabeth K. Englander, "Sexting at an Early Age: Patterns and Poor Health-Related Consequences of Pressured Sexting in Middle and High School," *Journal of School Health* 93, no. 1 (2023): 73–81, https://doi.org/10.1111/josh.13258.

13. Elizabeth K. Englander, "Sexting in LGBT Youth," *2020 Virtual Meeting* (presentation, American Academy of Child and Adolescent Psychiatry, Virtual Meeting, October 20, 2020).

14. Elizabeth Englander, "Bullying, Cyberbullying and Socio-Emotional Learning in 2023 and Beyond" (IV Global StopCyberbullying Telesummit, Virtual, October 3–31, 2022), https://cyberbullying.pt/.

15. Laura Hawks et al., "Association Between Forced Sexual Initiation and Health Outcomes Among US Women," *JAMA Internal Medicine* 179, no. 11 (2019): 1551, https://doi.org/10.1001/jamainternmed.2019.3500.

16. Englander, "Bullying, Cyberbullying and Socio-Emotional Learning."

17. Bianca Klettke et al., "Sexting and Psychological Distress: The Role of Unwanted and Coerced Sexts," *Cyberpsychology, Behavior, and Social Networking* 22, no. 4 (2019): 237–42, https://doi.org/10.1089/cyber.2018.0291.

18. Justin W. Patchin, "The Status of Sexting Laws Across the United States," *Cyberbullying Research Center* (blog), August 18, 2022, https://cyberbullying.org/the-status-of-sexting-laws-across-the-united-states.
19. Danah Boyd, "Digital Self-Harm and Other Acts of Self-Harassment," *DMLcentral* (blog), December 7, 2010, http://dmlcentral.net/blog/danah-boyd/digital-self-harm-and-other-acts-self-harassment.
20. LeAdelle Phelps and American Psychological Association, *Health-Related Disorders in Children and Adolescents: A Guidebook for Understanding and Educating* (Washington, DC: American Psychological Association, 1998).
21. Dillon T. Browne et al., "Children and Screens Research Update: How New Media Habits Impact Mental Health," *2020 Virtual Meeting* (presentation, American Academy of Child and Adolescent Psychiatry, Virtual Meeting, October 23, 2020).
22. Rebecca Lee, "What Is Digital Self-Harm?," *Psych Central*, June 6, 2018, https://psychcentral.com/lib/what-is-digital-self-harm.
23. Elizabeth K. Englander, "Achieving a Consensus on the Effects of Digital Media on Youth Mental Health," *2020 Virtual Meeting* (presentation, American Academy of Child and Adolescent Psychiatry, Virtual Meeting, October 23, 2020).
24. Elizabeth Englander, "Cyberbullying in 8- to 10-Year-Olds: Research on 12,000 Children" (presentation, International Bullying Prevention Association Annual Conference, Kansas City, MO, November 5, 2012), 10.
25. Q. Li, "Cyberbullying in Schools: An Examination of Preservice Teachers' Perception," *Canadian Journal of Learning and Technology* 34, no. 2 (2008).
26. Elizabeth Englander, "Cell Phone Ownership and Cyberbullying in 8–11 Year Olds: New Research," *Pediatrics* 142, no. 1_MeetingAbstract (2018): 724, https://doi.org/10.1542/peds.142.1MA8.724.
27. "Children and Parents: Media Use and Attitudes Report 2016," Ofcom, February 3, 2017, https://www.ofcom.org.uk/research-and-data/media-literacy-research/children/children-parents-nov16.
28. G. Mascheroni and K. Olafsson, "The Mobile Internet: Access, Use, Opportunities and Divides Among European Children," *New Media and Society* 18, no. 8 (2016): 1657–79, https://doi.org/10.1177/1461444814567986.
29. Charlotte Dodds, "How Is Cyberbullying Different from 'Traditional' Bullying?," *Cybersmile*, September 4, 2014, https://www.cybersmile.org/blog/how-is-cyberbullying-different-from-traditional-bullying.
30. Michele L. Ybarra et al., "Defining and Measuring Cyberbullying Within the Larger Context of Bullying Victimization," *Journal of Adolescent Health* 51, no. 1 (2012): 53–58, https://doi.org/10.1016/j.jadohealth.2011.12.031.
31. Kathryn DePaolis and Anne Williford, "The Nature and Prevalence of Cyber Victimization Among Elementary School Children," *Child and Youth Care Forum* 44, no. 3 (2014): 377–93, https://doi.org/10.1007/s10566-014-9292-8.
32. Brett Holfeld and B. J. Leadbeater, "The Nature and Frequency of Cyber Bullying Behaviors and Victimization Experiences in Young Canadian Children," *Canadian Journal of School Psychology* 30, no. 2 (2015): 116–35, https://doi.org/10.1177/0829573514556853.

33. Emily Vogels, "Teens and Cyberbullying 2022," *Pew Research Center: Internet, Science and Tech* (blog), December 15, 2022, https://www.pewresearch.org/internet/2022/12/15/teens-and-cyberbullying-2022/.

34. Monica Anderson, Michelle Faverio, and Colleen McClain, "How Teens Navigate School During COVID-19," *Pew Research Center: Internet, Science and Tech* (blog), June 2, 2022, https://www.pewresearch.org/internet/2022/06/02/how-teens-navigate-school-during-covid-19/.

35. Nikki Graf, "A Majority of US Teens Fear a Shooting Could Happen at Their School, and Most Parents Share Their Concern," *Pew Research Center* (blog), April 18, 2018, https://www.pewresearch.org/fact-tank/2018/04/18/a-majority-of-u-s-teens-fear-a-shooting-could-happen-at-their-school-and-most-parents-share-their-concern/.

36. Naaz Modan and Kara Arundel, "School Shootings Reach Unprecedented High in 2022," K–12 Dive, December 21, 2022, https://www.k12dive.com/news/2022-worst-year-for-school-shootings/639313/.

37. Englander, "Bullying, Cyberbullying and Socio-Emotional Learning."

38. Vogels, "Teens and Cyberbullying 2022."

39. Common Sense Media, "35% of Teens Admit to Using Cell Phones to Cheat," June 18, 2009, https://www.commonsensemedia.org/press-releases/35-of-teens-admit-to-using-cell-phones-to-cheat.

40. Elizabeth Englander, *Research Findings: MARC 2011 Survey Grades 3–12* (Massachusetts Aggression Reduction Center, Bridgewater State University, Bridgewater, MA, June 2012), http://webhost.bridgew.edu/marc/MARC%20REPORT-Bullying%20In%20Grades%203-12%20in%20MA.pdf.

41. Sharon Noguchi, "Nearly a Third of US Teens Use Electronics to Cheat, Survey Says," *Denver Post*, August 6, 2017, https://www.denverpost.com/2017/08/06/us-teens-electronics-cheat/.

42. Alex Mitchell, "Students Using ChatGPT to Cheat, Professor Warns," *New York Post*, December 26, 2022, https://nypost.com/2022/12/26/students-using-chatgpt-to-cheat-professor-warns/.

43. Tim Walker, "Technology Makes It Easier, But What Do We Really Know About Why Students Cheat?," National Education Association, 2017, https://www.nea.org/advocating-for-change/new-from-nea/technology-makes-it-easier-what-do-we-really-know-about-why-students-cheat.

44. "Teachers' Newest Online Worry: 'Cyberbaiting'," *ESchoolNews*, November 27, 2011, http://www.eschoolnews.com/2011/11/27/teachers-newest-online-worry-cyberbaiting/.

45. "Teachers' Newest Online Worry."

46. Meghan Mathis, "What To Do When Students Record You Without Your Permission," We Are Teachers, September 20, 2021, https://www.weareteachers.com/students-recording-teachers-without-permission/.

47. Mathis, "What To Do When Students Record You."

48. Richard Adams, "One in Five Teachers Abused Online by Parents and Pupils, Survey Says," Education, *Guardian*, April 21, 2014, https://www.theguardian.com/education/2014/apr/21/teachers-abused-online-parents-pupils.

49. Kamil Kopecký and René Szotkowski, "Specifics of Cyberbullying of Teachers in Czech Schools—A National Research," *Informatics in Education* 16, no. 1 (2017): 103–19, https://doi.org/10.15388/infedu.2017.06.

50. Sara Morrison, "When Teachers Are Victims Of Cyberbullying," *Vocativ* (blog), May 15, 2017, https://www.vocativ.com/419694/teachers-victims-cyberbullying-social-media/.

51. Xue-Chen Zhang et al., "Sensation Seeking and Cyberbullying Among Chinese Adolescents: Examining the Mediating Roles of Boredom Experience and Antisocial Media Exposure," *Computers in Human Behavior* 130 (2022): 107185, https://doi.org/10.1016/j.chb.2022.107185.

52. Fanny Carina Ossa et al., "Cyberbullying and School Bullying Are Related to Additive Adverse Effects Among Adolescents," *Psychopathology* 56, no. 1–2 (2023): 127–37, https://doi.org/10.1159/000523992.

53. M. Vimalkumar et al., " 'Okay Google, What About My Privacy?': User's Privacy Perceptions and Acceptance of Voice Based Digital Assistants," *Computers in Human Behavior* 120 (2021): 106763, https://doi.org/10.1016/j.chb.2021.106763.

54. Ellen Chang, "Messaging Apps That Are Secure: Signal vs. WhatsApp," *TheStreet*, July 23, 2022, https://www.thestreet.com/technology/messaging-apps-that-are-secure-signal-vs-whatsapp.

55. Baobao Zhang et al., "Americans' Perceptions of Privacy and Surveillance in the COVID-19 Pandemic," *PLoS ONE* 15, no. 12 (2020): e0242652, https://doi.org/10.1371/journal.pone.0242652.

56. Elizabeth Englander and A. Muldowney, "Just Turn the Darn Thing Off: Understanding Cyberbullying," in *Proceedings of Persistently Safe Schools: The 2007 National Conference on Safe Schools*, ed. D. L. White, B. C. Glenn, and A. Wimes (Washington, DC: Hamilton Fish Institute, George Washington University, 2007), 83–92.

57. Jun Zhao et al., " 'I Make up a Silly Name': Understanding Children's Perception of Privacy Risks Online," in *Proceedings of the 2019 CHI Conference on Human Factors in Computing Systems* (Glasgow, Scotland: Association for Computing Machinery, 2019), 1–13, https://doi.org/10.1145/3290605.3300336.

58. Mohsen Jozani et al., "Privacy Concerns and Benefits of Engagement with Social Media-Enabled Apps: A Privacy Calculus Perspective," *Computers in Human Behavior* 107 (2020): 106260, https://doi.org/10.1016/j.chb.2020.106260.

59. Elizabeth Englander, "Cyberbullying: New Research and Findings" (2012 National Cyber Crime Conference, Norwood, MA, April 30, 2012).

60. Katie Davis and Carrie James, "Tweens' Conceptions of Privacy Online: Implications for Educators," *Learning, Media and Technology* 38, no. 1 (2013): 4–25, https://doi.org/10.1080/17439884.2012.658404.

61. Allen St. John, "Warning Kids About Digital Privacy Doesn't Work. Here's What Does," *Consumer Reports* (blog), August 28, 2018, https://www.consumerreports.org/privacy/kids-and-digital-privacy-what-works-a7394637669/.

62. Chantal Faucher, Wanda Cassidy, and Margaret Jackson, "Awareness, Policy, Privacy, and More: Post-Secondary Students Voice Their Solutions to Cyberbullying," *European Journal of Investigation in Health, Psychology and Education* 10, no. 3 (2020): 795–815, https://doi.org/10.3390/ejihpe10030058.

63. Stephanie Pieschl and Torsten Porsch, "The Complex Relationship Between Cyberbullying and Trust," *International Journal of Developmental Science* 11, no. 1–2 (2017): 9–17, https://doi.org/10.3233/DEV-160208.

64. Lucy R. Betts and Karin A. Spenser, " 'People Think It's a Harmless Joke': Young People's Understanding of the Impact of Technology, Digital Vulnerability and Cyberbullying in the United Kingdom," *Journal of Children and Media* 11, no. 1 (2017): 20–35, https://doi.org/10.1080/17482798.2016.1233893.

Chapter 6

1. Rhona Lewis, "Recognizing the Types of Bullying and Potential Effects," *Healthline* (blog), January 22, 2021, https://www.healthline.com/health/childrens-health/types-of-bullying.

2. Marloes D. A. van Verseveld et al., "Teachers' Experiences with Difficult Bullying Situations in the School: An Explorative Study," *Journal of Early Adolescence* 41, no. 1 (2021): 43–69, https://doi.org/10.1177/0272431620939193.

3. Michael J. Boulton et al., "A Comparison of Preservice Teachers' Responses to Cyber Versus Traditional Bullying Scenarios: Similarities and Differences and Implications for Practice," *Journal of Teacher Education* 65, no. 2 (2014): 145–55, https://doi.org/10.1177/0022487113511496.

4. Li Ming Chen, Wen Cheng, and Hsiao-Chi Ho, "Perceived Severity of School Bullying in Elementary Schools Based on Participants' Roles," *Educational Psychology* 35, no. 4 (2015): 484–96, https://doi.org/10.1080/01443410.2013.860220.

5. J. Wang, R. Iannotti, and T. Nansel, "School Bullying Among Adolescents in the United States: Physical, Verbal, Relational, and Cyber," *Journal of Adolescent Health* 45, no. 4 (2009): 368–75, https://doi.org/10.1016/j.jadohealth.2009.03.021.

6. Elizabeth Englander, *Freshman Study 2011: Bullying and Cyberbullying* (Massachusetts Aggression Reduction Center, Bridgewater State University, Bridgewater, MA, June 2011), https://vc.bridgew.edu/marc_reports/.

7. Marian Wright Edelman, "Zero Tolerance Discipline Policies: A Failing Idea," *Huffington Post*, August 5, 2011, http://www.huffingtonpost.com/marian-wright-edelman/zero-tolerance-discipline_b_919649.html?view=print&comm_ref=false.

8. Elizabeth K. Englander, *25 Myths About Bullying and Cyberbullying* (Newark, NJ: Wiley, 2020), https://books.google.com/books?id=S7fRDwAAQBAJ.

9. Elizabeth Englander, "New Data and Findings: Cyberbullying, Bullying, and Youth" (School Administrators: New Resources; Virtual: Free Spirit Press, 2022).

10. "Study Shows Bullying Affects Both Bystanders and Target," *Penn State Live*, October 11, 2011, http://live.psu.edu/story/55627.

11. G. Gini et al., "The Role of Bystanders in Students' Perception of Bullying and Sense of Safety," *Journal of School Psychology* 46, no. 6 (2008): 617–38, https://doi.org/10.1016/j.jsp.2008.02.001.

12. N. Burrell, C. Zirbel, and M. Allen, "Evaluating Peer Mediation Outcomes in Educational Settings: A Meta-Analytic Review," *Conflict Resolution Quarterly* 21, no. 1 (2003): 7–26, https://doi.org/10.1002/crq.46.

13. R. Casella, "The Benefits of Peer Mediation in the Context of Urban Conflict and Program Status," *Urban Education* 35, no. 3 (2000): 324–55, https://doi.org/10.1177/0042085900353004.

14. S. Theberge and O. Karan, "Six Factors Inhibiting the Use of Peer Mediation in a Junior High School," *Professional School Counseling* 7, no. 4 (2004): 283–91.

15. Grethe Nordhelle, "Hidden Power Imbalance in the Mediation Process," in *Resolving Disputes in the 21st Century*, ed. Slávka Karkošková et al. (Budapest, Hungary: Lifelong Learning Programme, 2013), 118–27, https://vid.brage.unit. no/vid-xmlui/bitstream/handle/11250/99133/REDICT_%20book%5B1%5D. pdf?sequence=1#page=119.
16. E. Delisio, "Making Peer Mediation a Part of Campus Life," EducationWorld. com, 2004, http://www.educationworld.com/a_admin/admin/admin348.shtml.
17. C. Morgan, "Student to Student: The Use of Peer Mediation to Stop Bullying," Voices.Yahoo.com, June 1, 2010, http://voices.yahoo.com/student-student-peer-mediation-stop-6113012.html?cat=17.
18. R. J. Adams, "Bullying Basics for K–12 and the Workplace," Awesomelibrary.org, 2011, http://www.awesomelibrary.org/bullying.html.
19. US Department of Education, "Bullying: Peer Abuse in Schools," LD Online, 1998, http://www.ldonline.org/article/6171/.
20. Elizabeth Englander, "When Should You Hesitate to Mediate?," *Models of Respecting Everyone* 1, no. 1 (2005): 2–3.
21. Elizabeth Englander, "Cyberbullying: New Research and Findings" (2012 National Cyber Crime Conference, Norwood, MA, April 30, 2012).
22. US Department of Justice, "Want to Resolve a Dispute? Try Mediation," *Youth in Action Bulletin* (Washington, DC: National Crime Prevention Council, March 2000), https://www.ncjrs.gov/pdffiles1/ojjdp/178999.pdf.
23. H. Garinger, "Girls Who Bully: What Professionals Need to Ask," *Guidance and Counseling* 21, no. 4 (2006): 236–43, https://doi.org/Article.
24. Stephen Hackwell, "Teachers Tell Bullied Kids: Don't Be So Gay," *Echo*, November 2, 2011, http://www.echo-news.co.uk/news/local_news/9337363. Teachers_tell_bullied_kids__Don_t_be_so_gay/?action=complain&cid=9788420.
25. Englander, "New Data and Findings: Cyberbullying, Bullying, and Youth."
26. Kabir Dasgupta, "Youth Response to State Cyberbullying Laws," *New Zealand Economic Papers* 53, no. 2 (2019): 184–202.
27. N. Willard, *Safe and Responsible Use of the Internet: A Guide for Educators* (Eugene, OR: Responsible Netizen Institute, 2002), http://responsiblenetizen.org.
28. Willard, *Safe and Responsible Use of the Internet*.
29. Willone Lim, Bee Theng Lau, and Fakir M. Amirul Islam, "Cyberbullying Awareness Intervention in Digital and Non-Digital Environment for Youth: Current Knowledge," *Education and Information Technologies* 28 (2023): 6869–925.
30. Maria Rosaria Nappa et al., "Do the Face-to-Face Actions of Adults Have an Online Impact? The Effects of Parent and Teacher Responses on Cyberbullying Among Students," *European Journal of Developmental Psychology* 18, no. 6 (2021): 798–813.
31. Debra Pepler et al., "Witnesses in Cyberbullying: Roles and Dilemmas," *Children and Schools* 43, no. 1 (2021): 45–53.
32. Meghan McCoy, Elizabeth Englander, and Katalin Parti, "A Model for Providing Bullying 8 Prevention Programs to K–12 Education While Training Future Educators," in *Reducing Cyberbullying in Schools*, ed. Marilyn Campbell and Sheri Bauman (London: Elsevier, 2018), 109–24.
33. Elizabeth Englander, "That's Confidential," 2012, http://englanderdownloads. webs.com/thats%20confidential%202011%20small.pdf.

Chapter 7

1. R. Atlas and D. Pepler, "Observations of Bullying in the Classroom," *Journal of Educational Research* 92, no. 2 (1998): 86–99, https://doi.org/10.1080/00220679809597580.
2. P. O'Connell, D. Pepler, and W. Craig, "Peer Involvement in Bullying: Insights and Challenges for Intervention," *Journal of Adolescence* 22, no. 4 (1999): 437–52, https://doi.org/10.1006/jado.1999.0238.
3. US Department of Education, "Bullying: Peer Abuse in Schools," LD Online, 1998, http://www.ldonline.org/article/6171/.
4. Stan Davis and Charisse Nixon, *Youth Voice Project: Student Insights Into Bullying and Peer Mistreatment* (Champaign, IL: Research Press, 2013).
5. Elizabeth Englander, "Cyberbullying: New Research and Findings" (2012 National Cyber Crime Conference, Norwood, MA, April 30, 2012).
6. Amanda Lenhart, "Teens, Social Media and Technology Overview 2015," *Internet American Life Project*, Pew Research Center, April 8, 2015, http://www.pewinternet.org/2015/04/09/teens-social-media-technology-2015/.
7. Özlem Yesim Özbek and Pervin Oya Taneri, "Bullying Behaviors and School Climate Through the Perspective of Primary-School Students," *Eurasian Educational Research Congress 2022 Conference Proceedings* (2022), 265–384.
8. Mary Callaghan, Colette Kelly, and Michal Molcho, "Bullying and Bystander Behaviour and Health Outcomes Among Adolescents in Ireland," *Journal of Epidemiology and Community Health* 73, no. 5 (2019): 416–21, https://doi.org/10.1136/jech-2018-211350.
9. Elizabeth Englander, "Bullying, Cyberbullying and Socio-Emotional Learning in 2023 and Beyond" (IV Global StopCyberbullying Telesummit, Virtual, October 3–31, 2022), https://cyberbullying.pt/.
10. Dan Olweus, *Bullying at School: What We Know and What We Can Do* (Malden, MA: Wiley-Blackwell, 1993).
11. C. Salmivalli, "Bullying and the Peer Group: A Review," *Aggression and Violent Behavior* 15, no. 2 (2010): 112–20, https://doi.org/10.1016/j.avb.2009.08.007.
12. K. Konstantina and S. Pilios-Dimitris, "School Characteristics as Predictors of Bullying and Victimization Among Greek Middle School Students," *International Journal of Violence and School* 11 (2010): 93–113; Sally B. Palmer and Nicola Abbott, "Bystander Responses to Bias-Based Bullying in Schools: A Developmental Intergroup Approach," *Child Development Perspectives* 12, no. 1 (2018): 39–44, https://doi.org/10.1111/cdep.12253.
13. O'Connell, Pepler, and Craig, "Peer Involvement in Bullying."
14. M. Langevin, "Helping Children Deal with Teasing and Bullying" (International Stuttering Awareness Day Online Conference, Minnesota State University, October 22, 2001), http://www.mnsu.edu/comdis/isad4/papers/langevin.html.
15. A. Rolider and M. Ochayon, "Bystander Behaviours Among Israeli Children Witnessing Bullying Behaviour in School Settings," *Pastoral Care in Education* 23, no. 2 (2005): 36–39, https://doi.org/10.1111/j.0264-3944.2005.00330.x.
16. Callaghan, Kelly, and Molcho, "Bullying and Bystander Behaviour and Health Outcomes."

17. J. Carney, C. Jacob, and R. Hazler, "Exposure to School Bullying and the Social Capital of Sixth-Grade Students," *Journal of Humanistic Counseling* 50, no. 2 (2011): 238–53, https://doi.org/10.1002/j.2161-1939.2011.tb00122.x.
18. I. Rivers et al., "Observing Bullying at School: The Mental Health Implications of Witness Status," *School Psychology Quarterly* 24, no. 4 (2009): 211–23, https://doi.org/10.1037/a0018164.
19. Callaghan, Kelly, and Molcho, "Bullying and Bystander Behaviour and Health Outcomes."
20. Shu-Tzu Huang and Rebecca A. Vidourek, "Bullying Victimization Among Asian-American Youth: A Review of the Literature," *International Journal of Bullying Prevention* 1, no. 3 (2019): 187–204, https://doi.org/10.1007/s42380-019-00029-3.
21. Katri Blomqvist, Silja Saarento-Zaprudin, and Christina Salmivalli, "Telling Adults About One's Plight as a Victim of Bullying: Student- and Context-Related Factors Predicting Disclosure," *Scandinavian Journal of Psychology* 61, no. 1 (February 2020): 151–59, https://doi.org/10.1111/sjop.12521.
22. Lori K. Matuschka et al., "Correlates of Help-Seeking Behaviour in Adolescents Who Experience Bullying Victimisation," *International Journal of Bullying Prevention* 4, no. 2 (2022): 99–114, https://doi.org/10.1007/s42380-021-00090-x.
23. Elizabeth Englander, "Cyberbullying Among 11,700 Elementary School Students, 2010–2012," MARC Research Reports (Massachusetts Aggression Reduction Center: Bridgewater State University, 2012), http://vc.bridgew.edu/cgi/viewcontent.cgi?article=1005&context=marc_reports.
24. Rafael Miranda et al., "Adolescent Bullying Victimization and Life Satisfaction: Can Family and School Adult Support Figures Mitigate This Effect?," *Revista de Psicodidáctica* (English Edition) 24, no. 1 (2019): 39–45, https://doi.org/10.1016/j.psicoe.2018.07.001; Charisse L. Nixon et al., "Effects of Students' Grade Level, Gender, and Form of Bullying Victimization on Coping Strategy Effectiveness," *International Journal of Bullying Prevention* 2, no. 3 (2020): 190–204, https://doi.org/10.1007/s42380-019-00027-5.
25. M. Fekkes, "Bullying: Who Does What, When and Where? Involvement of Children, Teachers and Parents in Bullying Behavior," *Health Education Research* 20, no. 1 (2004): 81–91, https://doi.org/10.1093/her/cyg100.
26. Thérèse Shaw et al., "Telling an Adult at School About Bullying: Subsequent Victimization and Internalizing Problems," *Journal of Child and Family Studies* 28, no. 9 (2019): 2594–605, https://doi.org/10.1007/s10826-019-01507-4.
27. Debra Pepler et al., "A School-Based Anti-Bullying Intervention: Preliminary Evaluation," *Understanding and Managing Bullying* 6 (1993): 76–91.
28. L. Crothers, J. Kolbert, and W. Barker, "Middle School Students' Preferences for Anti-Bullying Interventions," *School Psychology International* 27, no. 4 (2006): 475–87, https://doi.org/10.1177/0143034306070435.
29. Miranda et al., "Adolescent Bullying Victimization and Life Satisfaction."
30. Nixon et al., "Effects of Students' Grade Level, Gender, and Form of Bullying Victimization."
31. Maria Rosaria Nappa et al., "Do the Face-to-Face Actions of Adults Have an Online Impact? The Effects of Parent and Teacher Responses on Cyberbullying

Among Students," *European Journal of Developmental Psychology* 18, no. 6 (2021): 798–813, https://doi.org/10.1080/17405629.2020.1860746.

32. Shaw et al., "Telling an Adult at School About Bullying."
33. Nixon et al., "Effects of Students' Grade Level, Gender, and Form of Bullying Victimization."
34. C. Murphy and V. Baxter, "Motivating Batterers to Change in the Treatment Context," *Journal of Interpersonal Violence* 12, no. 4 (August 1, 1997): 607–19, https://doi.org/10.1177/088626097012004009.
35. Elizabeth Englander, "New Data and Findings: Cyberbullying, Bullying, and Youth" (School Administrators: New Resources; Virtual: Free Spirit Press, 2022).
36. Murphy and Baxter, "Motivating Batterers to Change."
37. M. Camodeca et al., "Links Between Social Information Processing in Middle Childhood and Involvement in Bullying," *Aggressive Behavior* 29, no. 2 (2003): 116–27, https://doi.org/10.1002/ab.10043.
38. W. M. Craig and D. J. Pepler, "Observations of Bullying and Victimization in the School Yard," *Canadian Journal of School Psychology* 13, no. 2 (1998): 41–59, https://doi.org/10.1177/082957359801300205.
39. B. Stiller, M. S. Tomlanovich, and R. Nese, "Bully Prevention in Positive Behavior Support: K–8 Adaptations" (Northwest PBIS Conference, Oregon State University, 2011), http://www.pbisnetwork.org/wp-content/uploads/2011/02/Bully-Prevention-B-Stiller-1.4.pdf.
40. Crothers, Kolbert, and Barker, "Middle School Students' Preferences."
41. Davis and Nixon, *Youth Voice Project.*
42. L. Crothers, J. Field, and J. Kolbert, "Navigating Power, Control, and Being Nice: Aggression in Adolescent Girls' Friendships," *Journal of Counseling and Development* 83, no. 3 (2005): 349–54, https://doi.org/10.1002/j.1556-6678.2005.tb00354.x.
43. E. A. Stewart, C. J. Schreck, and R. L. Simons, "'I Ain't Gonna Let No One Disrespect Me': Does the Code of the Street Reduce or Increase Violent Victimization Among African American Adolescents?," *Journal of Research in Crime and Delinquency* 43, no. 4 (2006): 427–58, https://doi.org/10.1177/0022427806292338.
44. US Department of Education, "Bullying: Peer Abuse in Schools."
45. Davis and Nixon, *Youth Voice Project.*
46. G. Sugai, R. Horner, and B. Algozzine, "Reducing the Effectiveness of Bullying Behavior in Schools" (Office of Special Education Programs, Center on Positive Behavior Interventions and Supports, US Department of Education, April 19, 2011).
47. P. O'Connell, D. Pepler, and W. Craig, "Peer Involvement in Bullying: Insights and Challenges for Intervention," *Journal of Adolescence* 22, no. 4 (August 1999): 437–52, https://doi.org/10.1006/jado.1999.0238.
48. M. Demaray and C. Malecki, "Perceptions of the Frequency and Importance of Social Support by Students Classified as Victims, Bullies and Bully/Victims in an Urban Middle School," *School Psychology Review* 32, no. 3 (2003): 471–89.
49. E. Menesini et al., "Enhancing Children's Responsibility to Take Action Against Bullying: Evaluation of a Befriending Intervention in Italian Middle Schools," *Aggressive Behavior* 29, no. 1 (2003): 1–14, https://doi.org/10.1002/ab.80012.
50. Davis and Nixon, *Youth Voice Project*, 18.

Chapter 8

1. Renee Stepler, "5 Key Takeaways About Parenting in Changing Times," *Pew Research Center* (blog), December 17, 2015, https://www.pewresearch.org/fact-tank/2015/12/17/key-takeaways-about-parenting/.
2. Elizabeth Englander, "That's Confidential," 2012, https://englanderdownloads.webs.com/thats%20confidential%202011%20small.pdf.
3. Elizabeth Englander, "New Findings in Bullying and Cyberbullying Research" (keynote, Wellness Conference for Brevard County, Satellite Beach, FL, September 10, 2012).
4. Kristen L. Stives et al., "Understanding Responses to Bullying from the Parent Perspective," *Frontiers in Education* 6 (2021): 642367, https://doi.org/10.3389/feduc.2021.642367.
5. Emily Vogels, "Teens and Cyberbullying 2022," *Pew Research Center: Internet, Science and Tech* (blog), December 15, 2022, https://www.pewresearch.org/internet/2022/12/15/teens-and-cyberbullying-2022/.
6. E. Lawrence et al., "Is Psychological Aggression as Detrimental as Physical Aggression? The Independent Effects of Psychological Aggression on Depression and Anxiety Symptoms," *Violence and Victims* 24, no. 1 (2009): 20–35, https://doi.org/10.1891/0886-6708.24.1.20.
7. Sarah Lindstrom Johnson et al., "Parental Responses to Bullying: Understanding the Role of School Policies and Practices," *Journal of Educational Psychology* 111, no. 3 (2019): 475–87, https://doi.org/10.1037/edu0000295.
8. Lindstrom Johnson et al., "Parental Responses to Bullying."
9. Elizabeth Englander, "Cyberbullying: New Research and Findings" (2012 National Cyber Crime Conference, Norwood, MA, April 30, 2012).
10. Alicia Shevlin and Peter Richard Gill, "Parental Attitudes to the Australian Anti-Bullying Safe Schools Program: A Critical Discourse Analysis," *Social Psychology of Education* 23, no. 4 (2020): 891–915, https://doi.org/10.1007/s11218-020-09561-3.
11. Marloes D. A. van Verseveld et al., "Teachers' Experiences with Difficult Bullying Situations in the School: An Explorative Study," *Journal of Early Adolescence* 41, no. 1 (January 2021): 43–69, https://doi.org/10.1177/0272431620939193.
12. Englander, "That's Confidential."
13. van Verseveld et al., "Teachers' Experiences with Difficult Bullying Situations in the School."
14. V. Stuart-Cassel, "Analysis of State Bullying Laws and Policies" (US Department of Education, Washington, DC, December 2011), http://www2.ed.gov/about/offices/list/opepd/ppss/reports.html#safe.
15. Tracy Evian Waasdorp et al., "The Role of Bullying-Related Policies: Understanding How School Staff Respond to Bullying Situations," *European Journal of Developmental Psychology* 18, no. 6 (2021): 880–95, https://doi.org/10.1080/17405629.2021.1889503.
16. Elizabeth Englander, "Massachusetts Aggression Reduction Center," Massachusetts Aggression Reduction Center, Bridgewater State University, accessed June 30, 2012, http://webhost.bridgew.edu/marc/.
17. Elizabeth Englander, "New Data and Findings: Cyberbullying, Bullying, and Youth" (School Administrators: New Resources; Virtual: Free Spirit Press, 2022).

18. N. Darling et al., "Predictors of Adolescents' Disclosure to Parents and Perceived Parental Knowledge: Between- and Within-Person Differences," *Journal of Youth and Adolescence* 35, no. 4 (2006): 659–70, https://doi.org/10.1007/s10964-006-9058-1.

19. "Character Counts! Programs: Ethics of American Youth Survey: Josephson Institute's Report Card," The Ethics of American Youth: 2010, Josephson Institute, February 10, 2011, http://charactercounts.org/programs/reportcard/2010/installment02_report-card_honesty-integrity.html.

20. A. Vrij, L. Akehurst, and S. Knight, "Police Officers', Social Workers', Teachers' and the General Public's Beliefs About Deception in Children, Adolescents and Adults," *Legal and Criminological Psychology* 11, no. 2 (2006): 297–312, https://doi.org/10.1348/135532505X60816.

21. A. Lenhart et al., "Teens, Kindness and Cruelty on Social Network Sites," Pew Internet and American Life Project, November 9, 2011, https://www.pewresearch.org/internet/2011/11/09/teens-kindness-and-cruelty-on-social-network-sites.

22. Englander, "New Data and Findings: Cyberbullying, Bullying, and Youth."

23. Katherine Schaeffer, "Most US Teens Who Use Cellphones Do It to Pass Time, Connect with Others, Learn New Things," *Pew Research Center* (blog), August 23, 2019, https://www.pewresearch.org/fact-tank/2019/08/23/most-u-s-teens-who-use-cellphones-do-it-to-pass-time-connect-with-others-learn-new-things/.

24. Colleen McClain et al., "The Internet and the Pandemic," *Pew Research Center: Internet, Science & Tech* (blog), September 1, 2021, https://www.pewresearch.org/internet/2021/09/01/the-internet-and-the-pandemic/.

25. Lenhart et al., "Teens, Kindness and Cruelty on Social Network Sites."

Conclusion

1. K. R. Ginsburg, "The Importance of Play in Promoting Healthy Child Development and Maintaining Strong Parent-Child Bonds," *Pediatrics* 119, no. 1 (2007): 182–91, https://doi.org/10.1542/peds.2006-2697.

2. "Early Childhood Curriculum and Developmental Theory," in *International Encyclopedia of Education*, ed. S.M.-Y. Lim and C. Genishi (Oxford: Elsevier, 2010), 514–19, http://linkinghub.elsevier.com/retrieve/pii/B9780080448947000877.

Appendix B

1. Bonnie Benard, "The Case for Peers" (Opinion Papers, Western Center for Drug-Free Schools and Committees, Department of Education, Washington, DC, 1990).

2. Roger Rennekamp et al., "Reflect and Improve" (Takoma Park, MD: The Innovation Center, 2005).

Acknowledgments

My research and teaching is a source of great pleasure for me. I also greatly enjoy helping the tens of thousands of children that we reach every year through the Massachusetts Aggression Reduction Center (MARC). Writing about all this, though, is more laborious and (because writing is essentially a lonely activity) much less interactive. As my father once said to me, "Writing isn't nice. What's nice is *having written.*"

And so it is with this book, as it was with my first. I hope the book is helpful—that's how I'll derive my pleasure.

First, kudos go to my family, who tolerated a July where they didn't see much of me, and where we didn't go on vacation. Especially my husband, who doesn't need instructions and so readily picks up any baton I lay down. My three kids make good vetting sources, too.

Thanks also to Meghan McCoy and all of TeamMARC, who work so devotedly with educators and children in Massachusetts and beyond, and whose dedication gave me the brain-space I needed to conceptualize this book.

A third thanks goes to Molly Grab, Jayne Fargnoli, and the others at Harvard Education Press, for being consistently encouraging but not pulling punches.

Mostly, though, this book is dedicated to teachers—I know how corny that sounds, and I know how many of you have suffered through pabulum speeches about how Little Timmy was saved by a Special Teacher. But I will tell you that in my heart of hearts, I truly believe that nothing is more important than children. And the caregivers of children, for that reason, command a special respect and regard. Never let anyone convince you that you are simply teaching content. As Aristotle said, you are teaching children *how to live.*

About the Author

DR. ELIZABETH KANDEL ENGLANDER is an award-winning author and the founder and Executive Director of the *Massachusetts Aggression Reduction Center* at Bridgewater State University, a Center which delivers programs, resources, and research for the state of Massachusetts and nationwide. She is also a Founding Member of the *Social and Emotional Research Consortium* (SERC). As a researcher and a professor of Psychology for almost 30 years, she is a nationally recognized expert in the area of bullying and cyberbullying, childhood causes of aggression and abuse, and children's use of technology. She was named *Most Valuable Educator* by the Boston Red Sox and in 2018, Massachusetts Governor Charles Baker appointed her to his Juvenile Justice Advisory Council. She is on the Scientific Advisory Board for the Institute of Child Development and Digital Media, and in 2023, her 9th book (*You Got A Phone!*) was awarded a National Parenting Product Award.

Dr. Englander has served as a Special Editor for the *Cyberbullying* issues of the *Journal of the American Academy of Child and Adolescent Psychiatry-CONNECT* and the *Journal of Social Sciences*, and has authored more than a hundred articles in academic journals and books. She is also the author of nine books, including *You Got A Phone!*, the *Insanely Awesome* series for children, *Understanding Violence* (a standard academic text in the field of child development and violent criminal behavior), *Bullying and Cyberbullying: A Guide for Educators*, published by Harvard Education Press, and *25 Myths About Bullying and Cyberbullying* (Wiley press). She has also written a variety of research-based curricula and educational handouts for communities and professionals. Reflecting her interest in educating laypeople, Dr. Englander has answered questions in a column for the *New York Times* (online edition), and she frequently speaks to parents and the public.

During the global Coronavirus Pandemic, Dr. Englander conducted research with children and educators that has helped to shape the nation's pandemic response. Between 2020 and 2022, she authored and published five books, one for educators (*When The Kids Come Back*), two for children aged 8–11 years old (*The Insanely Awesome Pandemic Playbook: A Humorous Mental Health Guide For Kids* and *The Insanely Awesome POST Pandemic Playbook*), and two for younger children, all of which both feature supplemental guides and activities for teachers and parents.

Index

abuse behaviors, 7, 9–10, 56, 128
  bully use of anger to justify,
    67–68
  peer, 9, 33
  rationalization for, 68
administrators. *See* educators
adults. *See also* parents
  alliance emphasis in responding
    by, 143, 146
  consistent responding impact on
    social behavior by, 174
  cyberbullying lack of
    understanding by, 83–84
  digital technology messages
    from, 26
  gender differences on bullying
    response by, 144–145
  hesitancy of students to report to,
    139–142
  MARC surveys of, 180–181
  resiliency and non-school
    stressors awareness by, 50
  response to tattling by, 45–46
  screen time concerns of, 1
  socially inappropriate behaviors
    response by, 25
  strategy of supervision increase
    by, 143
  target response to offers to help
    by, 22–23
  tell an adult slogan and,
    13–14, 140

age-related shift, of bullying
    reporting, 140–141, 154–156
aggression
  alcohol impact on, 80
  body and language cues reduction
    of, 80
  child development and, 5, 69–70
  digital communication and, 5
  as normal life circumstance, 15
  parenting styles and, 69–70
  popularity and, 15, 46
  violent online game play impact
    on, 57
alcohol
  aggression and, 80
  digital communication
    disinhibition with, 80
  sexting and, 95
alliance
  adult responding with emphasis
    on, 143, 146
  value of peer, 149–151
Almon, Joan, 63
American Academy of Pediatrics, 177
anger
  as primary motive of bully, 66–69
  rationalization for, 68
  sexting and, 95
Angus Council Anti Bullying
    Policy, 73
anonymity, cyberbullying and,
    27–28, 79

Facebook, 29
Fahlman, Scott E., 62
false minimization, by victims, 32
family
  non-school stressors and, 50
  violence and resiliency in, 44–45
fear
  of retaliation for victim, 9–10, 32
  school shooting and high school
    students, 102
  victim defenseless feeling and, 8–9
formal discipline response, 11, 111,
  127–130
Formspring, 98–99
friendships
  between-friends bullying, 43–44,
    64–65
  bullying and preference of talking
    in, 141–142
  changes in nature of, 64–65, 81–82
  importance to girls, 64–65
  resiliency and, 43–44
  sexting and, 95
  social skills and, 64

gag factor, children and, 12–13
gateway behaviors, 6, 18
  dealing with, 24–26
  determination of bullying
    behavior, 21–24
  in digital environments, 26–27
  educator response to outward,
    25, 174
  evolution as preferred bullying
    tactic, 19–21
  intention assessment, 23
  MARC on, 110
  nonphysical attack methods
    today, 10–11, 20–21
  physical bullying rates compared
    to, 19–21

positive and proactive response
  to, 117–118
power imbalance assessment,
  21–23
psychological bullying
  significance to victim, 20–21
repetition assessment, 24
of rumors or lies, 20
gender differences. *See* boys; girls
girls
  anxiety over cell phone lack of
    connection, 70
  cell phone ownership, 101
  cognitive priming and, 65
  cyberbullying serious threats to, 27
  digital communication
    disinhibition and, 79
  emotion escalation susceptibility,
    65, 82
  friendship importance to, 64–65
  MERC on friendships and, 82
  nature of friendship changes,
    64–65, 81–82
  preference for reporting bullying
    to friends, 141
  privacy online understanding, 107
  reports of being pressured or
    coerced to sext, 94
  self-cyberbullying frequency, 99
  text message preference by, 82
  view of adult bullying response
    by, 144–145
  vulnerability to bullying, 50

harassment, 140
  bias-based, 42
  digital sexual, 90
  online, 28–29, 155
  public bullying and, 49
  sexting and, 96
hate speech, 14

criminal prosecution risk from,
  96–97
dating violence and, 95
frequency of, 91–92
LGBTQ youth and, 91
MARC on, 92, 95–96
mental health and, 94–95
motivation for, 92–95
negative- versus
  positive-pressured, 95–98
peers and relationship with,
  94–95, 97
pornography viewing and,
  93–94, 96
SERC study on, 90–92, 94,
  96–97
sibling bullying, 45
slogans, misleading
  involve bystanders, 14
  tell an adult, 13–14, 140
smartphones, 62–63, 90, 101
Social and Emotional Research
  Consortium (SERC), 5, 143, 183
  on bullying and cyberbullying
    discussion, 173
  on bullying support by
    friends, 136
  on bullying types, 42
  on cyberbully types, 29
  on LGBTQ youth, 22
  on parents, 167
  on repeat bully gender
    differences, 68
  on resiliency and strong social
    skills, 124–125
  resiliency study of, 41
  on serious threats in
    cyberbullying, 27
  on sexting, 90–92, 94, 96–97
  on social media, 102
  on strategies, 146–147

on technology and social
  relationships, 75
social behavior
  adult consistent responding
    impact on, 174
  of civility, 15–16
  different interpretations of, 33–34
  respect as, 16
social development
  coronavirus pandemic impact on,
    2–3
  digital communication impact on,
    2, 6, 57–60
social factors impacting bully
  changes in society as, 56–57
  electronics and child
    development, 57–60
  multiple cause answers for, 57
  violence in media as, 57
social lives, message and messenger
  about, 7, 12–15
social media, 13
  cruelty and conflict
    exacerbation, 82
  cyberbullying definition absence
    in, 11
  electronic devices and available
    information in, 62–63
  elementary level rates of, 74
  high school student connection
    with, 102–103
  increase in, 100–101
  public nature of, 107, 165
  SERC on, 102
  supervision of, 170–171
social power, 15, 22, 28, 46
social skills
  coronavirus pandemic decrease in,
    2, 54, 64
  educators on deficit of, 60
  electronic devices impact on, 6